Political Communication in the Era of New Technologies

STUDIES IN COMMUNICATION AND POLITICS

Edited by Bogusława Dobek-Ostrowska and Michał Głowacki

VOL. 1

Notes on the quality assurance and peer review of this publication

Prior to publication, the quality of the work published in this series is reviewed by an external referee appointed by the editorship.

BOGUSŁAWA DOBEK-OSTROWSKA /
JAN GARLICKI (EDS.)

Political Communication in the Era of New Technologies

PETER LANG
EDITION

Bibliographic Information published by the Deutsche Nationalbibliothek
The Deutsche Nationalbibliothek lists this publication in the Deutsche Nationalbibliografie; detailed bibliographic data is available in the internet at http://dnb.d-nb.de.

Library of Congress Cataloging-in-Publication Data
Political communication in the era of new technologies / Bogusława Dobek-Ostrowska, Jan Garlicki (eds).
pages cm. - (Studies in communication and politics ; Vol. 1)
Includes bibliographical references and index.
ISBN 978-3-631-64411-9
1. Communication in politics–Technological innovations. 2. Information technology–Political aspects. 3. Mass media–Political aspects. 4. World politics–1989- I. Dobek-Ostrowska, Bogusława II. Garlicki, Jan.
JA85.P65245 2013
320.01'4--dc23

2013034184

This publication was financially supported by
the Institute of Political Science, University of Warsaw and by
the Institute of Political Science, University of Wroclaw.

ISSN 21971684
ISBN 978-3-631-64411-9 (Print)
E-ISBN 978-3-653-02973-4 (E-Book)
DOI 10.3726/978-3-653-02973-4

Peter Lang – Frankfurt am Main · Bern · Bruxelles · New York · Oxford · Warszawa · Wien

This book is part of the Peter Lang Edition list
and was peer reviewed prior to publication

www.peterlang.com

Contents

Editors' Introduction

New technologies are a challenge for participants of the political communication process—political actors, the mass media and voters. Politicians, political parties, organizations, governments and state institutions can address society directly without mass media mediation. Citizens have obtained a strong instrument that helps them to be active in politics, to express their opinions and to formulate their expectations. The new channels of political communication limit the powerful role of the mass media successively, but this does not mean that their role will be reduced totally in the future. The traditional mass media still maintain an important position in politics.

Nowadays, new technologies not only create new ways of communication, but also make election campaigns more sophisticated and detail targeted. The Internet and social media along with the rapid development of polling and many other methods of public opinion may be used by politicians during election campaigns. This is relevant both for old, well-developed democracies (the American exceptionalism model and the Western European model of election campaign) and for young, unstable democracies in Central and Eastern Europe, Latin America, Asia and Africa (the new democracies model of election campaign). Current developments in the social, political and technological environments of national media systems create a strong need for new empirical and comparative studies that may help to illuminate similarities and differences in political communication and the usage of new technologies in different parts of the world.

All these problems are reflected in the fifteen chapters presented in this book. The first one, written by the editors of the book, is dedicated to the general application of new technologies in political communication. The authors try to answer the question of how the internet, social networking, blogging platforms, and mobile phone have changed the political landscape.

The book has been divided into four major thematic sections. The first one contains papers dealing with the issue of online political communication. The second section tackles the question of the development of social media and its influence on political communication. The articles concerning election campaigns in new media are included in the next section. Finally, the remaining papers, focusing on traditional forms of communication in the era of new technologies, are placed in the fourth section.

There are three papers placed in the first section entitled The Internet and Political Communication.

Barbara Pfetsch and Silke Adam discuss the inclusiveness and democratic potential of online communication. They try to explain why the potential of online communication has fuelled hopes and why the idea that the Internet would improve political communication has turned out to be naïve. Then the authors propose a new research perspective. They claim that only a new hybrid media system (the Internet combined with the traditional media) might be effective as a medium of empowerment and inclusiveness.

In his chapter, James Moir explores the ideological issues associated with the presentation of political information by analyzing examples of political communication drawn from web-based news media in Scotland. He argues that the idea that accessing such political information by individuals influences their perceptions and voting behavior is rooted in a neo-liberal ideology.

The next chapter in this section was written by Tendai Joseph Chari. The author analyzes the role of online political publications in Zimbabwe in order to assess the extent to which they have constituted alternative spaces for the mediation of national discourses. He argues that combinations of factors which limit Internet access in Africa are obstacles for online publications becoming a genuine alternative public sphere.

The Role of Social Media in Political Communication is the title of another section. Jakub Nowak analyzes in his chapter the case of an *adisucks* Facebook protest in order to demonstrate how social media may work as a tool of political communication and the sphere of modern civic engagement.

The chapter written by Ewa Krzątala-Jaworska focuses on the challenges and limits of the presence of local governments in social media. In her paper she examines the case of French municipalities promoting a specific project on Facebook and Twitter. The author argues that the use of social media by French municipalities is limited because of the lack of an elaborated strategy.

In their chapter, David J. Jackson and Brian Collins analyze the survey data in order to determine the use of social media for political purposes among university students. They try to answer how social media are used for politics by these young people and what differences there are between those who use social media for such purposes and those who do not. The paper also examines the effects of endorsement of a candidate for elective office by a celebrity.

German Espino Sanchez scrutinizes the case of the use of social media in political communication by political leaders in Mexico. He argues that although the Web 2.0 has great potential, Mexican politicians misuse social media. Instead of using them to create dialogue with voters, they use these channels of communication only to spread propaganda.

Four other chapters were devoted to the issue of Election Campaigns in New Media. The analysis and comparison of three studies on the European Parliament election campaigns in Germany (1999, 2004 and 2009) comprises the article written by Jürgen Wilke. He tries to trace the changes concerning the use of new technologies and new media occurring between these campaigns.

The article by Jan Garlicki and Daniel Mider analyzes the extent of the use of the Internet in election campaigns in Poland. The authors also examine the phenomenon of the permanent campaign and compare election campaigns in Poland to those in the US. They critically verify a thesis about the communication revolution in Polish election campaigns.

In her chapter, Ilona Grzywińska analyzes the relationships between voters and politicians in the case of two Facebook pages owned by two major political parties in Poland—the ruling Civic Platform and the main opposition Law and Justice. She endeavors to answer the question of whether these parties have built political dialogue with their voters and whether Facebook can be perceived as realization of the concept of the public sphere.

The 2009 presidential campaign in Romania was examined in terms of the use of new media by Antonio Momoc. The author focuses on the activity of the Romanian presidential candidates on blogs and social networks. The main aim of his article is to verify whether populist candidates are more interested in social-media marketing than others.

The three remaining chapters are put in the section entitled Traditional Forms of Communication in the Era of New Technologies. The paper by Ewa Nowak combines the theory of agenda-setting with an analysis of empirical data obtained in qualitative and quantitative research in order to verify whether the model in which the media agenda follows the policy agenda is changing towards a model in which the role of the media in making politics is growing.

Łukasz Wojciechowski, Peter Mikulas and Katarina Fichnova analyze the issue of the interactive character of billboards used in election campaigns. They argue that although an out-door ad is a form of the traditional media, its structure may encourage its audience to react or intervene, which is a characteristic of new media.

In the last chapter, Peter Szabo, Peter Mikulas and Lucia Spalova use discourse analysis to examine media coverage in the case of a chosen political event, namely the Hungarian president's visit to Komarno, Slovakia at the ceremony of unveiling the statue of St. Stephen in August 2009.

We present different experiences in political communication in many countries that represent three models of an election campaign—the American exceptionalism (chapter 5), the Western European model (chapters 2, 3, 5 and 9) and the new democracies model (chapters 4, 6, 8, 10, 11, 12, 13, 14 and 15). There are a lot of publications dedicated to new technologies in the American model, and less, but every year more, in Western Europe. Research in Central and Eastern Europe, Latin America, Asia and Africa are still limited and we do not know enough about the application of the new tools of communication in the new democracies model. This publication tries to diminish this gap. We publish nine chapters in this book in which the authors show fresh data and results of their studies in Poland, Slovakia, Romania, Mexico and Zimbabwe. The reader can find an interesting diagnosis of the development of new technologies in these countries and an answer to the question of how political actors use the new channels of political communication there.

Bogusława Dobek-Ostrowska and Jan Garlicki

1. The impact of new technologies on political communication. Western patterns and the case of Poland

Bogusława Dobek-Ostrowska
University of Wrocław, Poland
Jan Garlicki
University of Warsaw, Poland

Abstract: New technologies created new expectations among all participants of the political communication process. Interactive technologies are one way passive channels are complemented. Over the last ten years, the digital media have undergone a deep transformation. Computers with access to the Internet are being displaced gradually by mobile Internet and devices. Political actors not only use simple parties' or candidate's websites, they also have access to social network, blog and micro-blog platforms, and mobile internet accessible via their mobile devices 24 hours a day. The first part of this paper recognizes the role of new technologies in politics in western democracies. The analysis concerns the problem of whether these new tools destabilized the established political system. This part also presents the concept of the Fifth Information Age. The second part focuses on changes in political communication in a country where this political system transformation has taken place, Poland.

Keywords: campaign models, stage of campaigning process, new technologies, blog platforms, online campaigning, mobile internet, social network, tablet.

Introduction

Accessible technologies for political actors, the mass media and voters have always created a political landscape and have determined the forms of the relationships of political communication participants (Blumler and Gurevitch, 1995:82-83). Electoral campaigns have been a crucial point in the political process of democracy. Analyzing the electoral process can help us to appreciate the level of technology application.

One of the most useful concepts for this end has been presented by Farrell, Kolodny and Medvic (2001:12). They presented three main stages of the campaign process: the Newspaper Age (a pre-modern model of campaigning), the Television Age (a modern model of campaigning) and the Digital Age (a post-modern model of campaigning). They use some indicators to explain the evolution of this process such as technological trends, the dominant party model, the character of the electorate, the relationship between the party and the candidate, the character of the campaigning personnel, the type of consultants, the dominant forms of the candidate's communication with the electorate, and the orientation of political actors (party orientation, candidate orientation, political marketing and market orientation). The party model evolved from the mass party in pre-modern campaigning, through the electoral party in the modern campaign, to the cartel, issue or the political entrepreneur party in post–modern campaigning. A loyal electorate linked with a given party was typical of the first stage, while unstable voters are part of the political landscape in the second one. A dissatisfied and disappointed electorate appeared on a significant scale in the Digital Age. Parties and party machines played the main role in the first stage. Political leaders and party activists acted without any support from outside the party organization. It was changed in a visible way in the next age, when political consultants, marketers, and specialists in public relations entered politics and started to occupy an important place, which was reserved earlier for traditional political actors. In the third age, consultants and advisers began to emerge from the shadow, and nowadays they are the new type of political actors (Dobek-Ostrowska, 2011:66-67).

The main aim of the chapter is to recognize the role of new technologies in politics in the 21st century. The concept of the three main stages of the campaigning process helps us to explain a research problem and to answer the fundamental question of how new technologies change political communication and electoral campaigning.

Technology and its application in political communication

Technological trends are mentioned by Farrell, Kolodny and Medvic (2001:12) as the first indicator in their concept of the campaign process, and this is not by accident. Technological development creates and powerfully impacts other indicators. The dominant role was played by the mass press, radio, cinema, telegraph and telephone at the first stage. Terrestrial and cable television was used as the main channel of political communication in the next one. In the third stage, thanks to technological progress, political actors obtained new possibilities of communicating with voters. Farrell, Kolodny and Medvic could not predict the intensity and speed of the changes. One-way passive channels, typical of the 19th and 20th centuries, are complemented by interactive technologies in the 21st century. Over the last ten years, the digital media have undergone a deep transformation. Simple computers with access to the Internet are gradually displaced by laptops, tablets and mobile internet. Bill Clinton was the first one to use simple, one-way websites and e-mails in 1992 and 1996. Blogging started as a campaigning tool in 2003, the social network appeared in 2004, YouTube in 2006 and Twitter in 2008 (Johnson, 2009:12). Nowadays, political communication cannot exist without technological tools. Politicians not only use parties' or candidates' websites, but also have access to social networks, blog and micro-blog platforms, web videos, and mobile internet accessible with their smartphones 24 hours a day.

New technology has also changed the nature of advertising. The first online advertising was distributed in 1998 in the US. During the first eight months of the campaign in 2004, political actors and major organizations released about 2.6 million banner ads. The presidential election of Barrack Obama in 2008 was a crucial point in the development of the campaign process and it was the first full post-modern model of the electoral campaign.

There are no doubts that thanks to new technologies political communication has entered a new phase. The technological tools let their users generate the volume of information, allow them to communicate in real time and cross all boundaries and space. Additionally, senders of the news now know better who the receivers of their messages are. The role of viewers has also changed significantly. They are not merely a passive audience but active producers of the news. Finally, the traditional media have lost their power and the central position in the political communication process. They have given way to two-way communication which offers the audience an active role in politics.

Online revolution and democracy

We should agree with the opinion of Flatcher and Lynn Young who claim that:

> "The Internet and mobile communications technologies have, like most major innovations, destabilized the established system and opened up new opportunities." (2012:43)

The authors emphasize that new technologies of communication have changed and created new expectations among all participants of the political communication process, but above all, the audience and advertisers. Younger generations of voters look for easily accessible and short news, searchable and available on mobile devices (Flatcher and Young, 2012:43). New interactive ways of communication reinforce the defiant public who thanks to this technology can share (send and receive) ideas and opinions, taking part in the public discourse actively. New technologies are a kind of challenge (Drache, 2008:99-104), not only to democratic but also to non-democratic states, where control over the media and the public is strict. The examples of Russia, China, and other authoritarian and hybrid regimes (*Democracy index 2011*) show that the Internet there is the biggest winner of the competition among the media sectors in the countries where freedom of the press is limited. In this case, we should also ask about society's access to the Internet and purposes of the Internet usage.

Table 1: World internet usage and population statistics (June 30, 2012)

World Regions	Population (2012 Est.)	Internet Users Dec. 31, 2000	Internet Users Latest Data	Penetration (% Population)	Growth 2000-2012	Users % of Table
Africa	1,073,380,925	4,514,400	**167,335,676**	15.6 %	3,606.7 %	7.0 %
Asia	3,922,066,987	114,304,000	**1,076,681,059**	27.5 %	841.9 %	44.8 %
Europe	820,918,446	105,096,093	**518,512,109**	63.2 %	393.4 %	21.5 %
Middle East	223,608,203	3,284,800	**90,000,455**	40.2 %	2,639.9 %	3.7 %
North America	348,280,154	108,096,800	**273,785,413**	78.6 %	153.3 %	11.4 %
Latin America / Caribbean	593,688,638	18,068,919	**254,915,745**	42.9 %	1,310.8 %	10.6 %
Oceania / Australia	35,903,569	7,620,480	**24,287,919**	67.6 %	218.7 %	1.0 %
WORLD TOTAL	**7,017,846,922**	**360,985,492**	**2,405,518,376**	**34.3 %**	**566.4 %**	**100.0%**

Source: http://www.internetworldstats.com/stats.htm (July 1, 2013)

According to *the World Internet Usage and Population Statistics*, in 2012 only 34.3 per cent of the world population had access to the Internet (Table 1). The highest penetration was in North America (78 percent), Oceania and Australia (67.6 percent) and Europe (63.2 per cent). If we compare the data with tablet users we note that more than 44 percent of them lived in Asia (where paradoxically only 27 percent of the population has access to the Internet), in Europe (21.5 per cent) and North America (11.4 per cent) and a little bit less in Latin America and the Caribbean (10.6 per cent). Additionally, we observe a significant difference among countries in the same region, like in Europe (over 90 per cent in the Nordic countries and the Netherlands vs. 33 per cent in Ukraine).

Fenton claims that the process of democratization of the public sphere is linked with the accessibility of the Internet to producers (political actors among them) and users (Fenton, 2012:559). There is no doubt that a 'technical' access to the internet is one of the fundamental conditions for the development of the third stage of political communication, but it is not enough. The other one is the quality of the public sphere and civil society, citizen culture, and political education. Studies by Boulianne (2009) do not show a strong correlation between Internet usage and political activity of societies. This means that access to new technologies can be but is not always reflected in citizen motivation and political engagement. Fenton in her analysis tries to show the positive and negative sides of the new media and the news they disseminate. The author analyzes three areas which serve for her to suggest that the new media both reinvigorate and depress democracy.

Speed and space are the first area. New technologies help to expand news platforms and increase timelines. The news distributed by the new media cross geographical borders. However, unlimited speed and space also have negative consequences. The news created under the pressure of time is of worse quality, as fewer journalists gather information outside the newsroom.

The second area is the multiplicity and polycentrality that bring diversity and challenge news dominance. The plurality of news providers helps all political actors—strong parties and small ones, powerful and weaker ones—eliminate the monopoly of the major transnational corporation. Each citizen and politician has access to technologies which help them create and distribute their messages. The many to many model of information dissemination is a fact. But multiplicity and polycentrality can produce a negative effect, too. Recipients of the new media have more, but frequently, the same news. They are often shorter, personalized and polarized. It leads to the tabloidization and simplification of politics, but it also creates a high degree of social fragmentation (Fenton, 2012:562).

Interactivity and participation is the third area of Fenton's analysis. The author contrasts increasing civic intervention and citizen journalism with a limited and thin role of citizens. She presents three arguments which support the claim that interactivity and participation reinvigorate democracy. They lead to an increase in civic journalism, an expansion of citizens' access to public information and government services, and direct access to political and government sources (Fenton, 2012:561). She also finds some arguments which contradict the positive opinion. The new media can lead democracy towards depression. One of the most important problems is the lack of accountability and anonymity of messages. The news is not verified and accurate.

Having taken the arguments of Fenton into account, we cannot appreciate unequivocally the role of new technologies in democracy. They have both positive and negative consequences, but no doubt they have changed political communication in a radical way and thanks to it, political communication and campaigning have entered the Fifth Information Age (Bimber, 2003; Smith, 2010:168).

Campaigning in the Fifth Information Age

Smith, using Bimber's proposition of four information ages in the US (2003), has added the fifth one. The leading characteristic of the Fifth Information Age from 1992 to 2012 is a strong impact of the new technologies on each American election. The historical perspective confirms that major functions and tools of political communication were discovered and first used by politicians in the American 'Exceptionalism' model of electoral campaigning. Then, they were adopted or modified in countries classified in the Western European model and the New Democracies model (Latin America, East and Central Europe, former Soviet Union, parts of Africa) (Farrell, Kolodny and Medvic, 2001:19-23). This concept lets us predict that new instruments which were created and used for the first time by political actors in the Fifth Information Age in the US will be soon adopted or modified by politicians in other models of election campaigns.

The beginning of the Fifth Information Age is dated by Smith to 1992 during the Bush—Clinton–Perot race (2010:170-171). Political communication then entered a new phase thanks to 24-hour cable news, computer modems, faxes, e-mail, interactive satellites and the first online news services. Four years later in 1996, the World Wide Web was attached to campaigning tools. It was an exclusive way of communication because only 6.4 per cent of American households had access to the Internet, but websites started the process of campaign organization. In 2000, the American population with access to the internet increased significantly to 48 per cent (Whillock and Whillock, 2002). It was the first time that candidates used this tool for fundraising. Only 5 per cent of the total fund came online but it opened a new way of winning financial support in campaigns. The first full online campaign, called by Chadwick "the first real Internet election in the United States" (2006:162), took place in 2004. Bush and Kerry used their websites intensively, above all attacking and criticizing their political opponent. The candidates distributed their press releases, videos and political advertising on the Internet. Blogs were a new and weak instrument then, but started to create blogging communities which were an important part of the campaign four years later.

Barack Obama and his staff revolutionized campaign communication in 2008. It was the first full post-modernized online campaign where official interactive party's and candidate's websites, online advertising (banners and videos), social media, blogs, discussion fora, e-mailing, fundraising, mobile phone campaigns, phone banking, and call center services in English and Spanish were used together on a wide scale. David Axelrod and David Plouffe were the creators and organizers of Obama's innovate campaign, which was composed of five general pillars. The first one included the original interactive platform http://my.barackobama.com and the

Democratic Party website. Thanks to them, voters could, among a lot of possibilities, share videos, see the updates and donate money for the candidate. The second pillar was linked with social networks. There were more than a hundred specialists employed in the service of Facebook, Twitter, MySpace and Youtube. Obama's staff cooperated closely with Chris Hughes, the co-owner of Facebook. Mobile phones were the third pillar. It was a 'get out the vote' campaign. Voters received SMS reminders thanks to iPhones, Blackberries, Digg about the voting day with the address and phone number of the closely situated voting offices. The fourth pillar was dedicated to citizens' activity. Members of Obama's staff looked for activists and supported them in organizing discussion fora and discussion groups, in creating autonomous voter's blogs and photoblogs supporting the candidacy of Obama and distributed on barackopedia.com, allreaders.com or meetup.com. There were networks where the information about meetings and rallies was published, too. Fundraising was the fifth pillar of Obama's campaign. The new technologies created possibilities for candidates who did not want to be reliant on big corporations and businesses. Thanks to online tools like the platform My.barackobama.com, SMS campaign, advertising distributed by Google, Facebook, and Myspace, Obama raised half a million USD (with an average of about 80 USD per deposit), which constituted 43 per cent of all campaigning funds.

The presidential campaign in 2012 consolidated and developed the tools and techniques used earlier. Additionally, the landscape changed a little bit with older and more experienced users of new technologies that are universally accessible. Tools and methods used in American campaigns were immediately imitated in other parts of the world.

Johnson (2011:8-10) presents seven characteristics of the twenty–first century campaign model. The author indicates the dominant role of political consultants and stresses that the online component is an integral part of each campaign. Second, the new media encourage citizens to take part in political discourse: there are more ideas and opinions coming from society to politicians. Third, television is still a strong channel of political advertising but new ways of communication such as websites, Internet advertising, social networks, blogs, and microblogs have exploded. Fourth, campaigns speed up; all channels are used 24 hours per day, 7 days per week. The new media publish polling results and the news every hour. Fifth, campaigning research and data are accessible immediately. Sixth, new media offer new possibilities for fundraising, not only for big-dollar givers (Johnson, 2011:10), but also for small-amount donors. Seventh, thanks to online communication, citizens have obtained new ways of participation in politics. They can be mobilized by politicians, and then they can mobilize themselves and other voters.

No doubt these characteristics are typical of all democratic systems, both the Western European Democracy model and the New Democracies model of election campaigns. We can show how it works in Central and Eastern Europe with the example of Poland.

The growing role of new media in political communication in a country under political (systemic) transformation—the case of Poland

Polish politicians, political parties and electoral staffs recognized quite early the opportunities afforded by the use of new media in political campaigning. However, in the beginning their implementation was beyond the actual level of the development of new technologies and the level of the use of the Internet in Poland.

In using the term 'new media' we should remember that it cannot be limited to the Internet only. This term includes various forms of digital communication, such as satellite TV or mobile telephony with data transmission capabilities. Also within the Internet we can distinguish various technologies of communication. There are the Web 1.0 and the Web 2.0 (see chapter 10), as well as Usenet, Telnet or BBS, which are less known to the average Internet user. One feature of the digital revolution is the creation and intensification of a phenomenon that can be called the convergence of media. Communication carried out by various media is typically available in one of the new media, namely the Internet. A receiver can enjoy a variety of media that are available in one channel of communication. Another important feature introduced by the new media is its interactivity. These characteristics make the Internet a hypermedium (Nelson, 1965; Borsook, 1992).

The first attempts to use the Internet in political communication in Poland were made already in 1995 during the presidential election campaign. They were, however, incidental, mainly due to the very low number of Internet users in Poland. A group of people with access to the Internet did not exceed half a million at that time (see chapter 10; Krzemień, 2010).

In the parliamentary campaign in 1997 the Internet was used to a greater extent. Although then the use of new media was evaluated as a pioneer and unsophisticated, it should be noted that the first barrier was broken. Politicians recognized the opportunities offered by new media and started using them. It is worth mentioning that the first online debate was carried out during this campaign (Rafa, 2011).

Another qualitative change was brought by the presidential election campaign in 2000. At that time, a standard developed for the web pages of candidates in Poland. Such web pages contained the biographies of politicians, their pictures, electoral programs and slogans. Additionally, they started to present video materials. Despite all this, the use of new media in the election campaign of 2000 cannot be considered successful in terms of effective and efficient political communication. Opportunities created by new technologies were treated rather as supplements to traditional campaigning.

The presidential election of 2005 in Poland strengthened the position of Web 1.0 as a very significant tool for building the image of a political candidate. One can say that there was significant progress in this area (Dobek and Baranowski, 2012:130). The web pages of political parties began to be considered a good place for presenting programs and political agenda.

In the 2007 parliamentary elections, the use of communication channels classified as Web 1.0 already had a standardized and professional character.

It should be noted that although the parliamentary campaign of 2007 was conducted primarily using communication channels classified as the Web 1.0, some channels of the Web 2.0 such as blogs were also used. Nevertheless blogs and microblogs have not become significant and widely used channels of political communication in Polish campaigns (Biskup, 2011:87).

The widest range of the use of new media was observed in Poland during the presidential election campaign in 2010 and parliamentary elections in 2011.

The analysis of transformation in the use of new media in political communication, especially the Internet in election campaigns, leads to the conclusion that it was a rather abrupt and cascading increase, not a cumulative one. Election staffs and politicians recognized new possibilities in political communication, but the way of using new media was inconsistent. For example, politicians and their staffs focused first on the Web 1.0, and when they noticed the opportunities created by the Web 2.0, they moved their activity to those channels (e.g. social networks) forgetting that they had 'left something' in the Web 1.0. These were mainly web pages of candidates or political parties that were 'left alone'. In other words, they were not updated and usually did not have any qualities of interactivity.

New technologies—the nature of changes in political communication

Hardly anyone disputes the fact that new media have changed the nature of political communication. However, it is important to analyze the impact of the technological and information revolution, particularly in relation to the popularization of the Internet, on the development of political communication, especially its impact on the evolution of strategies of election campaigns. In recent years, there were several phenomena that have had a significant impact on the methods and dynamics of political communication, especially during election campaigns. Undoubtedly important in this regard are the effects of the development of new media. Many researchers of this process point to the variety of its actual or potential consequences. They name, among others, the following phenomena:

- the formation of so-called virtual communities (Rheingold, 2013)[1] and the empowerment of citizens in the media
- the change of the character of political communication, especially electoral communication due to the possibilities of personalization of communication (Sunstein, 2001; Mider, 2008:342-344)[2],
- the decentralization of mass communications (Chaffee and Metzger,2001),
- an increase in the possibilities of relationships and direct communication among political actors and voters (Riaz, 2010),
- the redefinition of the role of journalists induced by new relationships among politicians and voters, but also by new instruments to transmit messages (Kovach and Rosenstiel, 2001:24)[3],
- the availability of the content of election campaigns on Internet channels, i.e. a kind of modern political memory or, in other words, an archive of politicians' actions and statements (Mider and Maksimowicz, 2013:86-87)[4].

---

1 The term "virtual communities" was introduced by Howard Rheingold and refers to social communities that are created on the Internet, when a sufficient number of people is discussing long enough with a sufficient degree of mutual sympathy to form a network of personal relationships in cyberspace.

2 A key concept here is "Daily Me". This term was introduced by Nicholas Negroponte and developed by Cass R. Sunstein in the work *Republic.com*. C.R. Sunstein, discussing the phenomenon of Daily Me, sees it as convenient for both the customer (making it possible to obtain precisely defined types of data, and these unsolicited are not received) and the political sender (who can transmit highly personalized message), but also increasing the potential danger of atrophy of democracy. After some time citizens may begin to move in different extremely personalized perceptual spaces.

3 Bill Kovach and Tom Rosenstiel define this phenomenon as playing by a citizen or group of citizens an active role in collecting, delivering, analyzing and disseminating news and information. This kind of action is intended to provide independent, trustworthy, adequate and complete information. The fundamental value of participatory journalism is expressed in the formula: *Everyone is a reporter, everyone is a witness*. In the literature, there are also other terms used to describe this phenomenon, such as: We Media or Grassroots Reporting. A prime example of grassroots journalism is the South Korean online newspaper OhmyNews (www.ohmynews.com) established in 2000. In Poland some elements of participatory journalism are present in the web portal tvn24.pl.

4 Social and political attributes of such "memory" of the Internet are not subject to a systematic study. First attempts to define them were made by Daniel Mider.

Quite important are the questions of whether and to what extent the phenomena observed in the modern world have reached Poland. An explanation of these issues can be provided by analyzing political communication in the Polish election campaigns of 2010 and 2011.

The phenomenon of the empowerment of citizens is built on the shift from top-down communication, a one-sided transfer of information from political actors to voters, to two-way communication, which includes also a bottom-up component. The Internet can lead to the reintegration of social relationships; it becomes a unique and unmatched tool for reversing the processes of alienation, helping to create and enhance virtual communities. New media, especially Internet communication channels within the Web 2.0 such as social networking sites or blogs, resulted in the receiver becoming the sender because these media have enabled them to create and publish any content available to a theoretically unlimited number of people. Moreover, it has enabled and influenced the development of citizen (grassroots) journalism. However, research carried out in Poland leads to the conclusion that in the Polish system of political communication the opportunities given to new media are used only partially. In 2010, one third of Internet users declared that occasionally they become senders of information on political issues (Garlicki, 2011:34). During the 2011 parliamentary election campaign in Poland just over a fifth of Internet users considered themselves not only receivers, but also senders of political information. Most of them publish political information on Internet forums and about half of them on social networking sites (Garlicki, 2012:31-32). It is also important to mention that for those who use the Internet as the source of information about politics (only half of all Internet users) citizen journalism sites are the third source of information, after traditional news services on the Internet and web pages of parties and politicians (Garlicki, 2012:23).

In Poland, there is an ongoing debate on the phenomenon of personalization of communication due to the development of new media. The question is whether there was really a change from the one to all (media → receivers) to one to one (everyone can be a receiver and a sender at the same time) type of political communication? Opinions on this issue are diverse. In addition, we can also observe a communication phenomenon called few to many. Communication of information on the Internet in Poland has been dominated by news services of several traditional broadcasters who intensively enter new media, and receivers are those citizens who wish to use these sources of information. Internet users claim that in order to get information about politics they are more likely to use television, radio or even the national press. The Internet is an important source of information for them, but when it comes to politics it is neither the source of the most importance nor the one most frequently used. It is TV broadcasters who lead political communication in Poland. They also try to increase their influence by creating news sites on the Internet. Such sites duplicate or supplement news programs broadcast on TV. In general, powerful media groups are still trying to maintain their role in shaping the framework of the communication process and thus co-create the framework for political debate. To a significant extent, campaigning on the Internet in Poland reflects campaigning in the traditional media, especially on television. The results of the research allow us to conclude that there is no substantial difference in the use of the media between the people who use the Internet intensively and those who use it occasionally (Garlicki, 2011: 298).

The character and culture of political communication in new media

The role of the Internet during the 2010 presidential election campaign and the 2011 parliamentary elections campaign in Poland was undoubtedly significant, and to a greater extent than it had been before. However, it must be said that when it comes to the promotion of candidates, it was only a supporting medium, not the main campaigning tool. The presidential candidates and their staffs tried to take advantage of new media. New web pages of candidates and blogs were created. Political debate also took place in social networking sites such as Facebook and "Nasza Klasa". Undoubtedly, different channels of communication on the Internet allow wider access to information also about politics, but they are not yet widely used. The hypothesis that we are witnesses to the process of decentralization of communication seems to be true. At the present stage, this process is not dynamic, but clearly noticeable. The growing importance of citizen journalism sites can be observed. Although not many Internet users use the services yet, the number of these sites is already relatively significant and they express independent opinions on various issues. Taking into account all the analyses undertaken, it should be noted that the monopoly of traditional media, especially television, in Poland has not been yet overcome, but the processes of expansion of access to diverse information and further pluralization of the content are progressing. There is also a phenomenon of peculiar competition between new and traditional media. The competition concerns, among other things, the credibility of information, the speed of its transmission, and attractiveness of its presentation.

The development of new media created more ways of direct communication between politicians and voters grouped in social networks. This is one of the elements contributing to the weakening of the role of journalists as intermediaries and message senders. Also, the development of grassroots journalism may redefine the existing role of traditional journalism. On the other hand, traditional media journalists gained new channels of communication, which they began to use eagerly. Undoubtedly, the Internet channels of communication create an unlimited and indelible archive of actions and statements of politicians, a kind of modern political memory. Access to almost any information is possible basically at any time, anywhere. This allows us to compare different statements of the same politicians and their campaign promises with political practice.

There are quite noticeable differences in the manner of transmission of information between the Internet and the traditional media. The discourse on the Internet is much more emotional. Views and opinions are expressed more frankly and people are more prone to use abusive language. Even online editions of TV news or news portals radicalize their language and explicitness of communication. The relative (as emphasized by experts researching the communication in new media) anonymity of the discourse on the Internet makes participants rid themselves of inhibitions. Such conditions trigger aggression. For this reason, vulgarisms appear in the discussion, and in particular in the comments. However, in places where participants in a discussion appear under their real names (for example on Facebook), their language is sober. The Internet is in general a polarizing medium. In other words, the discourse on the Internet animates diehard supporters and radical opponents of a certain person, a specific issue or a political group. It can be observed that those who usually speak out are oriented extremely positively or extremely negatively towards some issue. This is the characteristic feature of political communication on the Internet. According to analyses, the most numerous group of participants in the debate on the Internet is the so called gladiators. These people both suffer (in the broad sense) and use violence against other Internet users. The Internet undoubtedly expands possibilities of searching and obtaining information, also on political issues. It is a medium which dynamizes political communication processes, and accelerates the pace of inducing social responses to political events, especially during election campaigns. The analysis of the use of communication channels on the Internet has shown that politicians make greater use of the opportunities created by the Web 1.0 (Garlicki, 2012). At the same time, Internet users are much more oriented towards and active in the Web 2.0. It has to be admitted that politicians also try to increase their activity in the Web 2.0, mainly by creating blogs and using social networking sites. Nevertheless, the activity of presidential candidates or rather their staffs (during the last presidential campaign) in social networks was not very coordinated or creative. For example, most of the posts were narrated in the third person. Campaigning on the Internet during the 2010 presidential election and 2011 parliamentary elections cannot be considered to have been run professionally. There were no creative or innovative solutions. There was no interactivity. None of the staffs attempted to create a social movement of Internet users supporting the campaign. It seemed that in most cases they probably were not professional companies, but rather teams of volunteers from youth organizations affiliated with political parties which were responsible for the organization and running of the campaign on the Internet.

The future of the Internet in political communication —neofuturism or dystopism

Since its creation, the Internet has aroused contradictory feelings of scholars of political phenomena: on the one hand a strong hope, on the other hand deep concerns about its influence on democracy. In the literature we can find numerous optimistic approaches: from moderate to utopian. Moderate optimists are strongly convinced that the Internet can revitalize and develop the political culture of democratic participation by strengthening and intensifying involvement in politics by participating in groups already active and by activating groups that were not extensively participating in politics before. Generally, in this regard, there are three approaches proposed and defined, among others, by Anthony G. Wilhelm (2000:14-23). The first, neofuturism, is based on a strong, optimistic belief that the Internet induces new forms of involvement in politics, different from traditional ones, and such new forms improve the quality and stability of existing democracies. It can even become a catalyst that will create conditions for the transition from representative democracy to direct democracy. The second approach is technorealism—a moderate, prudent approach to reflections on the influence of the Internet on society. It is based on a conviction that the Internet strengthens the involvement of the groups already participating in politics. However, it does not mobilize those who are passive and uninterested in politics. The third one is dystopism. This is an extremely pessimistic approach claiming that the involvement of the Internet into politics may result in a decrease in citizen participation in politics which will finally lead to atrophy of democracy. Followers of this approach go even further, claiming that the increased use of the Internet in politics may lead to transition from democracy to totalitarian rule.

On the basis of the Polish experience it might be concluded that we can rather expect technorealism. An increase in diversity in access to information about politics and an increase in diversity in the level of political participation should be expected. New media will also increase the ability of politically active citizens to obtain and transmit information. However, new media will probably not encourage those who are not very active and have little interest in politics to participate in it. Moreover, there is a significant group of citizens that do not use the Internet at all. This is a group of digital exclusion. For such people, possibilities regarding the spread of information and political participation created by new media are still utopian.

It is worth adding that although the majority of Internet users criticize aggressive behavior, which can be found in the new medium, more than half of them are convinced that we should not restrict and censor freedom of speech on the Internet.

Conclusion

The analysis presented in this chapter delivers some arguments to strengthen the opinion that new technologies do not merely provide new tools for political communication. They also provide new, different and often better ways to use the old campaign's functions (Smith, 2010:181). In the Digital Age, high-speed and low-cost ways of communication are accessible to all participants of the political communication process—political actors, voters, the mass media, individual citizens and formal organizations.

The historical perspective confirms that major functions and tools were discovered and first used by politicians in the American Exceptionalism model and then adopted or modified in countries classified in the Western European model and the New Democracies model (Latin America, East and Central Europe, former Soviet Union, parts of Africa). In the new Fifth Information Age from 1992 to 2012, we observe a strong impact of new technologies in each American election.

New technologies have also changed the means of political communication in a Central European country like Poland. Since the presidential election of 1995 the impact of new technologies has been constantly growing. However, there is lack of ingenuity and creativity among the dominant political parties. Politicians are simply copying Western solutions and mechanisms. Moreover, usually the copied solutions are those which are the cheapest and the simplest (e.g. their presence in social media). Many effective solutions still remain unused. On the other hand, although the number of participants of political communication processes in Poland is still increasing, we cannot diminish a significant group of people who do not have access to new technologies. Therefore, they are excluded from the new kind of political communication. Moreover, there is also a group of citizens who are not interested in politics and do not participate in it. In this case, new technologies might have a little impact on encouraging them to participate. Nevertheless, there is no doubt that the process of digitalization has been influencing politics and political communication in Poland.

References

Bergez, P. (2013). *Global Journalism. Theory and Practice*. NewYork: Peter Lang.

Bimber, B. (2003). *Information and American Democracy: Technology in the Evolution of Political Power*. New York: Cambridge University Press.

Bimber, B. (2012). Digital Media and Citizenship, in: Semetko, H. M. Scammell (eds.). *The SAGE Handbook of Political Communication*, Los Angeles, London: Sage, 115-126.

Biskup, B. (2011). Komunikowanie polityczne w tradycyjnych i internetowych serwisach informacyjnych—analiza przejawów kultury politycznej przed wyborami prezydenckimi w Polsce w 2010 r.[Political Communication in the traditional and online news channels in Poland in 2011]. in: J. Garlicki (ed.), Kultura polityczna Internautów w Polsce [Political culture of Polish users of the Internet]. *Studia Politologiczne,* vol. 21, 51-88.

Blumler, J, M. Gurevitch (1995). *Crisis of Public Communication*. London: Routledge.

Borsook T., N. Higginbotham-Wheat (1992). *A Psychology of Hypermedia: A Conceptual Framework for R&D*, Paper presented at the Annual Meeting of the Association for Educational Communications and Technology, Washington.

Boulianne, S. (2009). Does Internet Use Affect Engagement: A Meta-Analysis of Research. *Political Communication*, 26 (2), 75-89.

Chadwick, A. (2006). *Internet Politics: States, Citizens, and New Communication Technologies*. New York: Oxford University Press.

Chaffee, S.H., M.J. Metzger (2001). The End of Mass Communication?, *Mass Communication and Society*, 4/ 4, 365-379.

Davis, R.(2012). Blogging and the Future of News. In: H. Semetko, M. Scammell (eds.). *The SAGE Handbook of Political Communication*. Los Angeles, London: Sage, 49-61.

Dobek-Ostrowska, B. (2011). *Polski system medialny na rozdrożu. Media w polityce, polityka w mediach* [Polish Media System at the Crossroads. Media in Politics, Politics in Media]. Wrocław: Wrocław University Press.

Dobek-Ostrowska, B., P. Baranowski (2012). Witryny internetowe kandydatów jako narzędzie komunikowania wyborczego w kampanii wyborczej w 2011 r. [Websites of candidates as a tool of communication in the 2011 parliamentary elections campaign]. In: J. Garlicki (ed.), Elity polityczne a Internauci. Studium kultury politycznej w okresie wyborów [Political elites and the Internet users. Study of political culture during an election period], *Studia Politologiczne*, 24, 104-131.

Drache, D. (2008). *Defiant Publics: The Unprecedented Reach of the Global Citizen*. Cambridge: Polity Press.

Elmer, G., G. Langlois, F. McKelvey (2012). *The Permanent Campaign. New Media, New Politics*, New York: Peter Lang.

Garlicki, J. (2011. Kultura polityczna polskich Internautów [Political culture of Polish Internet users], in: J. Garlicki (ed.) Kultura polityczna Internautów w Polsce [Political culture of the Internet users in Poland]. *Studia Politologiczne,* vol. 21.

Farrell, D, R. Kolodny, S. Medvic (2001). Parties and Campaign Professionals in a Digital Age: Political Consultants in the United States and Their Counterparts Overseas. *The Harvard International Journal of Press/Politics*, September 2001 (6), 11-30. Fenton, N. (2012). News in the Digital Age. In: S. Allan (ed.). *The Routledge Companion to News and Journalism*. London and New York: Routledge, 557-567.

Flatcher, F., M. Lynn Young (2012). Political Communication in a Changing Media Environment. In: H. Semetko, M. Scammell (eds.). *The SAGE Handbook of Political Communication.* Los Angeles, London: Sage, 38-48.

Garlicki, J. (2012). Dynamika kultury politycznej i partycypacji politycznej Internautów w Polsce [Dynamics of political culture and political participation of the Internet users in Poland]. In: J. Garlicki (ed.) Elity polityczne a Internauci. Studium kultury politycznej w okresie wyborów [Political elites and the Internet users. Study of politcal culture during the election period], *Studia Politologiczne,* vol. 26.

Garlicki, J. (ed.). (2012). Elity polityczne a Internauci. Studium kultury politycznej w okresie wyborów [Political elites and the Internet users. Study of politcal culture during the election period],. *Studia Politologiczne*, vol. 26, Annex 1.

Rheingold, H. (2013). *The Virtual Community: Homestanding on the Electronic Frontier*, available at: http://www.rheingold.com/vc/book/, [accessed: April 2013].

Gibson, R., S. Ward (2012). Political Organizations and Campaigning Online. In: Semetko, H. M. Scammell (eds.). *The SAGE Handbook of Political Communication.* Los Angeles, London: Sage, 62-74.

Johnson, D. (2011). *Campaigning In the Twenty –First Century. A Whole new Ballgame?* New York and London: Routledge.

Kovach, B., T. Rosenstiel (2001). *The Elements of Journalism. What Newspeople Should Know and the Public Should Expect.* New York, Toronto, London: Three Rivers Press.

Krzemień, G. (2013). *Ewolucja Internetu. Początek* [The Internet evolution. The beginning]. http://blog. goldensubmarine.com/ 2010/05/ewolucja-internetu/ [accessed: April 2013].

Mider, D. (2008). *Partycypacja polityczna w Internecie. Studium politologiczne.* [Political participation in the Internet. Political science study] Warszawa: Dom Wydawniczy Elipsa, 342-344.

Mider, D. (2013). Ewaluacja wybranych metod badań społecznych w Internecie [Evaluation of some social sciences technics used in the Internet. In: D. Mider, A. Maksimowicz (eds.), *Cyberpolitologia. Badanie polityki w Internecie* [Cyber-political science in Internet. Study of politics in Internet] Warszawa Wydawnictwo ACAD, 86-87.

Nelson, T.H. (1965). *Complex information processing: a file structure for the complex, the changing and the indeterminate.* ACM '65 Proceedings of the 1965 20th National Conference, New York 1965, 84-100.

Rafa, J. *Wyborczy Internet* [Electoral Internet], available at:http://www.wsp.krakow.pl/papers/news-wyb.html, [accessed: December 2011].

Rantanen T. (2009). *When News Was New.* Malden, Oxford: Wiley-Blackwell.

Riaz, S. (2010). Effects of New Media Technologies on Political Communication. *Journal of Political Studies*, 1/ 2, 163-173.

Semetko, H. M. Scammell (eds.) (2012). *The SAGE Handbook of Political Communication.* Los Angeles, London: Sage.

Smith, C.A. (2010). *Presidential Campaign Communication. The Quest for the White House.* Cambridge: Polity Press.

Sunstein, C.R. (2001). *Republic.com.* Princeton: Princeton University Press.

Whillock, R.K., D.E. Whillock (2002). *Digital Democracy 2000. In R. Denton, Jr. (ed.) The 2000 Presidential Campaign: A Communication Perspective.* Westport, CT: Praeger 167-182.

Wilhelm, A. G. (2000). *Democracy in the Digital Age. Challenges to Political Life in Cyberspace.* New York and London: Routlege, 14 -23.

Part I
The Internet and Political Communication

2. Democratic Potentials of Online Communication for Political Debate

Barbara Pfetsch
Free University of Berlin, Germany
Silke Adam
University of Bern, Switzerland

Abstract: This chapter focuses on the democratization potential of online communication for political debate in Western democracy. We discuss the inclusiveness and democratic potential of online communication in two steps. The first section is devoted to the question of why online communication has fuelled hopes and how empirical studies cast doubt on the democratic potential of the internet. In the second section of the chapter, we propose a new perspective and argue that the internet might be effective as a medium of empowerment and inclusiveness only in interaction with the traditional media. We tackle the notion of a new hybrid media system and claim that political communication research must focus on this zone of interaction between old and new media in order to better understand and realistically assess the democratic potential of the internet.

Key words: democratic theory, internet, political debate, hybrid media system

Introduction

The democratic potential of online communication for political debate in Western democracy refers to the normative question of whether the internet can make up a better public sphere than traditional mass media. Reflection on this issue started immediately when the internet was introduced. Since then the idea that the internet would generally improve political communication has turned out to be too enthusiastic and also to some degree naïve. Therefore, the discussion of the democratic potential of online media in this chapter shall be narrowed to one specific aspect, namely the aspect of inclusiveness and plurality of voices in mass-mediated public debate.

Inclusiveness and plurality of actors have been of central importance for modern media systems. For instance, one strong criteria for the legitimization, public support and funding of public broadcasting media has always been that these media—if only by their freedom from political and commercial pressures—would feature the issues and opinions of a broad range of societal and political actors. While these norms still inform media laws, it is also true that mass communication research tells us that the selection of issues in the media is determined by professional standards of journalism. These are not guided by the idea of equal or balanced representation of societal groups but by the objective to reach a particular audience. Limited carrier capacity and the logic of news factors—such as social status, political office, or prominence—are reasons why the traditional media reveal a selection bias, so that elite actors and their issues enjoy privileged media access (e.g. Bennett, 1990). The consequence has been that reality as depicted in mainstream media has been restricted in its representation of standing actors, with the expected consequences for public debate. Mass media's selection bias produces what Gadi Wolfsfeld (1997: 24) called a "cumulative inequality." This means that those who depend the most on voice in the mass media to gain political influence have the most difficult barriers to its entry and access.

Against this background, we discuss whether online media are able to make up for this weakness of traditional media and whether one can expect the internet to be an inclusive medium which offers new opportunities for voice in politics. Thus, the question is whether the internet is challenging traditional mass media-elite linkages by offering those without easy access to public debate new venues for public recognition. If online channels are powerful enough to compensate for cumulative inequality, the internet would yield dramatic changes in contemporary political communication. First, it would threaten the most essential gate-keeping and agenda-setting roles of the traditional mass media. Second, it would change the set of actors and voices in public debate, with obvious consequences for political decision-making and mobilization.

The current chapter sets out to discuss the inclusiveness and democratic potential of online communication in two steps. The first section is devoted to a discussion of why online communication has fuelled hopes and of how empirical studies cast doubt regarding the democratic potential of the internet. In the second section of the paper, we propose a new perspective and argue that the internet may only be effective as a medium of empowerment and inclusiveness in interaction with the traditional media. In this vain Chadwick (2011: 2) recently proposed that the effect of online media has been that a new "hybrid media system" emerged that is "build upon interactions among old and new media and their associated technologies, genres, norms, behaviors and organizations." If this is true however—and this is still an open question—the idea of a mediated public sphere must be reconsidered. We also need to find out whether this hybrid media system produces more openness and inclusiveness with respect to challenging or new actors of public debate and, if so, how. Eventually, political communication research must focus on this zone of interaction between old and new media, if only in order to better understand and more realistically assess the democratic potential of the internet.

Expectations and empirical disillusions about the democratic potentials of the internet

Since the public sphere has been dominated by (traditional) mass media, the most pertinent problems of contemporary democracy relate to the inclusiveness of public debate. From a normative point of view the inclusiveness of public debate is a fundamental requirement of democracy. Authors like Jürgen Habermas, Benjamin Barber, Peter Dahlgren or Amitai Etzioni have argued extensively that a wide range of representatives of civil society and actors from the periphery of society need to be included in public debate. This normative claim however has always been in contradiction with the empirically observed "cumulative inequality" of access to media (Wolfsfeld, 1997: 24). Against this background the advent of online communication has fuelled the hope of an increase in the inclusiveness of public communication.

The democratic potential of online media is reflected simultaneously in open access, a seemingly unlimited carrier capacity, the availability of information that previously only journalists could access, and the interactivity and coexistence of horizontal and vertical communication (e.g. Bentivegna, 2002). As a result, online communication must be conceived as an indefinite reservoir of issues and frames which appeals to an undefined but also fragmented public. While the content of online communication bears the enormous capacity to overcome national, geographic and geo-political boundaries, the only remaining barriers are on the side of the user.[1]

Online communication—as Neuberger claims (Neuberger, 2009: 39)—threatens the gate-keeping role of traditional mass media. The qualities of the internet allow all kinds of actors to initiate communication and therefore act as potential agenda-setters and frame-builders and bypass the traditional media. For instance, established political actors easily profit from the make-up of the internet. They have the resources to exploit online communication and manage to avoid the filter of media selection (Baringhorst, 2008; Calhoun, 1998; Rethemeyer,2007). However, as everyone can, in principle, use the Web to address the public, the hope was that previously marginalized actors and arguments gain visibility in public (Gerhards and Schäfer, 2010). Therefore, the opportunities of online communication must be particularly important for outsiders and challengers like civil society actors and activists who do not necessarily fit the professional standards and rules of media selection. They are mostly deprived of

1 Studies on digital divide and media literacy refer to language barriers and social barriers (Marr, 2005; Schenk and Wolf, 2006).

direct access to institutional political decision-making and enjoy fewer opportunities than established actors to gain a voice in traditional media (Pfetsch, 2004; Wolfsfeld, 1997). Thus, online communication is particularly important for them (Castells, 2005; van de Donk, Loader, Nixon, and Rucht, 2004). Eventually, their access to the internet could improve the inclusiveness, the deliberativeness and the democratic quality of public debate.

Why does online communication possess such a challenging capacity? The main arguments in the literature refer to its decentralized architecture and the capacity and space for networks of new communicators, issue-centered communication and coalitions (Neuberger, 2009). It is above all these networks which increase peripheral actors' chances for greater visibility on- and offline (Koopmans and Zimmermann, 2003, 2007). Moreover, online communication provides alternative information and thus challenges the status of traditional media; it offers social movements—on the left and right side of the political spectrum—new possibilities to mobilize and coordinate offline activities (Koopmans and Zimmermann, 2003; Smith, 2000) and these movements have in turn been important in shaping the further development of the internet (de Wilde, 2003). Eventually these sometimes "subterranean" (Wright, 2004:80) channels of communication affect traditional participatory aspects of the political process, in particular when online networks successfully promote permanent campaigns and manage to communicate their ideas, counter-expertise and frames from desktops to offline media (Bennett, 2004).

What does empirical research tell us about the Internet's capacity to boost the inclusiveness of public debates and thereby challenge the traditional mass media-elite linkage? There are only few studies available that have addressed the question of the inclusiveness and democratic quality of internet communication. The scarce number of empirical studies is comprehensible since it is difficult to delineate what online communication is in the first place. The internet is an endless and multi-layered digital space which hardly lends itself to our empirical study designs. Nor are there easily available research tools and methods of media analysis that apply to the network architecture of the internet.

In order to come to delineate and research the online public sphere, researchers concentrate on issue publics in the internet. For instance Jürgen Gerhards and Mike Schäfer (2010) examine the US and German internet public debate on the issue of human genome research. Rucht, Yang and Zimmermann (2008) study the discourse surrounding the issue of genetically modified food. Ann Zimmermann (2006) concentrates on issues of European politics. All three studies compare online communication with print media coverage and analyze the actors, the framing of issues and arguments and the quality of the debate. With respect to the democratic quality of the debate and the actors the findings are quite sobering. Gerhards and Schäfer (2010, 148) write, "We do not see a more extensive popular inclusion of societal actors, especially civil societal actors, on the web pages. In the internet a small number of actors claim the bulk of standing for themselves, and, in this regard, communication online is even more one-sided than in the print media."

With respect to the range of argument, the same finding applies in the representation of actors, namely that the framing of political messages in internet communication is "even more one-sided" than in print media. (Gerhards and Schäfer, 2010: 153). The claim that the internet features more popular inclusion was neither corroborated in the study of the food issue nor in the investigation of European politics. According to Ann Zimmermann (2006) the working of search engines is responsible for the hierarchical structure of online debate. Search engines direct attention almost as hierarchically as in newspapers. One of the consequences is that "Civil society actors are systematically discriminated against as compared to governmental actors. […] The online communication is not more democratic than traditional mass media."

To conclude, the hints of criticism with respect to the democratic promises of the internet clearly prevail. It seems that the online public sphere is subject to similar power structures as offline media, at least from a user's perspective that strongly relies on the working of search engines to find relevant information on the web (Gerhards and Schäfer, 2010; Rucht, 2004; Rucht, Yang, and Zimmermann, 2008; Zimmermann and Koopmans, 2010).

The internet might not be successful in making the nature of public debate more inclusive and as a result more democratic from the perspective of a classical online user relying on the workings of search machines. Yet its enormous capacities for allowing all kinds of actors to communicate their ideas and form coalitions with allies might still be capable of changing political communication dramatically. First, online communication has the potential to successfully promote campaigns (e.g. the Occupy Movement) and thereby mobilize citizens whose activities are then taken up by traditional mass media. Second, online communication allows those who go beyond a simple Google search to dig for new and alternative information by using the abundance of online information available. Thereby, this abundance of online information might be especially important for journalists of traditional mass media. From this perspective, online communication may unfold its full democratic potential not against traditional media but with them: online and offline debates might reverberate and resonate with each other. If this is the case, we need to focus our attention on the space and the mechanism of interaction between online and offline communication. Consequently, the critical link regarding the impact of the internet on political communication relates to the *interplay and dynamics of online and offline communication.*

The interplay between online and offline media leads to a "hybrid media system" which is "built upon interactions among old and new media" in contemporary politics and society (Chadwick, 2011: 2). In his recent work, Andrew Chadwick elaborates on this idea of a hybrid media regime and applies it to cases of political communication that transgress boundaries that were formerly clearly delineated such as those, for instance, between formats (like entertainment and information), but also and most importantly between old and new media. Hybridization is seen as a process of both integration and fragmentation in communication. But the hybrid media system is mainly considered as the "outcome of power struggles and competition for preeminence during periods of unusual transition, contingency, and negotiability" (Chadwick, 2011: 10). Thus, the approach of hybridity claims to "shed new light on the relative power of actors in media systems. Attempts to control, police, and redraw boundaries, and the power struggles that crisscross domains are now defining features of political communication" (Chadwick, 2011: 10).

An example of the development of hybrid media systems is the British "bullygate" scandal, which refers to the media hype against the British premier Brown after the revelation of a then unpublished book about his conduct with personnel in his office. Another example Chadwick provides is the advent of Nick Clegg in UK politics after the debate in the election campaign of 2010. The most telling case, however, is that of the publication of Wikileaks documents and the debate over the behavior of Julian Assange. This communication involved civil rights activists, traditional media and the highest public officials in the US and UK. In all these cases real time news frames were mobilized and augmented and eventually became the subject of fierce contestation between members of the press or broadcast media and online activists organized in social networks such as Twitter. All the cases from the UK share one feature: the participants of the communication were

> "(…) composed of multiple, loosely-coupled individuals, groups, sites, and temporal instances of interaction involving diverse yet highly interdependent news creators that plug and unplug themselves from the news-making process, often in real time …. They include many non-elite participants, most of whom now interact exclusively online in order to advance or context news frames and fragments of information, sometimes in real-time exchanges but also during subsequent stages of the cycle of news that follows a major political event or the breaking of a story." (Chadwick 2011:15)

Another feature of the hybrid media system is that the traditional media make use of the communication in the internet for their own commercial and political purposes. Thus, what we see is that press and television and their online branches work together and develop their own genuine production routines and practices.

If we acknowledge that there is evidence for an emerging hybrid media system, we need to focus our attention on research about the spillover processes between online and offline media and their consequences (e.g. Zhou and Moy, 2007). Against this background the mechanisms of interaction and in particular the conditions and the nature of spillover processes of issues and frames between old and new media become a central research topic. Studies that systematically analyze the linkage between online communication and offline media are rare. The bulk of research here focuses on how traditional mass media set the issues and frames for online channels. The studies demonstrate that the old media are important agenda-setters for online blogs and other platforms. In their study of more than 90 million articles on political issues online, Leskovec et al. (Leskovec, Backstrom, and Kleinberg, 2009) find "that about 3.5% of quoted phrases tend to percolate from blogs to news media, while diffusion in the other direction is much more common." Other studies corroborate that offline-online agenda setting predominates (Ku, Kaid, and Pfau, 2003; Oegema, Kleinnijenhuis, Anderson, and Hoof, 2008).

However, from the point of view of democratic theory spillovers in the other direction are more significant. They allow us to understand under which conditions online communication actually lives up to its democratic potential. Thus, spillovers from the internet into traditional mass media are more conducive for the inclusiveness and participatory nature of public debate. Three types of spillover are particularly interesting:

- First, direct spillovers occur when messages from challengers' online networks are selected by journalists of the traditional media. As Baringhorst (2008) points out, this flow of communication is a viable strategy for challengers and in their eyes bears an enormous increase of access to the public. As Chadwick (2011) shows, in the hybrid media system, the traditional media deliberately use the information provided by challengers on the internet.
- Second, another type of spill over occurs when online outlets of the traditional media (e.g. *Spiegel-online*) or specialized online media (such as *Huffington Post*) get involved with challengers' online coalitions and online issue networks and feature their issues and frames. If these issues and frames are then taken up by the offline editions, we can speak of a *double media-focused spillover* in the sense of the paradigm of the two-step flow of communication in media effects research. The case of Wikileaks may serve as a good example here, as prominent online news platforms, such as Spiegel online in Germany or *the Guardian* in the UK or *the New York Times* in the USA, were in a symbiotic relationship with Wikileaks (Chadwick, 2011: 23-24).

- Third, spillovers from online to offline media might work via a campaign's mobilization of citizens. In this double *campaign-focused spillover*, a challengers' online coalition mobilizes citizens whose actions are then taken up by traditional mass media. The cases of the Occupy Movement or also the Arab revolution may serve as examples.

What do we know from political communication research[2] about these spillover processes and what does it say about the democratic potential of the internet? There are a number of studies that focus on the role of *individual actors such as the so-called* 'netizens' who are active in blogs, fora or social networks. Their aim is indeed to trigger spillovers into traditional media (Fuchs, 2007; Matzat, 2005; Mesch, 2007; Piotrowski, 2006). Particularly interesting is the work by Zhou and Moy (2007) who show that online discourse has an agenda- and frame-building effect on media reporting. This effect appears above all in latent stages of an issue's course. Zhou and Moy (2007) and also Peng (2005) not only find spillovers and thus changes in political communication modes but also link these spillovers to political change. In the case of post-Mao China, online fora have challenged the authority and the political agenda of the government (Yu 2006; Zhou and Moy 2007). Similarly Lee (2005) shows for Korea that online fora provoked an online, public, counter sphere, but more importantly fed into offline protest movements. The same arguments have been made about the role of online media in the revolutions in the Middle East such as the one in Egypt. Thus, spillovers from the net improve the democratic deficits of traditional media—particularly in countries where media freedom is severely restricted.

A study on Israel, however, does not support this view nor the idea of a hybrid media system. Vaisman (2009) contradicts the view that online communication—namely Hebrew left-wing blocs—affect traditional mass media. Unlike most American political blogs, which subscribe to norms of mainstream journalism, Israeli political blogs challenge mainstream journalism and as a consequence are largely ignored by it. Instead, blogs respond to the exclusion from coverage by bypassing the media and seeking direct access to politicians to generate public action.

2 The research that available here, can be distinguished according to the types of actors. For instance, quite a number of studies tackle with the role of established political actors in causing spill over processes to the offline world primarily during campaigns (Gonzalez-Bailon, 2009; Os, Wester and Jankowski, 2007; Stromer-Galley, 2000). Since we are interested in the challenging potential of the web, this strand of research is of minor relevance for our purpose.

A second strand of research refers to *collective actors* in the movement sector and their involvement in spillover processes. The few studies available demonstrate that challengers treat online communication as an important instrument within their action repertoire (Baringhorst, Kneip, and Niesyto 2007; Gillan, 2009; Lester and Hutchins, 2009; Richards and Heard, 2005). Research becomes sparse when we seek to understand the link between challengers' online campaigns and the traditional mass media. Lester and Hutchins (2009), in their study of an environmental campaign in the UK, find that the spillover from online communication to traditional media was a purposely planned and successful political strategy. Thus the spill over from online media to offline media pushed the issue onto the national political agenda. The strategy used the traditional media's power in political communication to provoke political change.

These studies indicate that in fact the interaction between old and new media, traditional press and the internet, produces an interesting new communication phenomenon with profound political consequences for politics and for the nature and quality of democracy and public debate. However, as charming the idea of a hybrid media system is, major questions about the mechanisms and conditions of spillovers and the political consequences thereof have yet to be researched.

Conclusion

Regarding the democratic potential of online communication, we have to cast doubts on the general assumption that the internet as such leads automatically to a broadening of the range of participants, issues, frames and arguments as well as to a better quality of political communication and public debate. Instead, from the few studies available we infer that the internet is reproducing the power structures that prevail in traditional media. However, we also see that the internet provokes fundamental changes in public sphere and in political communication insofar as the new media together with old media build up new structural communication networks which may be labeled a "hybrid media system". The interaction leading to the rise of this emerging communication structure involves outsiders who challenge the political elite as well as less tightly coupled groups and sites. The mechanisms of agenda building are spillovers between the online and offline media. In this respect online communication triggers completely new structures of political exchange and may indeed fulfill hopes for more inclusive, democratic public discourse. However, the hybrid public sphere may not automatically equal an enlightened debate. The hybrid media system may also be used for populist or unfair mobilization, for instance when the right wing or tabloid press jumps on campaigns on the internet.

The conclusion is that the hybrid media system has not yet been researched closely enough and has become a task for contemporary and future political communication research. We should particularly devote our attention to the nature and varieties of spillover effects and the mechanisms and conditions of interaction between old and new media and their consequences. However, since the analysis of the hybrid media system and particularly the interaction of online and offline media requires innovative research designs and rather complex and complicated methodological approaches, the task will be a rather demanding challenge.

References

Baringhorst, S. (2008). Politischer Protest im Netz—Möglichkeiten und Grenzen der Mobilisierung transnationaler Öffentlichkeit im Zeichen digitaler Kommunikation. In F. Marcinkowski and B. Pfetsch (Eds.), *Politische Vierteljahresschrift, Sonderheft 42/2009*. Wiesbaden: VS Verlag für Sozialwissenschaften, 609-634.

Baringhorst, S., V. Kneip, and J. Niesyto (2007). Anti-Corporate Campaigns im Netz: Techniken und Praxen. *Forschungsjournal Neue Soziale Bewegungen, 20*(3), 49-60.

Bennett, L. W. (2004). Global media and politics: Transnational communication regimes and civic cultures. *Annual Review of Political Science, 7*, 125-148.

Bennett, L. W. (1990). Toward a Theory of Press-State Relations in the United States. *Journal of Communication, 40*(2), 103-125.

Bentivegna, S. (2002). Politics and new media. In L. A. Lievrouw and S. Livingstone (Eds.), *Handbook of new media*. London: Sage, 50-61.

Chadwick, A. (2011). *The Hybrid Media System*. Paper presented at the 6th ECPR General Conference, University of Iceland, Reijkavik.

Calhoun, C. (1998). Community without propinquity revisited: Communications technology and the transformation of the urban public sphere. *Sociological Inquiry, 68*(3), 373-397.

Castells, M. (2005). *Die Internet-Galaxie. Internet, Wirtschaft und Gesellschaft*. Wiesbaden: VS Verlag für Sozialwissenschaften.

R. de Wilde, N. Vermeulen, and M. Reithler (2003). *Bezeten van Genen. Background study Netherlands Scientific Coucil for Government Policy* (No. 117). The Hague: Sdu Publishers.

Fuchs, B. (2007). Bollywood-Fans meeting online and offline: Filmkultur im Internet, auf Stammtischen und bei Clubbings. *Zeitschrift für Kulturwissenschaften*, 2, 69-84.

Gerhards, J., and Schäfer, M. S. (2010). Is the internet a better public sphere? Comparing old and new media in the USA and Germany. *New Media and Society, 12*(1), 143-160.

Gillan, K. (2009). The UK anti-war movement online. *Communication and Society, 12*(1), 25-43.

Gonzalez-Bailon, S. (2009). Opening the black box of link formation: social factors underlying the structure of the web. *Social Networks, 31*(4), 271-280.

Koopmans, R., and A. Zimmermann (2003). *Internet: A new potential for European political communication?* Berlin: WZB.

Koopmans, R., and A. Zimmermann (2007). Visibility and communication networks on the internet: The role of search engines and hyperlinks. In C. de Vreese and H. Schmitt (Eds.), *A European public sphere: How much of it do we have and how much do we need?*. Mannheim: CONNEX, 213-264.

Ku, G., L.L., Kaid, and M. Pfau (2003). The impact of web site campaigning on traditional news media and public information processing. *Journalism and Mass Communication Quarterly, 80*(3), 528-547.

Lee, E.-J. (2005). Das Internet und die Entstehung einer Gegenöffentlichkeit: Politische Mobilisierung in Korea zwischen 2000 und 2004. *Zeitschrift für Parlamentsfragen, 36*(4), 808-823.

Leskovec, J., L. Backstrom, and J.Kleinberg (2009). *Meme-tracking and the dynamics of the news cycle.* Paper presented at the ACM SIGKDD International Conference on Knowledge Discovery and Data Mining (KDD), Paris.

Lester, L., and B. Hutchins (2009). Power games: environmental protest, news media and the internet. *Media, Culture and Society, 31*(4), 579-595.

Marr, M. (2005). *Internetzugang und politische Informiertheit. Zur digitalen Spaltung der Gesellschaft* (19 ed.). Konstanz: UVK.

Matzat, U. (2005). Die Einbettung der Online-Interaktion in soziale Netzwerke der Offline-Welt. Möglichkeiten der sozialen Gestaltung von Online-Grupen. In M. Jäckel and M. Mai (Eds.), *Online-Vergesellschaftung? Mediensoziologische Perspektiven auf neue Kommunikationstechnologien.* Wiesbaden: VS Verlag für Sozialwissenschaften, 175-199.

Mesch, G. (2007). Social diversification: a perspective for the study of social networks of adolescents offine and online. In K. I. Bildung (Ed.), *Grenzenlose Cyberwelt? Zum Verhältnis von digitaler Ungleichheit und neuen Bildungszugängen für Jugendliche.* Wiesbaden: VS Verlag für Sozialwissenschaften, 105-117.

Neuberger, C. (2009). Internet, Journalismus und Öffentlichkeit. Analyse des Medienumbruchs. In C. Neuberger, C. Nürnberg and M. Rischke (Eds.), *Journalismus im Internet.* Wiesbaden: VS, 19-104.

Oegema, D., J. Kleinnijenhuis, K. Anderson and A. v. Hoof (2008). Flaming and blaming. The influence of mass media content on interactions in online discussions. In E. A. Konijn, S. Utz, M. Tanis and S. B. Barnes (Eds.), *Mediated interpersonal communication.* New York: Routledge, 331-358.

Os, R. v., Wester, F., and Jankowski, N. W. (2007). Presentations of Europe on political party websites during the 2004 EP election campaign. *Javnost, 14*(2), 63-82.

Peng, L. (2005). *The first ten years of internet media in China.* Beijing: Tsinghua University Press.

Pfetsch, B. (2004). Geschlossene Gesellschaft? Akteursensembles und Akteursbewertungen in Pressekommentaren. In C. Eilders, F. Neidhardt and B. Pfetsch (Eds.), *Die Stimme der Medien. Pressekommentare und politische Öffentlichkeit in der Bundesrepublik.* Wiesbaden: VS Verlag für Sozialwissenschaften, 74-104.

Piotrowski, K. (2006). Online - Offline. Soziale Netzwerke von Jugendlichen. In A. Tillmann and R. Vollbrecht (Eds.), *Abenteuer Cyberspace: Jugendliche in virtuellen Welten.* Frankfurt a.M.: Peter Lang, 1-63.

Rethemeyer, R. K. (2007). Policymaking in the age of the internet: Is the internet tending to make policy networks more or less inclusive? *Journal of Public Administration Research and Theory, 17*(2), 259-284.

Richards, J. P., and Heard, J. (2005). European environmental NGOs: issues, resources and strategies in marine campaigns. *Environmental Politics, 14*(1), 23-41.

Rucht, D. (2004). The quadruple "A": media strategies of protest movements since the 1960s. In W. van de Donk, B. D. Loader, P. G. Nixon and D. Rucht (Eds.), *Cyperprotest. New media, citizens and social movements*. London: Routledge, 29-56.

Rucht, D., Yang, M., and Zimmermann, A. (2008). *Politische Diskurse im Internet und in Zeitungen: Das Beispiel Genfood*. Wiesbaden: VS Verlag für Sozialwissenschaften.

Schenk, M., and Wolf, M. (2006). Die digitale Spaltung der Gesellschaft: Zur politikorientierten Nutzung des Internet und der traditionellen Medien in den sozialen Milieus. In K. Imhof, R. Blum, H. Bonfadelli and O. Jarren (Eds.), *Demokratie in der Mediengesellschaft* (9 ed.). Wiesbaden: VS Verlag für Sozialwissenschaften, 239-260.

Smith, C. F. (2000). British political parties: continuity and change in the information age. In I. Horrocks, J. Hoff and P. Tops (Eds.), *Democratic Governance and New Technology: Technologically Mediated Innovations in Political Practice in Western Europe* London: Routledge, 72-87.

Stromer-Galley, J. (2000). On-line interaction and why candidates avoid it. *Journal of Communication, 50*(4), 111-132.

Vaisman, C. L. (2009). Public property media meets the online workers' union: the roles and influence of Israeli political blogs. *Megamot, 46*(1-2), 222-253.

van de Donk, W., Loader, B. D., Nixon, P. G., and Rucht, D. (Eds.). (2004). *Cyberprotest. New media, citizens and social movements*. London: Routledge.

Wolfsfeld, G. (1997). *Media and political conflict. News from the Middle East*. Cambridge: Cambridge University Press.

Wright, S. (2004). Informing, communicating and ICTs in contemporary anti-captialist movements. In W. van de Donk, B. D. Loader, P. G. Nixon and D. Rucht (Eds.), *Cyberprotest. New Media, Citizens and Social Movements*. London: Routledge, 77-93.

Yu, H. (2006). From active audience to media citizenship: the case of post-Mao China. *Social Semiotics, 16*(2), 303-326.

Zhou, Y., andMoy, P. (2007). Parsing framing processes: The interplay between online public opinion and media coverage. *Journal of Communication, 57*(1), 79-98.

Zimmermann, A. (2006). *Demokratisierung und Europäisierung online?* Freie Universität, Berlin.

Zimmermann, A., and Koopmans, R. (2010). Transnational political communication on the internet: Search Engine results and hyperlink networks. In R. Koopmans and P. Statham (Eds.), *The making of a European public sphere: Political communication and collective action in an era of European governance*. Cambridge: Cambridge University Press, 171-194.

3. Mediating Politics in Scotland: Information and Ideology

James Moir
University of Abertay Dundee, United Kingdom

Abstract: Much of the research in the field of political communication rests on foundational assumptions about how attitudes and behaviours relate to one another. Research that examines variation in political attitudes often presumes that they drive key behaviours such as voting patterns. This is often manifested through attempts to explain attitude variation through communication exposure and attention variables, as in research on media framing, or through the overall tone and content of political communication. This chapter seeks to problematize this linkage through an examination of a set of exemplars of political communication in the news media that exploits web-based interfaces. These are primarily drawn from BBC webpages because of the authoritative nature of this broadcaster in the UK and its in-depth coverage of Scottish politics. The aim is to provide a critique of cognitive approaches to political communication by considering the growth of this form of communication as part of a wider ideological association with neo-liberalism in which the individual is thought to access 'information' through various new media as the basis for action.

Keywords: opinion polling, web-based interfaces, news, attitudes, ideology

Introduction

It is evident that internet-based communication is transforming the political communication landscape. One issue that is of interest is the extent to which audiences engage with new media in understanding and evaluating political communication. This is particularly the case with respect to the treatment of politics as information within the news media. It is often the case that the treatment of politics here is one of communication that aids in the shaping of political attitudes and opinions. However, the linkage between forms of political communication such as, for example, blogs and tweets, and their persuasive effect in changing attitudes and opinions, is difficult to assess. Bull sums this up when he states, "Analysis of the major dimensions of traditional persuasive communication research—message source, message characteristics, message, receivers, and cognitive models of persuasion—would benefit greatly from the application of techniques used in the study of political language" (Bull, 2007: 273).

This is a laudable aim in that it yields new insights into how such communication 'works'. However, the study of political communication as cognition and persuasion can easily ignore ideological issues, and in particular the neo-liberal focus on the individual who is the subject of such communication. The atomism that can be argued to occur when politics is considered in such terms is occluded in the attempt to 'inform' the public.

The aim of this chapter is to offer an exploration of the ideological issues associated with the presentation of political information through examples drawn from web-based news media, especially through the BBC given its authoritative institutional status in the UK. The key issue under consideration is whether or not a communication model of the 'issues', in which messages are packaged, transmitted and received, is in force. It is argued that such a model is rooted in a neo-liberal ideology that rests on the idea of individuals accessing packaged information and weighing it up in a way that potentially influences their perceptions and voting behavior.

Packages, Polls and Perceptions

There is little doubt that online political news is now a central feature of the coverage of political communication. Indeed this form of coverage blurs the line between reporting and active participation. Many news websites, such as the BBC in the UK, offer extensive online coverage, particularly in the run-up to an election (Figure 1). These websites not only focus on providing reports of election coverage (i.e. the passive receipt of information) but also offer ways for users to engage in finding out more and testing and comparing their own political opinions. This is particularly germane to Scotland where there is considerable political differentiation, not only in relation to UK-wide party politics but also Scottish nationalist representation. Voters are therefore faced with the 'localization' of traditional UK-wide party politics as well as the issue of distinctive nationalist representation in the devolved Scottish parliament.

Figure 1: BBC Front Page for Coverage of the Scottish Parliamentary election, 18/09/11

An aspect of this coverage is the presentation of packaged information on political issues. These packages are designed to offer comparisons across the political party spectrum on a range of issues that are considered as being of importance to the electorate. Indeed what seems to be a key assumption is that individual voters are concerned with comparisons of the parties on various issues. Furnishing them with such 'information' is therefore paramount in order that they may weigh up the various stances on these issues in arriving at a particular voting intention (Figure 2). This offers a rationalist view of how voters respond to such information and is akin to a cognitive model of mind in which mental operations are involved in arriving at a single-minded view.

Figure 2: BBC Webpage Comparison of Election Issues, 18/09/11

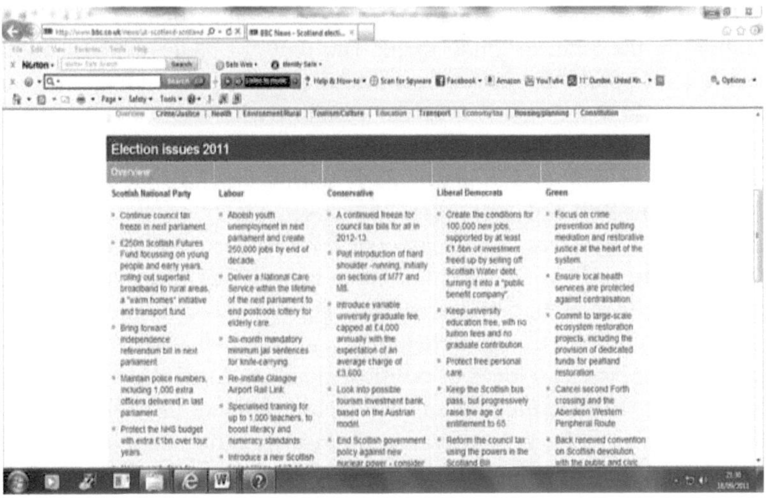

The packaging of these issues in this way is presented as a heuristic device to enable easy and straightforward cross-comparison. For example, in the above screenshot the positions of the five main political parties are outlined through brief bullet points. It is evident that there is a mix of UK-wide and local Scottish issues that are presented side-by-side (e.g. National Health Service budget, referendum on independence, university education, council tax, Glasgow airport rail link, etc.). However, in communicating complex political arguments in this way there is the danger of over-simplifying matters and of assuming that comparison rather than commitment is the over-riding concern. In other words, such packaging presents neat and tidy summaries without much in the way of a nuanced exploration of the issues. Moreover, it presents politics as if it were to be engaged in as a consumer choice in which comparisons are made, pros and cons are weighed up, and a selection made. Such a means of engaging in politics therefore turns it into a kind of online shopping experience, and one that is rooted in the individual psyche of the website viewer. Such websites are designed to be visually appealing and 'user-friendly' and therefore it is no wonder that they appear to portray political information in a 'packaged', easy-to-view and arguably simplified manner. To do justice to the intricacies and nuances of political arguments would be beyond the bounds of this kind of presentation, and yet the danger is that such a presentation runs the risk of over-simplifying matters.

It can be argued that far from helping users to gain a handle on political issues of the day, such websites may well lead users to consider themselves as viewers of products on shelves in a kind of 'political supermarket', with only the information on the label to guide them. This kind of static view of politics is rooted in the idea that the user requires information in order to help make up his or her mind on how the political parties stand or what they have to offer. It is unlikely that these websites are the only sources of mediated political information that people will consult, particularly during the run up to an election. Indeed, most people will watch or at least catch some sight of television programs showing political speeches and debates, read newspaper reports or see political leaflets and posters. However, the main point being made here is that in comparison to these other sources, a 'click-and-compare' mind-set is encouraged rather than considering politics as a live rhetorical and argumentative domain in which there are varying hues and tones of political standpoint and underlying ideological commitment. The gratification of such websites comes through their convenience since they provide easy-access, ready-to-hand information that is presented in a stylistically simple format (e.g. bullet point comparison) that in turn may run the risk of leading to a corresponding simplicity of political engagement. Quick and easy access to packaged, bite-sized pieces of information does not necessarily do justice to political ideas and debates.

Whilst such news websites offer relatively static information, it is nonetheless possible to take a more active stance with regard to the 'conversations' concerning comparisons of the policies of the major parties (Figure 3).

Figure 3: Compare the Parties Webpage, 18/09/11

Such comparisons again typically focus on thematic issues such as education, health and housing and again encourage a 'shopping basket' approach to understanding political matters. In the above example, the user is offered a slightly greater degree of interactivity through entering parties or topics on drop-down menus that allow for comparison (e.g. selection of first and second choice party and their positions on education, health etc.). Users can gain access to summaries of party policy updates, submit blogs or use a website Twitter feed. However, despite claiming to offer involvement in politics, the problem again is one of compartmentalization of issues and a lack of any sustained comment or overview of political party ideology. It would be hard not to come away with a view of political parties as simply offering policy commitments on an issue-by-issue or theme-by-theme basis without any connecting thread of ideological commitment. Moreover, such issues and themes tend to reify political engagement as weighing up one party's stand on, for instance, education, with another, or in arriving at some kind of aggregate view on the topics presented as being the basis for voting.

However, it is possible to take this personalized approach further still through Voting Advice Applications (VAA), which allow for comparison of one's own stance with the positions taken by political parties (Cedroni and Garzia, 2010). In effect this offers the user guidance on his or her political direction (Figure 4).

Figure 4: Scottish Vote Compass VAA, 18/09/11

Note that in the above front page entry of the website users are invited to 'express preferences' on a series of questions that will then allow for an unspecified matching process to take place that will show how a given user's profile matches up with the main political parties. What is presented is the idea that the expression of individual 'views' and 'opinions' are converted into indices of political alignment and that this in turn maps onto political allegiance in terms of voting behavior. The naturalization of this individualistic notion of political engagement is ideological in itself in that it reinforces a neo-liberal association with expression of views and choice. That political engagement may be more than the aggregate of individual views and that there may be a collective aspect to this process are in effect sidestepped. Instead, the user of such a website is confronted with a process of engagement that has an in-built ideological assumption but is disguised as a neutral mechanism by which the site acts as a broker between individual views and preferences and political party policies. This brokerage service is offered as tool or aid for finding one's political direction but is nonetheless far from being something that is simply in the hands of the user. The tool is in and of itself also something that shapes political engagement and how people view the nature of the political process. Such websites are therefore not simply a means of clarifying one's political commitment and direction; they are also active agents themselves in the political process.

By way of example (Figure 5) the following question provides an indication of the types of question and the mode of responding within the website.

Figure 5: An example question for the Scottish Vote Compass, 18/09/11

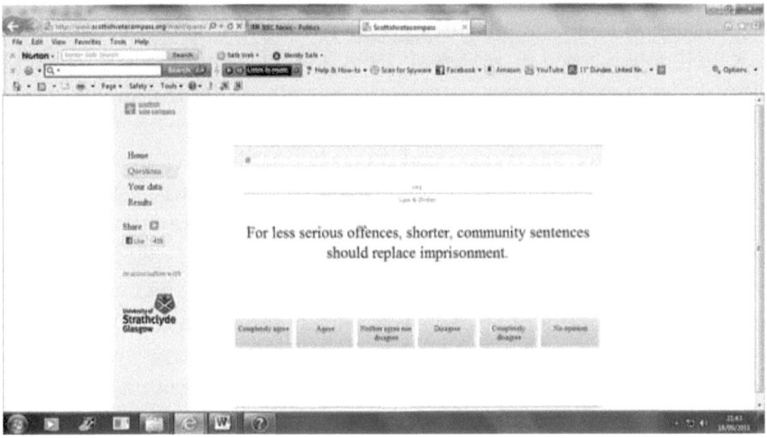

There are a couple of interesting features within this question and response format. Firstly, note the short nature of the statement that one is invited to respond to. This is typical of the kinds of statements that are presented throughout the series. Such statements are relatively simple with regard to their readability and overall length. In other words, they do not present much in the way of text and as such can be regarded as 'user-friendly', being easy to read and comprehend. Nevertheless, perhaps more so than their paper-based counterparts, such a presentation of short statements is problematic with a consideration of their lack of information or elaboration. In the example above, what might constitute "less serious offences" is arguably vague and this turn of phrase could be open to considerable leeway of interpretation. Secondly, note the response categories which are typical of Likert scales of this kind. Such a categorical response mode is in effect based upon the assumption that people are literally 'single-minded' on such issues. In other words, this mode of response may allow for easy translation into 'strength' of opinion, typically through conversion of responses into numerical ratings, but they do not permit people to hold contradictory or equivocal standpoints. As such they close off the very thing that political engagement can be said to be based upon: argumentation and challenge and even perhaps struggling with dilemmas and contradictory positions. So, it would appear that ease of online presentational format and a one-click response modality arguably make such websites complicit in promoting a one-sided, single-minded view for the voter.

Opinion polling and Opinionation

The sophistication and centrality of opinion polling and its representation in the media is well documented (e.g. Herbst, 1998; Lavrakas and Holley, 1990; Mancini, 1999). Most countries have witnessed a growth in the frequency of surveys, particularly those directly commissioned by the media. There has been a phenomenal growth in polling techniques and analyses, particularly through the use of computerized systems. However, notwithstanding the greater degree of sophistication of these polls they have remained rooted in certain key assumptions about the nature of voting psychology. Indeed, it could be argued that the use of these polls has served to promote an ideology of opinionation in which an inner state of mind (i.e. *having* an opinion) is taken as a warrant for action (i.e. casting a vote in an election). In this way the individual psychology—how someone thinks about a particular issue or political party—is seen as the focus of attention.

Thus *having* a set of opinions is conventionally associated with how people 'think' and with the way their thinking relates to their actions. To express an opinion is to possess the quality of having thought about some issue or other and to demonstrate that one *thinks* before engaging in the electoral process. This is the political actor whose actions are reasoned and have some basis which others can understand and assess. Thus expressions of opinions can be considered with respect to an association between how people account for matters and seeing their agency as belonging to sentient beings. In this way a major cultural dualism is maintained: taking people's 'outward' accounts and actions and considering these as representations of what they are like 'inside' as rational agents. However, opinionation can be considered as the ideological outcome of people's engagement within social practices rather than as something they bring to the political process as best sense representations of parties and their politics. The whole notion of opinionation is based upon viewing people as rational agents and derives from accountability within practices rather than from some sort of cognitive processing and exchange of representations.

A perceptual-cognitivist view of opinionation is, of course, the basis of much of the psychological investigation which trades on the assumption that people are concerned with interacting with one another in order to understand what they are thinking and feeling. This is part of a wider cultural commonplace, an 'inner/outer' dualism, and is integral to a range of social practices. The notion of these two separate realms is therefore a major rhetorical feature that is incorporated into how people interact with one another. It provides a means of trading on notions of 'sense-making' as well as the portrayal of people's inner mental states. There is a huge cultural imperative to be seen, to be intelligible and to be able to convey one's 'thoughts' in the form of judgments, reasons, and evaluations as the outcome of some kind of deliberative mental *process*. Seeking opinionative judgments about political parties and their politics implies the lone individual is bringing to bear his or her internal mental apparatus to these external matters in a way that involves some mental effort. And once having worked on it there is an outcome: in cognitive processing terms an 'input-process-output' model in which the outcome is voting behavior.

This model is oriented to reflect social practices that people engage in, in particular practices that encourage people to consider political engagement as an individual psychological act. Opinionation is something to which people orient themselves through how they portray their political views and actions. Notice here that orienting oneself to something does not necessarily involve an explicit mention of these psychological terms but rather of how people treat such a process as natural. In effect, this orientation is one of perceptual-cognitivism as process, as something that is normatively attended to as a means of accomplishing social practices, in this case the dynamics of online political engagement.

The nature of this engagement is founded upon opinionative practices that generate what individuals 'think' about certain political issues. In this way these issues are placed prior to this operation, being the "just-so" nature of what politics is about and of needing to be communicated and understood as the basis for individual voting intentions and behavior. In this communication model people are placed in a realm of political issues and a realm of mental operations that necessitate being brought together. The giving of opinions about these matters is associated with the psychological notion of *perception*, which is in turn related to *behavior* through a psychological linkage between the two. This assumption about political engagement positions persons as lone agents who reach 'decisions', *have* opinions, have deliberated matters to some extent, and who can account for how they vote in a way that 'makes sense' of the issues. We can see why a person might have a certain political opinion given their perception of political issues or party leaders and their performance. This is the basis of opinion polling and of course its representation in the media; people are assumed to want to know what others *think* about the political issues of the day.

As noted above, the testing of public opinion through polling typically trades on a sense-making rhetoric in which the mind is theorized as a mental system that operates upon an external reality in order to produce a rational account of it. However, the de-coupling of cognitive activity from opinionation as a social practice through the use of such polling methods is what makes this activity easier to portray as the outcome of some individualistic inner sense-making process. People's views are rendered as individual opinions, evaluations and judgments rather than as the result of an ideological practice rooted in the elicitation of such opinions. This sustains the view that we make electoral choices via our own individual opinions, and that this is no more than what is representative of the aggregate will of the electorate. Everything comes down to a matter of individual choice.

Although this kind of voluntarism and model of mind is very much the lifeblood of modern cognitive psychology, it can also be found in less explicit ways within other, more unlikely, realms which accord more theoretical weight to social practice. As Potter and Edwards (2001) point out, the social theorist Pierre Bourdieu may be considered an unlikely advocate of cognitivism but his theorization of *habitus* (e.g. Bourdieu, 1977; 1992) trades on an unreflexive 'inner/outer' dichotomy. This presupposes the development of a psychological system in which dispositions associated with membership of social and cultural groups come to generate practices, perceptions, attitudes and opinions. This system is then able to produce 'meaning' (i.e. make sense), store and process it. This in turn can be related to people's partisanship and voting behavior. Now whilst Bourdieu gives more weight to social practice and culture than to cognitive psychology, he cannot rid himself of this 'inner/outer' dualism and the reification of 'mind' as a perceptual system.

But whilst academic disciplines such as psychology and sociology trade on this dualism, it is also, of course, constructed and maintained as noted above in the everyday practice of opinion polling and its representation in the media. There is a commonplace discursive currency of reference to what people think about political matters and how they might or might not be influenced by what others think. This can be seen in the amount of media coverage given over to representations of political issues and opinion poll data. Much of this is presented in terms of opinion poll survey, pie charts and other visual techniques. Shifts in public opinion are charted, discussed and assessed. This becomes all the more intensive and frenetic at election time as poll information is updated on an almost daily basis. However, there has been an increasing trend to include polls in the coverage of political stories as a means of displaying public opinion towards 'live' issues and events. This is perhaps part of what can be considered a wider trend of 'lifestyle politics' (Shah *et al.,* 2007), in which people express their politics, not via the ballot box, but through their consumer choices. Political action in this sense is 'down' at the level of direction and interaction with others. However, the interplay between the public's interest in party politics and their issue-focus is perhaps less well understood. The explosion in media coverage of political issues through, for example, dedicated television news channels or interactive websites is a testament to the fact that political news is itself a product that is consumed in an increasingly on-demand fashion. Add to this the personalization or presidentialization of politics (Hazan, 1996; Maddens and Fiers, 2004; Mughan, 1993; Poguntke and Webb, 2005) as a feature of media focus in terms of popularity ratings and it appears to lend support for a move away from straightforward party political allegiance and towards individual opinionation. Indeed the presentation of polls is now a routine feature of political news (Figure 6).

Figure 6: BBC Poll Tracker Webpage, 18/09/11

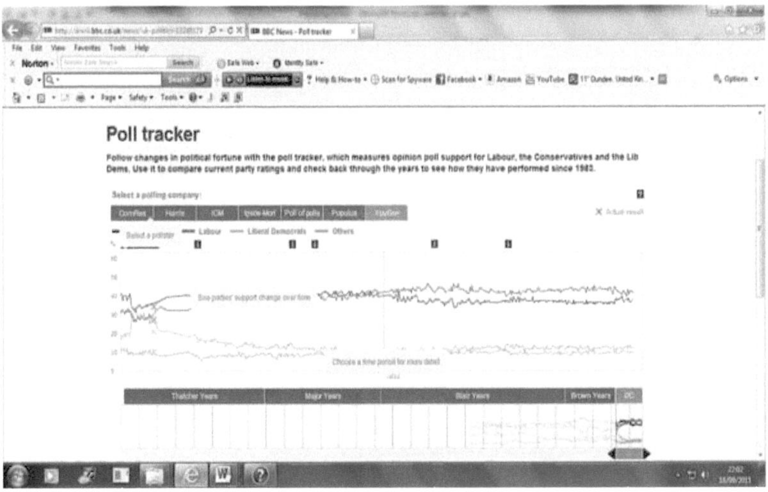

In the above example, the website visitor is presented with a representation of the percentage support the major political parties have attracted over time. The interactivity of the website can be accessed through the selection of a particular polling company or 'poll of polls', by selecting time periods to track changes in support, by selecting particular prime ministers and tracking changing support during their time in office, by clicking on a link to see how current percentage support may affect 'marginal' seats, or by clicking on another link to see how the votes percentages would translate into seats in parliament via a 'seat calculator'.

Whilst such information may be useful for political pundits and *their* interpretations of the changing fortunes of the parties, it is perhaps harder to see what voters would make of such information. There seems to be an assumption behind this sort of interactive provision that voters will want to know the minutiae of the percentage ups and downs of political parties in the polls. Indeed, it may even be assumed that this knowledge of aggregate support will in turn influence how voters themselves consider the parties at a given moment in the polls. In other words, there seems to be an assumption that the interactivity of this polling information will somehow influence voters' views of the parties. If this is correct then this assumption trades on the idea that people want to know what others think about the parties in terms of percentage expressed support, and that this will in turn affect their own views. However, there is danger in all of this that the polls begin to overtake the policies: that they come to be seen as an important driver of voter behavior.

However, it is also possible again to play a more active role in such polling through reacting to political communications in real time. This 'information' is treated as the expression of reactions with any fluctuations and changes as the result of some sort of social influence process. Figure 7 below is a case in point where a 'perception panel' is set up such that viewers can react in real time to a political speech and then see how others reacted overall, depending on which party they support.

Figure 7: BBC Perception Panel Webpage, 18/09/11

The viewer is able to 'see' others' opinions as reactions to the unfolding speech. This provides an interpretation of these opinions based on declared party allegiance and a kind of reflexive engagement with the process of opinionation. This is a case in which making opinions visible is taken as being just what politics is about. This is indeed short-term politics taken to a new level: instantaneous reaction to others and their opinions. In all of this there is the danger of reducing political matters down to the level of individual psychological operation. This results in a displacement of the *political* aspect of political opinions by a focus on opinionation. In other words, what the polls show about what others 'think' becomes privileged over a discussion of the actual political issues themselves.

Caveats, Counter-Arguments and Conclusions

The foregoing analyses and arguments have suggested that political news and other websites designed to engage voters are ideological in the way that they implicitly turn political engagement into a matter of personalized and individualized choice. This is expressed through the 'user-friendly' way that information is presented or the disguised ideological nature of the interactivity such that it occludes the underlying assumption that voter behavior is founded upon the aggregate of individual expressions of views and opinions.

There is a concern that the growth of new media has led to increasing audience fragmentation and the decline in social discourse. Indeed some have suggested that this trend "will deprive societies of shared information and experiences, leaving us less able to discuss issues, less exposed to diverse viewpoints, and more inclined to connect primarily, or only, with those with whom we agree (Bollinger (2010: 119). The argument here is that the danger to political engagement and democracy is not the long held traditional concern of 'supply-driven' potentially biased news coverage bur rather 'demand-driven' bias based on the consumption of news that aligns with pre-existing opinions. This selective exposure view (Stroud, 2007) of people's use of online news argues that people seek information that is consonant with their worldviews and avoid dissonant information. However, it has been found that people are willing to take information at face value regardless of the source of that information or political perspective (Murphy and Auter, 2012).

Taking the above into account, the argument being made here is that it is not simply the case that 'demand-driven' internet use is a threat to political engagement, but rather that the *design* of political news websites is based on the assumption that information and interactivity are necessarily key to individual choice. Such a critique is also founded upon the view that the landscape of new media is now becoming well-trodden ground, and moreover that it is one that is influencing the way in which people engage with politics and ultimately vote in elections. This assumption seems reasonable given that new media offer greater choice and control over content than traditional media such as newspapers or television. It is also the case that given that people's finite time and money to spend on media consumption, they will devote fewer resources to older media in favor of Internet-based media.

There is some support for the hypothesis that the Internet supplanting older forms of media. For example Dimick et al. (2004) have conducted some of the most extensive research on this topic and found that around a third of their respondents reported using newspapers and television less often once they started to use the Internet. Their study compared the gratifications by the Internet and traditional media. However, Gaskins and Jerit (2012) point out that whilst the replacement hypothesis has some support in terms of the Internet being considered as superior to traditional news media the picture is complicated by other studies that suggest that the Internet in some cases is considered to have a supplemental role. Their own extensive study does indicate that people are replacing traditional media sources, and in particular newspapers, with the Internet. They also note that most Internet usage involves websites rather than blogging, posting comments or sending political e-mails. In other words there is more of a passive usage than an active usage. Gaskins and Jerit argue that convenience and the capacity to personalize news consumption are the main factors in this. However they also point out that those who describe themselves as cable or mainstream television news viewers are less likely to say that they are replacing the Internet. Finally, the authors note that their study does not support the view that people are becoming less informed as they gravitate from mainstream media to the Internet or that replacement has a uniform effect on people's political knowledge.

These results are interesting in that they provide evidence of a complex and overlapping pattern of old and new media usage with respect to accessing political information. Gaskins and Jerit argue that the choice between the two forms of media depends on how well an outlet satisfies users' interests and needs. They also suggest that as the access to the Internet has become more commonplace, a more personalized form of engagement has arisen. However, perhaps most interesting of all is that their results indicate that political allegiance may affect replacement behavior with conservatives abandoning newspapers and liberals abandoning radio.

Taken as a whole, these results seem to suggest that there is not a move en masse towards replacing old media with new sources of political information. This may therefore at first seem to cast doubt on the thrust of the arguments made in this chapter. After all if people are using a variety of sources then they are more likely to be exposed to contradictory or at least different 'takes' on political issues. However, there is a counter-argument to be made. Note that Gaskins and Jerit focus on the gratifications of Internet news and political information with respect to convenience and control. This seems a perfectly reasonable research direction to pursue but what it does not do is hold up these apparently technical reasons to ideological scrutiny. This is something that has been developed in this chapter in that the aim has been to show how these are not just technical concerns and that behind them is a neo-liberal ideology of individual choice as being in and of itself the paramount concern The issue at stake here lies in examining how such convenience and control reflects and perhaps even amplifies the ideological focus of political engagement as something that occurs 'down' at the individual level. Indeed it is possible to speculate that the trend towards greater use of news and other political websites may well be an accelerant of this trend.

Therefore, this argument seeks to probe such gratifications through an examination of the ways in which what counts as, for example, being user-friendly, is not just about a set of indices that can be read off what people do in an online environment, but rather what such a focus tells us about the assumed nature of political engagement. Making things 'easy' to navigate in an online environment, giving the user various 'options' or including links and social networking tools may all seem to lead to the sense that interactivity is of paramount concern. However, the argument here is that this is ideological through and through, leading to the assumption that such interactivity is all there is to political engagement, and that it is nothing more than a kind of aggregate of individual opinions.

A 'single-minded', opinion-driven model of the person is implicitly presented within these various genres of new media with respect to political issues. Indeed, aggregates of what individual people 'think' about political matters are in turn presented as newsworthy. The extracts presented in this chapter illustrate the extent to which issues are converted in opinions for consumption in an ever more fast-paced and complex means of representation. This is ideological insofar as attempts are made to forge connections between message source and recipients' identifications with political parties. The interesting point here is that this kind of work could potentially come under the heading of 'message characteristics' within the communication model of persuasion preferred by Bull. However, this information is not a neutral presentation of political matters and indeed these various modalities of engagement are wedded to a neo-liberal view of the person as trying to make best sense of the issues as they are packaged.

The image of the website user is that of building and maintaining something like a loose-leaf folder of opinions that can be updated, and that informs voting behavior at a given point in time. However, it can be argued that this restricts the way people approach such matters as short-term reactions to political issues and does not allow for them to be in several minds about an issue. In other words, it assumes people have fairly clear and consistent views about these discrete issues and plays down political commitment to a party political doctrine. Rather than taking perception and its shaping of attitudes and opinions as the engine of political engagement we should consider how the media is implicated in the relentless pursuit of opinionation as a form of social life and the charting of its shifting patterns as the collective focus of attention.

References

Bollinger, L. (2010) *Uninhibited, Robust and Wide-Open: A Free Press for a New Century.* Oxford University Press: New York.

Bourdieu, P. (1977) *Outline of a Theory of Practice.* Cambridge; Cambridge University Press.

Bourdieu, P. (1992) *Language and Symbolic Power.* Polity Press.

Bull, P. (2007) Political language and persuasive communication. In *Language, Discourse and Social Psychology*, A. Weatherall, B. M. Watson and C. Gallois (eds), Basingstoke, Hampshire, U.K. and New York, U.S.A.: Palgrave.

Cedroni, L. and Garzia, D. (2010) *Voting Advice Applications in Europe: The State of the Art*, Napoli: ScriptaWeb.

Dimmick, J., Chen, Y., and Li, Z. (2004) Competition between the Internet and Traditional News Media: The Gratification Opportunities Dimension. *Journal of Media Economics*, 17, 19-34.

Gaskins, B. and Jerit, J. (2012) Internet News: Is it a Replacement for Traditional Media Outlets? *The International Journal of Press Politics*, 17, 2, 190-213.

Hazan, R.Y. (1996) Presidential parliamentarism: direct popular election of the prime minister. *Electoral Studies* 15, 21-38.

Herbst, S. (1998) *Reading Public Opinion. How political actors view the democratic process.* Chicago, Chicago University Press.

Lavrakas, P. and Holley, J. and Miller, P. (1990) (Eds.). *Polling and Presidential Election Coverage,* Newbury Park, CA, Sage.

Maddens, B. and Fiers, S. (2004) The direct PM election and the institutional presidentialisation of parliamentary systems. *Electoral Studies,* 23, 769-93.

Mancini, P. (1999) New frontiers in political professionalism. *Political Communication,* 16, 231-46.

Molder, H. te and Potter, J. (2005) (eds.) *Conversation and Cognition.* Cambridge: Cambridge University Press.

Mughan, A. (1993). Party leader and presidentialism in the 1992 election: A post war perspective. In David Denver, Pippa Norris, Colin Rallings, and David Broughton (Eds.), *British Elections and Parties Yearbook, 1993.* Hemel, Hempstead: Harvester Wheatsheaf, 193 -204

Murphy, J. C. and Auter, P.J. (2012) The Politics of Source: How the Credibility of a News Source Changes Based on the Political Perception of Blogs. *American Communication Journal*, 14, 1, 1-17.

Poguntke, T. and Webb, P., (2005) (Eds.) *The Presidentialization of Politics in Democratic Societies*. Oxford: Oxford University Press.

Potter, J. and Edwards, D. (2001) Sociolinguistics, Cognitivism and Discursive Psychology. In N. Coupland, S. Sarangi and Ch. N. Candlin (eds.) *Sociolinguistics and Social Theory.* Harlow, Essex: Pearson Education, 88-103.

4. Online news media and the limits of the alternative public sphere: the case of Zimbabwe

Tendai Chari
University of Venda, South Africa

Abstract: Online media have reconfigured relations between the state and the citizen globally. In Zimbabwe, restrictive legislation resulted in the constriction of media space, prompting the mushrooming of online publications operating from outside the country. These online publications have become platforms for undercutting the state's monopoly in the media, thus ensuring that views that counter state hegemony are guaranteed space. However, the real impact of these 'new public spheres' on the Zimbabwean society in general and the democratization discourse in particular remains a matter of conjecture rather than scholarly inquiry. This paper assesses the extent to which these online publications have constituted alternative spaces for the mediation of national discourses. Data were elicited through focus group interviews, in-depth interviews and textual analysis. The paper argues that professional shortcomings and a combination of technical, social and economic factors limiting Internet access prevent online publications from becoming a genuine alternative public sphere.

Keywords: alternative public sphere; consumption habits; democratization; online publications; participation; Zimbabwe

Introduction

The technological revolution of the mid-1990s witnessed the phenomenal mushrooming of online publications in Zimbabwe at the turn of the millennium. Stringent media laws, a debilitating economic and political crisis epitomized by hyperinflation, high unemployment rates and general social decay resulted in the closure of a number of privately owned newspapers. This triggered an exodus of journalists, who emigrated to neighboring countries, mainly South Africa and Botswana, as well as European countries and the United States of America. Some of the journalists started online publications with a distinct focus on Zimbabwe to act as outlets for alternative views. Some of these publications carried the mantle of closed newspapers, albeit online.

This article examines the role of online publications in the democratization project in Zimbabwe in order to assess the extent to which they have constituted real 'alternative public spheres' in the post-colonial context. The study examines consumption habits of online publications by Zimbabwean citizens living in the country, their perceptions of online publications and the roles they ascribe to them. Ethical practices that act as obstacles to the execution of these media's democratic mandate are also considered. The study hopes to open pathways to reconsider the democratic imperatives of online media in an African context. A key question spotlighted in this paper is whether online publications are able to broaden the democratic spaces or are simply 'private spheres' to a few who are able to access them.

The Media-State Interface since 1980

In 1980, Zimbabwe inherited from Rhodesia a fairly diversified media characterized by a vibrant state-owned media and a blossoming privately-owned press which reflected the dominance of white capital in the economy. For the first ten years of independence the new ZANU PF government, under the leadership of Robert Mugabe, maintained a dual media policy characterized by a tight grip on broadcasting and "tactical indifference" towards the press (Chuma, 2007; Ronning and Kupe, 2000). Repressive laws which had been used by the colonial regime to muzzle the media remained on the statutes, but were rarely used. No fundamental restructuring or nationalization of either the economy or the media was to be undertaken consistent with the policy of reconciliation.

The second decade of independence (1990-1999) witnessed phenomenal growth in the newspaper industry in the country. The absence of a codified media policy and a liberal economic environment occasioned by the state's adoption of the IMF and World Bank supported the Economic Structural Adjustment Policy (ESAP) in 1990, as well as the emergence of a vibrant civil society yearning for alternative outlets to voice concerns about the harsh economic conditions occasioned by ESAP, spurred the growth in the private media sector. These newspapers were instrumental in galvanizing marginalized groups and civil society around issues of governance, politics and economics (Chuma 2007).

The formation of the *Daily News* in 1999 by the Associated Newspapers of Zimbabwe (ANZ) and a consortium of local and foreign investors (Waldahl 2004; Ronning and Kupe, 2000) marked a watershed in the social and political history of the country. This also coincided with the formation of a formidable opposition political party, the Movement for Democratic Change (MDC), with roots in the trade union movement. The deleterious effects of a government-led land reform program triggered the worst economic hardships in the history of the country. The *Daily News* and its "allies" in the private press carried the mantle of venting popular discontent, inevitably colliding with a weakening state.

Government promulgated an array of stringent media laws such as the Access to Information and Protection of Privacy Act (AIPPA, 2002) and the Broadcasting Services Act (2001), in order to tame the privately owned media.

The Daily News and its sister publication, *The Daily News on Sunday*, refused to comply with the requirements of AIPPA and were closed in September 2003, resulting in the constricted media space in the country.

A restructuring exercise in the public media and the closure of privately owned newspapers due to a combination of political and economic factors drove thousands of journalists into exile in neighboring African countries, Europe and the United States of America, where they started online publications, websites and pirate radio stations. Spurred by technological convergence, these media coalesced into one big block representing opinions alternative to those of the state.

Although the popularity of these online publications and websites, both inside the country and abroad, is apparent, very little is known about their real impact on the country's body politic, and claims that they are opening the country's democratic spaces have not been tested. The few studies available (Mabweazara, 2011; Moyo, 2007; Morgan, 2004) focus on their production structures and journalistic practices. This study, therefore, seeks to fill the gap pertaining to the democratic potential of these online publications by examining the manner in which readers interact with and consume them.

Zimbabwe's Online Media Context

Zimbabwe has made significant strides in the development, application and use of new communication technologies. In 2005, the government adopted an ICT policy whose vision and mission is to transform the country into a knowledge-based society by the year 2020 (Isaacs, 2007; Government of Zimbabwe, 2005). There is currently one fixed telephone network subscriber, the state-owned TelOne, and three mobile subscribers, one of which is state owned and two of which are privately owned. In addition, there are three public data service providers, one state-owned broadcasting signal transmission and one public broadcaster. There are over 30 Internet Service Providers (IPSs) in the country.

While the fixed phone sector has experienced marginal growth, the mobile phone sector has experienced phenomenal growth, with subscriber base increasing from 2 million to 6.9 million by mid-2010 (Mansfield 2011). The country's tele-density increased from 67% in 2010 to 75% by December 2011 (*The Sunday Mail* 2012). The country ranks number 10 in Africa in terms of Internet use, with the number of users estimated to be about 1,481,000 (13% of the population) (Internetworldstats 2010).

However, access to the Internet is hindered by, among other factors, an antiquated telecommunication infrastructure, prohibitive costs, and low electricity generation. This often results in a malfunctioning Internet system. Costs of accessing the Internet are very high relative to people's earnings. As of June 2011, rates for accessing the Internet in the capital city, Harare, ranged between USD1 and USD1.40 for 30 minutes. This is very high considering the fact that the average worker in the country takes home between USD165 and USD250, amounts which are far below the poverty datum line, which is about USD500 (*The Standard,* 4 September, 2010).

Media and Democracy Nexus: Conceptual Considerations

Although there is an outpouring of literature on the broad subject of media and democracy (see Curran, 1991; Kean, 1991; Ronning and Khupe, 2000), literature on online news media and democracy, particularly on Africa, is rather fragmented. A cross-cutting feature of literature on media and democracy is its location of the mass media in the realm of the "public sphere", implying that the media are, in principle, open "to all receivers and senders" and are answerable to the wider society (McQuail, 1994: 11). Online media lend themselves to this kind of analysis, not least because of their vast potential to facilitate many-to-many communication, but also their capacity to accommodate marginalized voices, what some scholars refer to as "alternative public spheres" (Atton, 2002; Sandoval and Fuchs, 2010).

Habermas (cited by McCarthy, 1989: xi) conceives the public sphere as the space between civil society and the state, where "critical and robust discussion of general matters is institutionally guaranteed". He notes that the liberal public sphere developed in specific historical circumstances of a developing market economy. In such a public sphere, state authority was monitored through informed and critical discourse by the people. This bourgeoisie "public sphere" was exclusive of other "classes of men". The resultant intertwining of state and society in the 19th and 20th centuries led to the collapse of the liberal bourgeoisie public sphere, which was later replaced by the public sphere of the welfare state. It is significant to note how the expansion of the public sphere is reciprocally linked with economic progress and distribution of wealth. However, the fact remains that the "post-liberal" era envisaged by Habermas, where the public sphere is inclusive of all and sundry, is still utopian in much of the developing world.

Questions have been raised about the appropriateness of referring to newspapers and television as "mass media" given the fact that in many developing countries the "mass media" remain inaccessible to the generality of the masses, or are used less as organs of public information than "technologies for managing consensus and promoting consumer culture" (McCarthy, 1989: xii). Without a critical mass of middle class people, how appropriate can the concept of "public sphere" be applicable to the developing world, particularly Africa?

Some scholars argue that technological developments of the 1990s, such as the Internet, have given the concept of the public sphere a new lease of life (Kellner, n.d.; Dott, 1998). Kellner argues that in contemporary high-tech societies, there is a significant expansion and re-definition of the public sphere which goes beyond the one conceived by Habermas. For technological optimists like Kellner, this expanded public sphere is a site of "information, discussion, contestation, political struggle and organization that includes the old and the new 'new cyberspace', as well as the interactivity of everyday life" (Kellner, n.d.: 12). The implication for this is a reformulation of the concept of the public sphere.

Chae (2005) sought to understand the culture and social conditions of the public sphere in the United States of America through an analysis of public forums in twenty-five U.S. online newspapers. He describes online public forums as a "conversational arena" in which people talk with each other in public settings about public issues (2005: 3).

His argument that the culture of the public sphere differs in accordance with the development of the socio-economic structure is instructive (Chae, 2005: 26). Thus, the culture of the public sphere of a country, such as the U.S., which is the most advanced information society, cannot be the same as that of a developing, socially bifurcated and economically struggling country like Zimbabwe.

A study by Morris (2002), which compared coverage of American politics by "new" and traditional media, observed that more than the traditional media, the new media tend to sensationalize issues, resulting in the erosion of public trust for the new media. The observation by Morris that the presentation of political news has been changing because new media lend themselves to sensationalism is instructive. The present study, however, differs from Morris's in the sense that it focuses on the audience's experiences with new media in order to understand the utility value of these media in democratization.

To date, much scholarly work on how online media impact on democracy has largely focused on the experiences of the established democracies of the West, while similar studies on the African continent are far in between. The few studies available have tended to focus on how new media are impacting on journalistic practices, rather than on the broader society (see Burger, 2005; Mabweazara, 2010). The few existing studies do not delve deeper into the contributions of new media in national discourses since they narrow their focus to institutional aspects of these online media (Moyo, 2007).

Online Media: 'Alternative Public Spheres' or "Private Spheres"?

The Internet and other "new" communication technologies have been described as "alternative public spheres" on account of their capacity to give space to previously marginalized voices. However, there is lack of consensus on the meaning of the term 'alternative media', with some scholars defining it as non-mainstream media that are independently operated. These include community-focused media such as pirate radio stations, online discussion boards and broadcast companies and publications owned by activists (Coyer *et al:* 2007). O'Sullivan *et al.* (1983: 8) defines alternative media as "those forms of mass communication that avowedly reject or challenge established and institutionalized politics, in the sense that they all advocate change in society, or at least a critical assessment of traditional values". For O'Sullivan et al., alternative media (also referred to as "radical" or "underground media") stand in opposition to mainstream productions by representing political and social doctrines that "lie outside the defined limits of parliamentary consensus and debate" (ibid.). Lewis (cited by Banda, 2006: 10) argues that alternative media serve a specific ideological purpose and identifies, among other things, access by minorities, decentralized production and interactivity as some of the key tenets of alternative media. Couldry and Curran (cited by Moyo, 2007: 87) conceive alternative media as media whose production challenges 'concentration of media power, whatever forms those concentrations may take in different locations'. Thus, Couldry and Curran accentuate structure rather than professional practices as the defining features of alternative media.

Sandoval and Fuchs (2010: 141) warn against being too optimistic about concepts like "civil media", "community media", "alternative media", "grassroots media", "participatory media" or "participatory culture". They argue that in contemporary society, which is characterized by structural inequalities, our understanding of alternative media is insufficient. They conceive "alternative media" as "critical media" (ibid.). The argument that democracy should not only be limited to the political realm, but that it also embrace other systems like an economy based on participatory ownership and decision-making is plausible. One finds merit in the view that alternative media should be committed to pointing out the unequal, dominative and non-participatory democracy. This means that by providing "critical content" alternative media will be able to advance social transformation and contribute towards the attainment of genuine democracy. This is because critical media expresses progressive political interests and acts as an outlet for suppressed possibilities. Sandoval and Fuchs (2010: 148) argue that:

> "...the discourse on alternative and participatory media should be situated within the context of the analysis of capitalism. Capitalism brings about structural inequalities that shape the limits and potentials of alternative media projects".

Sandoval and Fuchs's conceptualization of alternative public spheres appears much broader and devoid of the sentimentalism associated with technological determinists who often view technology as "an emancipator", which, by itself, will bring freedom, prosperity and enlightenment (Lenert, quoted in Mabweazara, 2010: 17).

Methodological Discussion and Data Collection

Data for the study were elicited through a focus group discussion, in-depth interviews and textual analysis. The focus group comprised a group of 18 part-time journalism students at a privately-owned college in the capital Harare. Their ages ranged between 21 and 40. Given the variability of access to online media among the Zimbabwean population and the complexity of the issues under discussion, journalism students were deemed appropriate to participate in the focus group discussion. Many had the experience of reading news online and were able to present their responses articulately and in a more focused way. The "cross-flow of communication" (Darlington and Scott, 2002: 61) arising from group interaction enabled the author to glean in-depth qualitative data on opinions, feelings and experiences of the participants about the democratic potential of online media.

In order to obtain more focused responses on consumption patterns of online publications, in-depth interviews were held with twelve purposively selected readers of online publications who had not participated in the focus group. The idea was to access deeper personal experiences and insights about the topic at hand beyond the influence of dominant views. Thus, the in-depth interviews were meant to corroborate data obtained from the focus group, as well as obtain broader perspectives on consumption practices of online publications and their democratic potential. As pointed out above, the use of purposive sampling was justified on the grounds that access to online media is uneven in the country and largely confined to urban areas. Patton (1990: 81) points out that the logic and power of purposive sampling lies in selecting information rich cases that help to address the research questions.

In addition, data pertaining to the ethical practices of online publications were retrieved from some of the online publications' websites and subjected to textual analysis. The idea was not only to confirm the views of participants in the focus group and in-depth interviews, but also to generate new data that could help ascertain and evaluate the ethical practices of online publications and the implication on the public sphere. Data from the focus group and in-depth interviews were transcribed, coded thematically and interpreted using the hermeneutic approach (Kvale, 1996), while textual data were content analyzed.

Online Media Consumption Practices

Findings from the in-depth and focus group interviews indicate that the most popular online publications and websites are *Zimsituation.com, NewZimbabwe.com, ZimOnline.com*, *Zimdaily.com* and *TheZimbabwetimes.com*. Levels of awareness about the existence of online publications and news web sites available in Zimbabwe are very low. This could be linked to the erratic and almost opportunistic access to the Internet reported by the respondents. Some of the respondents said they only read online news after being tipped by friends about a 'juicy' story online or if they come across an interesting story while sending email or browsing the Internet. The 'opportunistic' access to online news is reflected in the following statements by some respondents:

> "I only read online news publications when I go to the University of Zimbabwe where I can access the Internet for free. If I do not go to the University I will not be able to read online news."

These statements suggest that the utility of online publications in Zimbabwe is mediated by a complex web of factors linked to the economy. Limited access to the Internet and the prohibitive costs of accessing news online implies that online news media have a limited impact on Zimbabweans residing in the country. This is consistent with earlier literature which showed that online media have a limited impact on democracy (Norris and Curtice, 2005; Moyo, 2011).

The fact that some respondents merely stumble on some stories while searching for other information also suggests that online news stories do not rank that highly in the priority lists of people who access the Internet in Zimbabwe. This is perhaps linked to the fact that many people are unemployed (the unemployment rate is over 80%) and would be looking for jobs, trying to link up with relatives and friends in the Diaspora, or trying to get some other information which has an immediate impact on their socio-economic conditions.

Even those who have access to the Internet at work may not have enough time to read stories because they would be too busy to do so and would rather go on email first before reading the news. A certain university where this author worked for close to ten years had a policy of blocking the Internet during working hours (8:00 AM to 4:00 PM) and unblocking it during lunch hour (1:00 PM to 2:00 PM). The author observed that immediately after the expiration of the

Internet 'embargo', people would start by checking and sending emails before doing anything else, hoping to beat the load shedding time, which was usually around 5:00 PM. This practice was still in place at the time of writing and the author observed that a number of lecturers had laptops and 3G modems in order to circumvent this problem. What is therefore instructive is that limited access to the Internet has a strong bearing in shaping online news consumption habits. This means that economic imperatives are a key determinant on the impact of the online publications' potential to promote democratization in contemporary Zimbabwean society.

As a result of the limited access to the Internet, the downloading of news stories from websites and reading them later is now a common phenomenon. This came out clearly during the focus group discussions. Respondents who access the Internet at work find it difficult to read news online during lunch hour because most people would be using the Internet, resulting in the system slowing down. Cost is not necessarily the most crucial factor in inhibiting people from reading news online. Even those who have easy access to the Internet at work said that reading news usually comes last after checking email, jobs or study opportunities.

During the height of Zimbabwe's economic crisis in the late 2000s, there was a popular joke that everybody, including people who were working, was looking for a job and that the Internet was the first port of call if ever the opportunity presented itself. It was common for employers to deliberately limit access to the Internet for their employees as a strategy of limiting the "brain drain". There was speculation among workers that the Internet policy of the university mentioned above was a strategy to limit the employees' access to job opportunities abroad. This suggests that while people would have liked to read online publications, prevailing socio-economic conditions in the country, where politics of the belly dominated, disengaged the citizenry from national debates such as those championed by online publications.

In terms of content, some respondents who read online publications, cited sensational content, e.g. rumors and gossip about celebrities, sports personalities and politicians, as things that exert a strong magnetic pull on them. Other than sleazy news, online publications are able to report on controversial topics shunned by the mainstream press because of the restrictive legal environment which imposes stiff penalties for "falsehoods", or libelous stories. One respondent talked about online publications as "having more leverage to report on sensitive stories because they operate outside the perimeter of legal restrictions such as AIPPA and POSA". In addition, they are also better positioned to report breaking news since they have a shorter news cycle than mainstream media, which would have to wait until the next day to report on an event. This means that their information is considered "more up to date" than that of mainstream newspapers.

A case in point is the reporting of the 2008 elections, when online publications became part of what has been described as a 'parallel market of information' (Moyo, 2010: 54). News websites and cell phones moved in to fill the gaps left by the mainstream media as a result of an embargo imposed on reporting the presidential results. One such blogger, The Bearded Man (http://thebeardeman-blogspot.com/2008/03/Zimbabwe-election-results.2008.html) compiled the running tallies of election results before they were officially announced, thus undercutting the mainstream press.

What is instructive is to note that even this "positive" attribute of online publications was not necessarily shared by all the respondents since some cited the "sensational nature" of online publications and their tendency towards gossip as a negative attribute. In the words of one male participant in the focus group interview, "these gossip stories tend to undermine the credibility of online publications". This shows that just like mainstream newspapers, the context in which online news media are consumed is complex, and so is their readership. In order to understand their actual impact on democracy in Zimbabwe, one would require a thorough investigation of the myriad of complex socio-economic, ideological and political factors which mediate their consumption.

Online civic engagement

Gauging from the views of participants in the focus group discussions, participation in online chat forums and opinion columns among respondents is very low, mainly due to lack of time. The same reasons attributable to a low readership of online news (lack of adequate access to the Internet, load shedding, high costs) were also cited as reasons for not participating in online chat forums. The following statements from some respondents shed light on the consumption habits of online publications:

> "I have never participated in online forums because most of the time when I am using the computer there will be several people waiting to use the same computer."

> "I never participate because our computers are so slow. At times I get to hear about what is online newspapers through friends who have better access to the internet."

> "When I go to the Internet Cafes, I start by checking my emails. Usually the time is not even enough to reply all emails because I don't check my email every day. This means that I have no time at all to participate in online debates even if I would have wanted."

These statements show that lack of participation in online chat forums is linked to resource constraints (e.g. shortage of computers connected to the Internet, high costs, shortage of time), technical reasons (such as slow speed of the Internet as a result of a smaller bandwidth) and the actual content of online publications (i.e. stories that do not reflect the reality on the ground). The low levels of participation on online chat forums means that the range of views discussed on these forums is limited, thereby making them a medium for the privileged elite who have access to the Internet. Interactivity and the potential for a cross pollination of ideas is the hallmark of online media but when the majority of people are shut out for one reason or the other, it means that the medium becomes a preserve of the few.

The democratization potential of online publications

Opinions on the role of online publications in the democratization process of the country are rather mixed. While the majority of the respondents accentuated the limitations faced by online publications in prosecuting their democratic mandate, the minority view online publications as playing a positive role. Some respondents in the interviews said they regard online publications as alternative spaces for different voices, and that they set the agenda for mainstream newspapers, while also acting as surveillance antennas on behalf of the citizens. The following statements are illustrative of these roles:

> "I would say to a certain extent they have expanded the media space in terms of being outlets for voices oppositional to the Zanu PF government. The only problem I have is that their news is generally more of the same stuff and more of the same voices. They have not made attempts to deal with various issues dogging the nation as they have tended to restrict their news to the same handful of (sic) political protagonists. What I would have expected are well researched stories that are diverse and inclusive of the broader citizenry."

> "Most of these online publications carry mostly political stories while other important issues like health, development etc. are marginalized. As a result, they tend to be read by a small fraction of the society."

> "They have the potential to become genuine alternative platforms if only there is connectivity on a nationwide scale. As it stands, connectivity and logistical problems of acquiring the computer and the cost of paying for the computer and the cost of paying for the internet restrict online news publication to a few well- to-do people."

These sentiments suggest that the democratic role of online publications is viewed as constrained by the lack of diversity in their content, the limited range of discourses (e.g. obsession with politics as mentioned by one of the respondents) and their elite orientation, both in terms of content and target. As observed earlier, the mission and vision statements foreground the desire to fill the lacuna left by closed mainstream newspapers, showing that the content of online publications and websites is not different from that of privately owned print newspapers. As a result, their ability to transcend the polarization which characterizes the public and privately owned media is limited.

Although the online publications publish sensitive political stories, which mainstream newspapers would hesitate to publish because of harsh media laws, their political ideologies and the manner in which they approach key national issues such as the economy, land reform and others is not very different from mainstream privately owned newspapers. A few respondents mentioned the failure by these online publications to operate above political polarization as a huge inhibition to their democratic mandate. There had been an expectation that national discourses would transcend the ruling party-opposition dichotomy, but this has not happened, resulting in the neglect of views falling between the two sides.

It was observed that the 'no-holds barred' approach of online publications acts as a bait for readers since they are able to publish sensational stories that 'tickle' a news starved audience. This sentiment was echoed by one respondent who said:

> "I like reading online publications because they tell it like it is. They do not hold back any information. We now know who among our ministers, is corrupt, who is having an extramarital affair. Even those who have HIV or Aids, we now know them. We would have never read such stories in The Herald."

This implies that, while some of the stories covered by the online publications might be interesting to the public, they would not necessarily be in the public interest because they do not enhance the informational base of the citizens, but are meant to increase ratings in a market characterized by stiff competition. Elsewhere, the ability of new media to present news in a manner that is more appealing to the reader has been noted (Morris, 2002). Morris notes how online media in the United States of America are attracting more readers because of their 'unique' packaging of the news, which borders on sensationalism, dramatization and conflict, in order to attract more audiences and make profit (7).

Some citizens perceive online publications as 'antennas' to alert citizens about the goings-on in the dark alleys of officialdom, particularly those stories that mainstream newspapers would not be able to report on for fear of reprisals. Such issues include allegations of human rights violations during the 2008 elections, allegations of killings in the Marange Diamond fields and other corruption scandals involving government officials. One respondent had this to say:

> "It is through online publications that we got to know about the killings at the Marange diamond fields. The state media was silent about the whole issue. Online websites picked the story and it was broadcast to the whole world."

Thus, online publications were able to put the country on the international spotlight during national crises such as the 2008 cholera crisis. This resulted in an overwhelming humanitarian response by the United Nations agencies and other international donors.

Besides monitoring institutions of the state and ensuring accountability, online publications are also perceived as agenda setters on important national developments, particularly breaking news. The mainstream media take a cue from online publications, particularly on the sensational news discussed above. A case in point is Prime Minister Morgan Tsvangirai's involvement in a car accident in March 2009, in which his wife died. Online publications picked up the story before the mainstream media could publish it.

In some situations, the mainstream media are forced to respond to a story that would have appeared in an online publication, either to "set the record straight" or refute it. Examples include rumors about the alleged ill health of President Mugabe, which appeared in some online publications in September 2010. The online publications alleged that Mugabe was "losing the battle against cancer and had started looking for a successor". Mugabe later dismissed the rumor when he was interviewed by Reuters (Chinaka, 2010). However, online news publications only set the news agenda on stories that seemingly interest the public (sensational stories, gossip and rumors) rather than on substantive stories that enhance democracy such as economic policy, governance issues, indigenization policy, the constitution-making process, the land issue and others.

It could also be argued that there is a reciprocal agenda setting process which takes place between the mainstream media and online publications. For serious national issues, online publications collect stories (sometimes unedited) from mainstream media and post them on their websites. Sometimes they publish opinion polls on a matter that could have been covered in the mainstream media. There is, therefore, a complex network of relationships that are created between online media and mainstream media and also among online publications themselves.

Ethical pitfalls and implications for democracy

In spite of their great potential to open spaces for voices different from that of the state, there are concerns that online publications fail to adhere to basic journalistic ethics and professional standards, thus undermining their contribution to the democratization process. Respondents blamed online publications for various transgressions, the main ones being inaccuracies, falsehoods, lack of balance and objectivity, use of anonymous sources, to mention but a few. The following statements are instructive:

> "Online publications do not have enough correspondents in the country to monitor what will be happening. They mostly employ freelance journalists, who are out to make quick money by publishing as many stories as they can, even if they have not cross-checked the veracity of those stories."

> "The internet is a jungle where anyone can write anything and get away with it. Of the online publications I have read, ethics seem to be very low on their priority list. Some of their stories are too sensational, and they seem to derive pleasure in maligning certain personalities without giving the individual concerned the right of reply, which is a fundamental aspect of ethical journalism."

It is noteworthy that mistrust of online publications primarily emanates from perceptions about their organizational practices, their style of journalism and actual content. During the interviews, some respondents claimed online publications face difficulties in cross-checking stories and sometimes rely on relatives, acquaintances and friends for news tips and information about what is happening in different parts of the country. That online publications are viewed as detached from reality because they are domiciled abroad echoes an observation made by Lush and Kupe (2005: 10) that

> "The further you are from the story, the more difficult it is to be objective in tune with the often complex dynamics of a story unfolding thousands of kilometers away…Distance alone makes it extremely difficult for journalists outside the country to fill the information void created by the state's propaganda machinery…"

The tendency to rely on informal sources for news has been the online publication and news website's Achilles heel on several occasions. A case in point is the publication by ZimOnline.com of a story in February 2005, alleging that three journalists working for foreign news organizations, Brian Latham, Angus Shaw and Jaan Raath, had been arrested by government police for practicing journalism without being accredited by the Media and Information Commission (MIC). The story was found to be untrue and Zimonline.com retracted and apologized.

Although Zimonline.com retracted the story, millions of people had read it and most probably believed it. Thus, Arrant (2000: 3) notes that 'the crushing demand for fresh news items to fill up airtime twenty-four hours a day, makes accuracy and balanced reporting more difficult. Such challenges manifested themselves during the March 29, 2008 harmonized elections when online publications were competing to be the first with the news of the results. In the process, some of them became hostages of the rumor mill that Harare, the capital city, is famous for.

A textual analysis of some websites shows that during the March 2008 election, some websites misrepresented some election results. Different websites published conflicting sets of results, with one website inaccurately stating that opposition leader, Morgan Tsvangirai, had received 50.3% of the vote, while the incumbent, Robert Mugabe, was reported to have garnered 42%, and independent candidate Simba Makoni 6.8%. The House of Assembly results were also inaccurately represented as MDC-Tsvangirai (99 seats), Zanu PF (95 seats) and MDC-Mutambara and independent candidates (12 seats) (Independent Election Results Centre). Zimonline.com, another news website based in South Africa, also erroneously reported that that one of the Vice Presidents, Joyce Mujuru, had lost to an opposition candidate, and that the late Zanu PF political commissar, Eliot Manyika, had lost his seat, resulting in him shooting and killing a Movement for Democratic Change (MDC-Tsvangirai faction) supporter in frustration (Zimonline.com 2008).

The prolonged delay in announcing the official results helped fuel speculation and the rumor mill and the "parallel information market" went into an overdrive. There was apprehension in some quarters that the rush to announce erroneous results by these online publications could trigger violence similar to that witnessed after Kenya's 2007 elections, whereby both the incumbent and the opposition leader were claiming victory. When media get implicated in such bloody events, their democratic credentials come under close scrutiny.

There is also a perception among some citizens that online publications specialize in rumor-mongering and, therefore, are not sources of serious news and information. An example is a rumor about the alleged death of the Reserve Bank Governor, Dr. Gideon Gono, in June 2010. The story is believed to have originated from a "UK based Zimbabwe online publication". On the 24th of June, 2010 *ZIMEYE*, an online publication published a story on its website, headlined 'Gideon Gono dies'. The story was accompanied by Gono's photograph and a caption which read thus:

> "Harare: (ZIMEYE) Reserve bank Governor, Dr. Gideon Gono, died in a car accident Wednesday, which occurred along Chiredzi road. However, no other details are available as the Zimbabwean government has not declared the news official. ZIMEYE will keep readers informed of the new development."

Gono was later quoted dismissing the story as 'malicious trash' (NewZimbabwe.com, 25 June 2010). However, the story had travelled the whole world through the Internet and social networks. On an online encyclopedia, Wikipedia, Gono's profile had already been edited reflecting that he had died. The perception that online publications are purveyors of rumors engenders cynicism among the citizens. A respondent had this to say with regard to the 'rumor-mongering' tag associated with online publications:

> "Some of their stories are so weird that you really wonder where they get them from. The other day I read in *The Zimbabwean* that 60 000 people had died during a doctors' strike. More recently there was also a story in the Zimbabwean claiming that 41 victims of the June 27 political violence had been buried at Chitungwiza

> cemetery disguised as paupers. One really wonders where such stories originate from. To be frank with you sometimes you really wonder whether these guys are journalists or political activists."

This demonstrates the extent to which online publications can engender cynicism among some readers. Some online publications have gone so far as publishing medical records of certain individuals, thus invading individual privacy. For instance, in 2006, *NewZimbabwe.com* published a story alleging that a certain government official had infected his wife with HIV. The official is alleged to have nearly killed his wife in a scuffle after the wife accused him of infecting her with the virus. Although the general approach in journalistic practice is that public figures do not have an absolute right to privacy by virtue of their stature, publishing someone's medical condition without his or her consent, whatever the stature of that person is, is inexcusable.

Similarly, some online publications treat children of government officials as "fair game", thus violating children's rights. For example, in February 2010, a number of online publications published the grade seven results of President Robert Mugabe's youngest son, who is a minor, claiming that he had "dismally failed". Some even suggested that he had "inherited his mother's IQ' (Nehanda Radio, 2 February, 2010). The story is an example of a violation of children's rights. The use of pseudonyms by online journalists provides a shelter of anonymity which encourages these kinds of ethical transgressions. Moyo (2007: 102) argues that the use of pseudonyms has, to some extent, eroded the credibility of online publications and websites.

Such practices demonstrate the serious limitations faced by online media in enhancing the democratization process in Zimbabwe. Lack of accountability on the part of these online publications undermines their ability to enforce accountability on political institutions in the country since they would be distrusted by the citizenry.

Conclusion

This article evaluated the democratic potential of online publications in Zimbabwe. The results are rather a mixture of hope and skepticism. The hope is derived from the observation that online publications are providing an outlet to voices and opinions alternative to the state in a climate characterized by tight governmental control of the mainstream media. Unlike mainstream newspapers that are constrained by legal impediments, online publications are able to focus their searchlights on the activities of the state, thereby ensuring accountability.

However, this democratic mandate is contingent upon levels of access, content and consumption practices. The observation in this study that the awareness of online publications among Zimbabwean citizens is low, access opportunistic and online citizen engagement low, confirms findings of earlier studies that show that new media have limited impact in altering politics (Norris and Curtice 2005). However, conclusions need to be tampered considering the fact that the study focused on the general consumption patterns of online publications rather than on acquisition of political information per se. The democratic potential of online publications was inferred from respondents' perceptions of the content of online publications, their ethical practices and consumption practices. Norris and Curtice (2005) rightly observe that the democratic potential of online media cannot adequately be evaluated on the basis of the direct flow of information from online publications and websites to the citizens, but that there is also need to take into account the "two-step flows" of information from opinion leaders and partisans to citizens.

In order to fully map out the impact of online publications on democratization, future studies may focus on the interaction between readers of online publications and fellow citizens. In the context of the present study, it was interesting to hear some respondents say that they read online publications after being "tipped" by friends, an indication that there is high demand for information from online publications and websites. This also signals emerging forms of "opinion leadership" and interactions which need further investigation. Similarly, it would be interesting to know whether respondents who claimed that they download stories from websites to read later, share them with others, and if so with whom? Such an investigation represents a radical break from previous studies' preoccupation with direct communication flows to more concrete understanding of the interaction between online media and interpersonal communication. Only then shall we have a solid understanding of the transformative potential of online publications. For now, their status as "alternative public spheres", particularly in developing contexts, remains contestable.

References

Atton, C. (2002). *Alternative Media. London:* Sage Publications.

Banda, F. (2006). Alternative Media: A viable option for Southern Africa, *Openspace,* 1 (5), 80-83.

Burger, G. (ed.), (2005). *Doing Digital Journalism: How Southern African News gatherers are Using ICT.* Grahamstown: Rhodes University.

Blumler, J.G. and Gurevitch, M. (1995). *The Crisis of Public Communication*. London: Routledge.

Chuma, W. (2007). *Mediating the Transition: The Press, State and Capital in a Changing Zimbabwe, 1980-2004*, Unpublished Dphil Thesis, University of Witwatersrand.

Chinaka, C. (2010). Mugabe dismisses rumours of poor health, *Rueters*, 9 September.

Curran, J. (1991). Mass media and democracy: A reappraisal. In J. Curran and M. Gurevitch (Eds.) *Mass media and democracy,*. London: Edward Arnold, 67-284

Chae, Y. (2005). *An aspect of the culture of the public sphere in U.S.: The Analysis of online public forums in local online newspapers*, Paper presented at the annual meeting of the International Communication Association, Sheraton New York, NY. Retrieved on 3 August 2010 from http://wwwallacademic.com/meta/p13770_index.html.

Darlington, Y., D. Scott (2002) *Qualitative Research in Practice: Stories from the field. Crows Nest:* Allen and Unwin.

Dzamara, I. (2007). Doctors' strike: 60000 dead. *The Zimbabwean*. I February, 2007.

Government of Zimbabwe (2005). *E-Readiness Survey Report*. Ministry of Information and Communication Technology, Harare: Printflow.

Habermas, J. (1989). *The Structural Transformation of the Public Sphere: An inquiry into Category of Bourgeoisie Society*. Cambridge, MA: Polity Press.

Internetworldstats.com (2010), *Internet use in Zimbabwe*, Retrieved on 25 August, 2010 from http://www.internetwordstats.com.

Kean, J. (1991). *The Media and Democracy*. Cambridge: Polity press.

Kellner, D. (n.d.) *Habermas, the public sphere, and democracy: A critical intervention*. Retrieved on 15 July 2010 from http://www.gseis.ucla/faculty/kellner/papers/habermas.htm

Kvale, S. (1996). Interviews: *An introduction to Qualitative Research Interviewing*. Thousand Oaks, Carlifonia: Sage Publications.

Lush, D. and Kupe, T., (2005). Crisis? What crisis? *Report on International Conference on Media Support Strategies for Zimbabwe, International Media Support (IMS)*. The Netherlands Institute for South Africa, (NIZA), Media Institute for Southern Africa, (MISA), Open Society Institute. Retrieved March 3 2008 from http://www.i-m-s.dk/media/pdf/Zimbabwe.

Mabweazara, H.M. (2010). "New" technologies and journalism practice in Africa: towards a critical sociological approach. In N. Hyde-Clarke (Ed.), *The Citizen and Communication: Revisiting Traditional, New and Community Media Practices in Southern Africa*. Claremont: Juta and Co. Ltd., 11-30.

Mabweazara, M.H. (2011). News making Practices and Professionalism in the Zimbabwean Press. *Journalism Practice*. Vol. 5 (1), 100-117.

Mansfield, I. (2011). *Mobile Broadband to Ensure Continued Vibrancy of Zimbabwe's Telecommunications Market*. ITU-Cellular News, 10 May, Retrieved from htt://cellular-news.com/story/49100.php?=h Accessed on 16 June 2011.

McCarthy, T. (1989). Introduction. In J. Habermas. *The Structural Transformation of the Public Sphere: An Inquiry into Category of Bourgeoisie Society*. Cambridge, MA: Polity Press, xi-xiv.

McQuail, D., (1994). *Mass communication theory: An introduction*. London. Routledge.

Morris, J.J. (2002). *The New Media and the Dramatization of American Politics*, Paper presented at the annual meeting of the American Political Science Association. Boston Marriott Copley Place, Sheraton Boston and Hynes Convention Centre, Boston, Massachusetts, August 28, 2002. Retrieved on 30 September 2009 from htt://www.allacademic.com.meta/p66276_index.html.

Moyo, D. (2007). Alternative Media, Diasporas and the Media of the Zimbabwean crisis. *Ecquid Novi: African Journalism Studies,* Vol. 28 (1,2), 81-105.

Moyo, D. (2010). We're all story tellers: Citizen Journalism in the age of digital 'pavement radio' In N. Hyde-Clarke (Ed.) *The Citizen and Communication: Revisiting Traditional, New and Community Media Practices in Southern Africa,*. Claremont: Juta and Co. Ltd, 50-74.

Moyo, L., (2011). Blogging down a Dictatorship: Human Rights, Citizen Journalists and the Right to Communicate in Zimbabwe. *Journalism,* 12 (6),745-760..

Nehanda Radio (2010), *Mugabe's Son Inherits Mother's IQ*. Retrieved on 21 July, 2010 from http://nehandaradio.com/2010/02//02/mugabes-son-inherits-mothers-iq

O'sullivan, T.M., Hartley, J., Saunders, D., J. Fiske, J. (1983). *Key Concepts in Communication.* London: Routledge.

Ott, D. (1998). *Power to the People: The Role of Electronic Media in Promoting Democracy in Africa, First Monday*. Retrieved from http://131.193.153.231/www/issues/issue3_4/ott/. Accessed on 15 August 2010.

Patton, M. (1990). *Qualitative Evaluation and Research Methods*. Beverly Hills, CA: Sage.

Ronning, H., T. Kupe (2000). The Dual Legacy of Democracy and Authoritarianism: The Media and the State in Zimbabwe. In J. Curran and M.J. Parker, (Eds.) *De-westernizing Media Studies*. London: Routledge, 157-177.

Sandoval, M., C. Fuchs, C. (2010). Towards a Critical Theory of Alternative Media. *Telematics and Informatics*. 27,171-150.

SW Radio (2007). [Radio Programme Transcript]. Hot Seat: foreign correspondent Peta Thornycroft on Media in Zimbabwe. Retrieved from http://www.swradioafrica.com/pages/hotseat. Accessed on 20 February 2008.

The Standard (2010, 4 September). Power cuts give Econet connectivity nightmares.

Waldahl, R., (2004*), Politics and Persuasion: Media Coverage of Zimbabwe's 2000 Election*, Harare: Weaver Press.

Zimdiaspora (2010). *Gono death report false*. Retrieved July 10 from http://www.thezimbabwean.co.uk/index.php?=com_content&view_article&id=3213.

ZIMEYE (2010). *Gideon Gono dies'* Retrieved August, 12, 2010, from http://wwwnewzimsituation.com/5415k2/breaking-news-gideon-gono-dies-htm.

Zimonline.com.ac.za (16 February, 2005) *We got it Wrong,* Zimsituation.com Retrieved 15 March 2010 from http://www.zimbabwesituation.com/nov26a_2004.html

Websites visited

ZimOnline.com: http://www.zimonline.co.za/Mission.aspx Accessed 12 June 2011

ZimDaily.com: http:///zimdaily.com/news2/staticpages/index.php/about_us Acessed12 June 2011

Zimbabwejournalists.com:http://www.zinmbabwejournalists.com/about.phpAccessed 17 June 2011

Internet World Stasts.com: http://www.internetworldstats.com/af/zw.htm Accessed 18 June 2011
NewZimbabwe.com: http://www.newzimbabwe.com Accessed 14 June 2011
Zimbabwe Elections Results.com: http://www.zimelectionresults.com Accessed 9 may 2010
Internet WorldStas.com http://www.internetwordstats.com Accessed 17 June 2011.

Part II
The Development of the Role of Social Media and its Influence on Political Communication

5. Social Media, Entertainment and the Politics of Young People in the US

David J. Jackson
Brian Collins
Bowling Green State University, USA

Abstract: Survey research of US university students analyzed here allows us to draw a number of conclusions about the political significance of social media and entertainment media. Large numbers of relatively affluent and educated youths are shown to use email, texting, Facebook and Twitter for political purposes. Ideologues and partisans are the most engaged, presumably because they care about politics in general and the outcome of elections in particular. Also, there appears to be a group of highly politicized young people who use both traditional and social media for political purposes—the two kinds of media do not appear to be at cross-purposes. Finally, a significant percentage of young respondents admit the possibility of their vote for US President being influenced by the endorsement of a candidate by a celebrity. Familiarity and likability appear to matter, as fans of the kind of music performed by the celebrity are more likely to be influenced.

Keywords: celebrities, endorsements, entertainment social media, youth politics

Introduction

This paper uses survey data of university students to examine a number of important questions about media use among young people and the effects of non-traditional media on young people's political beliefs. Specifically, the media habits of US university students are examined to determine how social media are used for political purposes and what political differences there are between those who use social media for politics and those who do not do so. Also, this paper contributes to our understanding of entertainment media's role as an agent of political socialization and general influence. Specifically, it examines the effects of celebrity endorsements of candidates for elective office as compared with more traditional media and pundit endorsements.

New Media Theory

There is a burgeoning literature on the uses of new (social) media by young people for political purposes. In fact, things are changing so fast here that even to write a short review of the literature is to run the risk of becoming hopelessly outdated between the time such a review is written and the time a work appears in print. However, the research does show a number of important tentative findings about the uses of social media.

Pempek et al. (2008) examine how college students use social networking sites like Facebook to cultivate human interaction online. The main objectives of their research were to explain how much time college students spend on social networking sites, why they use social networking sites, and how they use social networking sites. They used 92 undergraduate students (mostly female and on average 21 years old) and looked at their usage of Facebook over the course of one week. The students were given a diary-like measure which contained seven time-use questions, a seven-day activities checklist, and a survey about their use of Facebook which was to be completed by the next day. Their research found that students spent on average 27.93 minutes per day during weekdays and 28.44 minutes per day during weekend days on Facebook, logging on a few times a day. Students also tended to log on between the hours of 6:00PM and12:00AM. Most also said that the week examined was a typical for their usage. The majority of students recorded that they use Facebook to "communicate with friends, most frequently friends who are not on campus" (Pempek et al.: 231). Other reasons were having fun, taking a break from work, and fighting boredom. The authors were surprised to see that expressing identity/opinions was seldom selected. Students were found mostly to observe (almost 50% responded this way) or wall-post rather than send private messages while on Facebook. Students belong on average to 24.58 groups on Facebook, however, half of the students surveyed said they had no interaction with said groups during the average week on Facebook.

Levy (2011) discusses how new media is being used politically by young people. Levy claims that new media allows for users to participate during speeches via chat rooms, whereas before they could only watch (if they could even do that) and vote. Levy writes:

> "Built into these applications is an awareness of group activity and networked communications. That's how you organize people for politics, advocacy groups, or anything where you want to build groups of people and create community awareness. But instead of networking with a few dozen people, you can quickly grow groups to thousands, or even hundreds of thousands of people, because of the way information on these sites spreads like wildfire."

Levy also suggests that young people understand that they network globally, but take it for granted and fail to see the political ramifications of their online actions. "They may not even know that they are engaging in politics when they 'friend' Barack Obama on Facebook or MySpace. But I think they most certainly are (aware), and are increasing political awareness among their network through that act," says Levy. He goes on to say that Twitter was the most important technology of the 2008 campaign because of the one million users (at the end of March 2008) and the fact that users publish multiple tweets a day; if a small fraction of those tweets were devoted to the presidential election, it would definitely increase political awareness. A website was created for this sole purpose of these political tweets called *www.politweets.com*. Levy also writes that Barack Obama "is really the only candidate who really understands that the important stuff happens online" (16). Levy then claims, "Although I would argue the Internet is not a media equivalent to television, it's a platform that's growing more important every day. It doesn't mean print, television, or radio journalism will go away, but the way we interact with it today will change, and increasingly that's going to happen by traditional media adapting to the Internet" (ibid.).

Ladhani (2011) discusses citizens' efforts to make government information more public through Twitter accounts. Citizens created *tweetcongress.org* as a first initiative to get members of Congress active online. The site lists over 560 political figures and party accounts on Twitter and ranks the members by followers and level of activity. Another site with the same mindset is *guvluv.org* where users enter an address and *guvluv.org* compiles tweets from other politically active citizens. The site also categorizes trending tags and makes a dashboard of related tweets. Clay Johnson, Director of Sunlight Labs and one of the founders of the agency that created *mybarrackobama.org*, said that "providing tweets' location along with messages to government officials will serve as a clearer mechanism to understand how their voters truly feel about certain issues" (Ladhani: 45). Twitter was even used by President Obama to help promote health care reform in the summer of 2009. Users entered their zip code on an interactive map and sent a tweet to their member of Congress supporting health care reform.

Donnelly-Smith (2011) asks college students questions regarding their political activity and the use of social networking. When the students were asked the question "Are social networking websites like Facebook and MySpace useful for encouraging student political engagement?" most responded positively, saying that they were great tools to get people involved in politics. Kelson Mosier from Brigham Young University said that social networking sites were "vital—not only because it's made a difference in campaigning, but because we've got groups all over the Internet that people join because it's an amazing forum for political opinion that couldn't exist elsewhere" (Donnelly-Smith: 39). On the contrary, Gave Barouh from Montgomery College said "If someone sends me a Facebook invite to a political event I might not go, but if someone invites me directly, I'm much more likely to go… I don't think people use [these sites] for a political purpose that much" (37). When asked how they learn about politics, most said that they learn from family and friends while others said they learn through media and school.

Smith (2011) examines how Twitter users used the site in the wake of devastating earthquake that hit Haiti in January of 2010. For weeks after the earthquake, hundreds of tweets regarding Haiti were published every hour. Smith looks at these tweets and tries to answer the following questions: how do Twitter users communicate their involvement with Haiti relief efforts, and what public relations relationship strategies are represented by Twitter users. Smith collected over 1,400 tweets between January 22 and February 11, 2010 over six different sessions. He found that people used Twitter to "connect with a community of supporters, promote involvement, and personalize issues" (Smith: 331). He then went on to give examples of these themes. "Made another donation to Haiti today! Feels good to do my good deeds!!" (connecting with a community), "EVERYONE REACHING OUT TO #HAITI MUST GET THIS TRENDING! GET THE PIGS OUT OF THE YARD! #STOPHAITICORRUPTION" (promoting involvement/call to action), "Donated to Haiti, almost completed Zelda and discovered a new funeral doom band. Overall productive day" (personalize issues; Smith: 331). Regarding his second question, Smith writes, "users also reflect public relations relationship cultivation strategies in their tweets, including communicated relational commitment and conversational human voice" (Smith, 331). His example of relational commitment is "Honestly, I have NOT yet given money to Haiti relief—don't trust the donate via text thing but during tonite's telethon, I will call it in!" (Smith: 332).

Golbeck, Grimes and Rogers (2011) look at how members of the United States Congress use Twitter. They observed and collected the 200 most recent posts by each Congressperson on Tweet Congress on February 9, 2009, which totaled 69 people (the number of tweets collected was due to the maximum number of tweets one can observe on the site). The total number of tweets collected was 4,959. They conducted a follow up using the same procedures in June and August to check for patterns. This time they collected 1,516 tweets. The number of Congresspersons on Twitter had grown as well by this time, increasing to 159. They find that in both Houses Republicans outnumbered Democrats (102-57). The states with the most Congresspersons on Twitter are California (11) followed by Texas and Ohio (both with nine). Ten states did not have any Congresspersons on Twitter (Maryland and Massachusetts most notably). The average number of tweets per Congressperson is 125.3 with Rep John Culberson having the most posts at 2,076. Most tweets were information based, making up 54.7% of the total. After information were communication to people outside Congress (7.4%) and official business (5.1%). Just under 45% of all tweets contained links. Retweeting was a rare occurrence; out of the 4,626 tweets collected, only 5 were retweets.

Zhang et al. (2011) discuss how social networking sites have increased political and civic activity in the populace. In a *Pew Internet and American Life Project* survey, it was shown that 40% of people who use social networking sites had at one point used them for a political purpose. They define civic participation as "activities that address community concerns through non-governmental or electoral means, such as volunteering for building a homeless shelter or working on a community project." They define political participation as "activities that aim at directly or indirectly influencing the selection of elected officials and/or the development and implementation of public policy" (Zhang et al.: 76). Later they discuss how the mass media (television and the internet) affects civic and political participation (can deter or encourage participation). They conclude that interpersonal communication can greatly encourage political participation. Social networking sites may also encourage bonding and bridging of social capital. As stated earlier, 40% of social networkers have accounts on social networking sites for political information, while 20% use them to find the political beliefs of their friends and 22% search for campaign information. As for young voters, almost half have accounts for political information. Individual political factors such as political interest, political efficacy, political trust and party identification can also influence political and civic participation.

Zhang et al. then telephone-surveyed the US Southwest "to examine the extent to which reliance on social networking sites such as Facebook, MySpace, and YouTube has increased users' confidence in government and political and civic participation" (Zhang et al.: 76). They survey 998 respondents chosen at random with a 30.2% response rate. Just under 65% of respondents were female and were on average 52 years old. Just over 74% were White, 15.8% Hispanic, 6.7% Black, 2.2% Native American and 0.9% Asian. As for political ideology, about 50% considered themselves as conservative, 37.2% as moderate and 12.5% as liberal. Respondents also said that they rarely or never rely on social networking sites for political information. Overall, social networking sites were found to positively correlate with civic participation but not with political activity or confidence in government, due to the fact that those sites are "geared toward maintaining relations with their friends and can have the potential for stimulating community involvement" (87). Interpersonal political conversation also correlated with civic participation as well as political participation; however, it did not correlate with confidence in government.

The evidence is clear for a number of conclusions about the role of social media in politics. For example, most college students have a Facebook account to "communicate with friends, most frequently friends who are not on campus"

(Pempek et al.: 231), few using them to express identity or opinions; almost half of all young voters have social media accounts for political information (Zhang et al., 2011). It was also found that experts and non-experts suggest that new media (e.g. Facebook, YouTube, Twitter) are very important tools to get young people involved in politics, allowing them to participate in ways other than just voting. Another finding suggests that new social media makes it easier for government information to become public and makes communication easier between public officials and citizens. The last finding from these articles suggests that there is a positive relationship between social networking sites and civic participation but not, however, with political activity or confidence in the government, because social networking sites are "geared toward maintaining relations with their friends and can have the potential for stimulating community involvement" (Zhang et al.: 87). These articles go a long way in helping understand new social media's place in the political world, however significant gaps exist in terms of what kinds of youths use social media for political purposes. Yet another survey of university-aged students is necessary to get a clearer picture of the demographic and political differences between political users of social media and others.

The Sample

Approximately 10,000 students enrolled at Bowling Green State University (BGSU) were asked to participate in an on-line survey. BGSU is a large, regional state university located in Northwest Ohio. As such, even a representative sample of BGSU students would not produce a nationally generalizable sample in terms of sex, age, race, education, region and income. However, when considering the uses and effects of social media and entertainment media in politics, such a sample is still useful for a number of reasons. First, young, affluent and educated people are the group most likely to use social media. Therefore it makes sense to investigate whether they use them for political purposes. Also, young people are the most likely to tune in to the new hybrid news and entertainment shows such as *The Daily Show with Jon Stewart*, which have received much scholarly attention about their effects on young people's political beliefs and actions, an investigation of the effects of which takes up the greater portion of the second part of this chapter.

Finally, a positive argument may be made for examining the attitudes of university students as well. Political science scholarship demonstrates that likelihood of voting increases with the attainment of higher levels of education (Wolfinger and Rosenstone, 1980). Therefore, in examining the attitudes of young people enrolled at university we are learning about the beliefs of those most likely to vote and therefore to influence the political process. Moreover, scholars have also found that elites, defined mainly as those who work full-time in politics or public affairs, such as the U.S. President, governors, members of Congress and so on, but sometimes defined more broadly to include prominent members of communities such as corporate CEOs or community leaders, influence the opinions of others (Paul and Brown, 2001; Mondak, 1993). Those with a university education are more likely to be found among the elite, and therefore to influence the beliefs of others.

Of the approximately 10,000 BGSU students asked to participate, 461 completed all or some of the survey, for a response rate of approximately 4.6%. Thirty-one percent (31%) described themselves as seniors, or in their fourth year of university, while the mean age of respondents was 21.43 with a standard deviation of 4.12. Only 4.2% of respondents described themselves as African American, while 2.5% described themselves as Hispanic, and 2.9% categorized themselves as Other. This means 90.4% described themselves as white, which is skewed even for the majority white population of students enrolled at BGSU. Just under sixty percent (58.9%) of the respondents are female. In terms of estimates of family income, the modal category was $50,000 to $74,999, with 27% placing themselves there. Only 10.5% estimated their annual family income at less than $20,000 while only 18.5% estimated it at $100,000 or more.

Political Social Media Use Habits

Respondents were asked a number of questions about their use of social media for political purposes. Just under 20% (19.7%) report ever receiving a text message aimed at persuading them to vote either for or against a particular candidate for office, while only 10.5% report ever sending such a text. This parallel's a Pew Center report from the 2010 elections which found that, "10% of adults sent text messages relating to the election to friends, family members and others." (Smith and Rainie, 2010). Exactly 20% report following candidates or elected officials through email, while 25.2% follow them through Facebook and 12.4% do so through Twitter. 19.4% report regularly or sometimes following news or news headlines through Twitter. Again, these findings roughly parallel Pew findings from the 2010 elections, which found that, "Some 21% of online adults used social networking sites such as Facebook or MySpace in the months leading up to the November 2010 elections to connect with a campaign or the election itself, and 2% of online adults did so using Twitter" (Smith, 2010).

Are there differences among various political party preferences and use of social media for political purposes? In terms of following candidates or elected officials through Facebook, Democrats, Republicans and supporters of another party are statistically significantly more likely to do so than those with no party or preference or who do not know their party preference. Republicans are the least likely to follow a politician through Twitter, with Democrats, Independents and those who support a third party being much more likely. Those who do not know their party preference or do not have one are substantially less likely than Democrats, Independents, and supporters of third parties to follow politicians through email. Partisans are also much more likely to have ever sent a text message supporting or opposing a candidate, while the differences are smaller in terms of having ever received such a message.

Does sex matter? There are some interesting differences. Men are statistically significantly more likely than women to follow a politician through Facebook (31.3% to 21.7%), to have ever sent a text message encouraging someone to vote for or against a candidate (14.9% to 7.9%) and to have ever received such a text message (26.3% to 16.2%).

Ideology appears to matter too. Conservatives (27.3%) and Liberals (29.9%) are more likely than moderates (15.7%) to follow a politician through Facebook. The same pattern holds for email, with ideologues being about twice as likely to follow a politician through email. Ideologues are nearly four times as likely ever to have sent a text message urging a vote either for or against a candidate, and they are moderately more likely ever to have received such a message.

Traditional News Media Use Habits

As for the number of days looking at a newspaper per week, the modal category was zero days, with 25.3% of respondents. The mean number of days reading a newspaper was 2.69 with a standard deviation of 2.34, which suggests that there is extreme variation in the number of days spent reading a paper among the respondents. Many read a paper frequently while likely equally many do not read a newspaper ever. The modal category for number of days watching news on TV was also zero, with 28.9% of respondents, while the mean number of days was 2.42 with a standard deviation of 2.37, again suggesting a wide distribution that includes many fervent news television watchers and equally as many non-viewers. The modal category for number of days talking with friends or family about politics was one day (24.3%), but again the mean number of days was low (2.44 days) and the standard deviation high (2.19), again suggesting a very widely varied distribution. Together these data suggest a sample that is not overall very engaged with the traditional news media such as TV or newspapers or with talking about politics with family or friends, but the existence of a small cadre (about 10% in each variable) who spend seven days a week reading a paper, watching news on TV and talking with family and friends about politics.

There may be a relatively small cadre of highly politicized youths who read the newspaper, watch the news and communicate about politics via social media. If this is in fact the case, we would expect significant positive relationships among these variables. In other words, talking to friends about politics and news media use ought to correlate with each other, and with political use of social media. There are moderate, statistically significant positive correlations among days reading a newspaper, days watching news on TV and days talking to friends and family about politics. Social media use for politics is measured as a dummy variable ("yes" or "no" to following candidates through email, Facebook, Twitter and sending or receiving political texts), so to check for relationships between these variables and the traditional news media variables differences in means and chi-square tests is appropriate.[1] There are some significant findings. For example, those who follow candidates or officials through email spend statistically significantly more days reading a newspaper, watching the news on TV and talking with family and friends about politics than others. The same significant differences hold for having ever received a political text message, having sent such a text, and following candidates or officials through Facebook and Twitter. As expected, youths who say they plan to vote in the next national elections read a newspaper more frequently and talk to friends and family about politics more frequently. Finally, those who plan to vote also are more likely than others to have received or sent a political text message and to follow candidates through Facebook. In other words, there does seem to be a highly politicized cadre of youths who use both traditional and newer social media to remain informed about politics, talk about it, and influence others.

Effects of Endorsements: Traditional and New Endorsers

Respondents were asked to estimate the effect on their vote for President of the endorsement of a number of traditional sources (*The New York Times*, *Cleveland Plain Dealer* newspapers), political commentators (Rush Limbaugh), and celebrities of varying levels of political credibility (country star Toby Keith, pop star

1 For clarity of presentation, specific statistical measures are not presented, but are available from the lead author upon request.

Lady Gaga, actress Lindsay Lohan, superstar musician and social activist Bono, and rap star Kanye West). The results appear in Table 1.

Table 1. Effect of Endorsement on Potential Presidential Vote

Endorser	Much or Somewhat More Likely to Vote For (%)	No Effect (%)	Much or Somewhat Less Likely to Vote For (%)
Toby Keith	3.9	83.8	12.4
Rush Limbaugh	5.4	60.7	33.9
Lady Gaga	4.8	71.3	24.0
Lindsay Lohan	0.2	67.4	32.4
Cleveland PD	7.3	90.6	2.2
Bono	7.0	84.7	8.2
Kanye West	2.6	73.1	24.3
The New York Times	19.2	75.8	5.0

Clearly the overwhelming majority of the respondents believe that none of the endorsements would have any influence over their vote. However, there are some important differences among the endorsers. In terms of a potential positive effect among the respondents, no endorser comes close to *The New York Times*, where just under 20% believe the endorsement could have a positive influence over their vote choice. On the other hand, almost no respondents admitted that Lindsay Lohan's presidential endorsement could have a positive effect on their choice. Interestingly, both Rush Limbaugh's and Lohan's endorsement could negatively affect the vote choice of just about a third of the respondents, but I suspect for very different reasons. As a polarizing conservative commentator, Limbaugh is likely to have a positive effect on conservatives, but no effect on others. As a drug-addled starlet, Lohan's credibility is so low that her endorsement could be taken as a signal that something is wrong with the candidate she endorsed. Both Kanye West and Lady Gaga would turn away about a quarter of the respondents. Interestingly, each has taken noted political stands including West's famous claim during a live broadcast to help the victims of Hurricane Katrina that "George Bush doesn't care about black people," and Lady Gaga's support of gay rights, including the ending of the "Don't Ask, Don't Tell" policy that barred gays from serving openly in the U.S. military.

Marketing and other scholars have developed several explanations of how the process of celebrity endorsement works to convince people to buy products, or to hold certain beliefs. Early research indicated that the perceived "trustworthiness" of the source of information influenced the level of agreement with ideas. Hovland and Weiss (1952) showed that "high credibility" sources such as the *New England Journal of Medicine* were more persuasive than "low-credibility" sources such as the former Soviet Union's official newspaper *Pravda*, or U.S. gossip columnists. Media and politics scholars have noted the prevalence of "experts" on television news broadcasts, while calling into question their reliability (Soley, 1992). Nevertheless, scholars have found experts and news commentators do influence public opinion (Page et al., 1987).

Dholakia and Sternthal (1977: 230-231) differentiated between influence on attitudes and behavior and found that highly credible sources positively influence attitudes, but may actually reduce the likelihood of inducing behavior, such as consenting to a product trial. This may support Petty and Cacioppo's (1986) suggestion that behavior is more likely to be motivated by attitudes born of issue-relevant argumentation than those derived from more peripheral and affective cues. Sternthal, Dholakia and Leavitt (1978: 259) also found that recipients' predisposition toward an issue influenced the impact of credible sources, with those favorably disposed toward an issue to be more influenced by a moderately credible source than a highly credible one. They also found that those predisposed negatively were more likely to be influenced by a highly credible source.

Scholars have examined the impact of the physical attractiveness and "likeability" of the source as well and found that attractive sources are generally more effective than unattractive ones (Kahle and Homer, 1985). However, Baker and Churchill (1977: 553) found that attractive sources are not always more successful celebrity endorsers, and argued advertisers should consider the match between the product and the spokesperson, because unattractive models may be more convincing than attractive ones with regard to selling non-romantic items. McGuire (1985) found that increased familiarity, likeability and resemblance between source and perceiver increase a message's effectiveness.

McCracken (1989: 311) found these "source credibility" and "source attractiveness" models wanting, because their interpretation of the persuasiveness of celebrities has "everything to do with the celebrity and nothing to do with the product." He developed "meaning-transfer theory" to account for the characteristics of the celebrity and how they interact with those of the product to make for a more effective endorsement.

McCracken contended that the effectiveness of a celebrity endorsement depends in part on the meanings the endorser brings to the process, including social status, class, gender, age, personality and lifestyle. Celebrity endorsement of a product will succeed only if an association is formed between appropriate aspects of the celebrity's meaning and the endorsed product. After the celebrity has transferred the meaning(s) to the product, consumers transfer the meaning(s) from the product to themselves (314). Importantly, McCracken argues that those who are moving from one age category to another would be especially keen to take on meanings created by celebrities.

Applying McCracken's theory, Jackson (2007) and Jackson and Darrow (2005) found substantial effects of celebrity endorsements of political ideas. Utilizing a sample of 456 English-speaking Canadian university students, Jackson and Darrow found that celebrities can make popular ideas more popular and unpopular ideas less unpopular. For example, Wayne Gretzky's endorsement of the highly unpopular belief that President George W. Bush was a great president lead to a decrease in the level of strong disagreement with the belief. Jackson's 2007 results were similar, utilizing a survey of U.S. university students. For example, among country and western music fans, the very popular position that the U.S. government should do more to help farmers was even more popular when endorsed by a popular country and western musician.

Celebrity endorsement theory would lead us to a number of hypotheses about the presidential endorsements analyzed above. For example, we would expect that fans of the particular music performed by the artist would be more likely to find the musician credible, and therefore be positively influenced by their presidential endorsements. Among those who say rap is their favorite musical style, 18.9% would be much or somewhat more likely to vote for a presidential candidate if Kanye West endorsed him or her; among fans of other kinds of music, the number is only 1.3%. Among Country music fans, 14.7% would be more likely to support a presidential candidate because of Toby Keith's endorsement, while among non-fans only 1.9% would be more likely. Clearly, preferring the kind of music performed matters at least for even knowing who the musician is and possibly for endowing them with greater credibility.

Similarly, among those who identify themselves as conservatives, 18.5% would be at least somewhat more likely to vote for a presidential candidate who had Rush Limbaugh's endorsement, whereas for non-conservatives the number is a miniscule 0.6%. Also, whether fairly or not, *The New York Times* is considered by many to be a liberal or left-leaning newspaper. Would liberals be more likely than others to be influenced by the paper's endorsement? Whereas 20% of non-liberals would be influenced positively by the *Times*, 22.8% of liberals would–not a large difference. Perhaps the political party of the respondent is more important. *The New York Times* is generally considered a newspaper sympathetic to the Democratic Party. Among those respondents who describe themselves as Democrats, 27.5% would be positively influenced by the *Times*' endorsement, while only 15.9% of non-Democrats would be.

Conclusion

Social media are here to stay. Significant numbers of relatively affluent and educated youths are shown to use email, texting, Facebook and Twitter for political purposes. Ideologues and partisan are the most engaged, presumably because they care about politics in general and the outcome of elections in particular. Also, there appears to be a group of highly politicized young people who use both traditional and social media for political purposes. Finally, a significant percentage of young respondents admit of the possibility of their vote for President being influenced by the endorsement of a celebrity. Familiarity and likability appear to matter as fans of the kind of music performed by the celebrity are more likely to be influenced. Further research should attempt to differentiate between the effects of low- and high-credibility celebrity endorsers.

References:

Baker, M.J. G.A. Churchill. 1977. The impact of physically attractive models on advertising evaluations. *Journal of Marketing Research* 14(4), 538-555.

Dholakia, R.R., v B. Sternthal. Highly credible sources: persuasive facilitators or persuasive liabilities? *The Journal of Consumer Research* 3(4), 223-232.

Donnelly-Smith, L. (2008). Political engagement in the age of Facebook: student voice. *Peer Review,* Spring/Summer 2008. Retrieved 7 November 2011 from http://www.aacu.org/peerreview/pr-spsu08/pr-spsu08_Donnelly.cfm.

Golbeck, J., J.M. Grimes, A. Rogers. Twitter use by the U.S. Congress. *Journal of the American Society for Information Science and Technology,* Aug. 2010. Retrieved 7 November 2011 from http://onlinelibrary.wiley.com/doi/10.1002/asi.21344/abstract.

Hovland, C.I. W. Weiss. (1952). The influence of source credibility on communication effectiveness. *The Public Opinion Quarterly*, 15(4), 635-650.

Jackson, D. (2009). *Entertainment and politics: The influence of pop culture on young adult political socialization.* Second Edition. New York: Peter Lang.

Jackson, D.J. and T.I.A. Darrow. (2005). The influence of celebrity endorsements on young adults' political opinions." *The Harvard International Journal of Press/Politics,* 10, 80-98.

Kahle, L.R., P.M. Homer. (1985). Physical attractiveness of the celebrity endorser: A social adaptation perspective. *The Journal of Consumer Research,* 11(4), 954-961.

Ladhani, N. (2010). Making a difference: 140 characters at a time. *Social Policy,* 40(1).

Levy, J. (2008). *Beyond 'Boxers or Briefs?' Phi Kappa Theta Forum*, retrieved 7 November 2011 from http://findarticles.com/p/articles/mi_qa4026/is_200807/ai_n27997929/.

McCracken, G. (1989). Who is the celebrity endorser? Cultural foundations of the endorsement process. *The Journal of Consumer Research,* 16(3), 310-321.

McGuire, W.J. (1985). Attitudes and Attitude Change. In *The Handbook of Social Psychology*, ed. Gardner Lindzey and Elliot Aronson. Third Edition. New York: Random House.

Page, B.I, R.Y. Shapiro and G.R. Dempsey. (1987). What moves public opinion?" *American Political Science Review,* 81(1), 23-43.

Pempek, T., Y.Yermolayeva and S.L. Calvert. (2009). College Students' Social Networking Experience on Facebook. *Journal of Applied Developmental Psychology*, 30(3), 227-238.

Petty, R.E. and J.T. Cacioppo. (1986). *Communication and persuasion: Central and peripheral routes to attitude change*. New York: Springer-Verlag.

Soley, L.C. (1992). *The news shapers: The sources who explain the news*. New York: Praeger.

Smith, A. (2011). *Twitter and social networking in the 2010 midterm elections*, retrieved 4 November 2011 from http://pewresearch.org/pubs/1871/internet-politics-facebook-twitter-2010-midterm-elections-campaign.

Smith, A. and L. Rainie. (2010). *Politics goes mobile,* retrieved 4 November 2011 from http://www.pewinternet.org/Reports/2010/Mobile-Politics.aspx.

Smith, B.G. (2010). Socially distributing public relations: Twitter, Haiti, and interactivity in social media. *Public Relations Review,* 36(4), 329-335.

Sternthal, B., R. Dholakia andC. Leavitt. (1978). The persuasive effect of source credibility: Tests of cognitive response. *The Journal of Consumer Research,* 4(4), 252-260.

Wolfinger, R.E. and S.J. Rosenstone. (1980). *Who Votes?* New Haven: Yale University Press.

Zhang, W., T.J. Johnson, T. Seltzer, and S.L. Bichard. (2010). The revolution will be networked: The influence of social networking sites on political attitudes and behavior. *Social Science Computer Review*, 28(1), 75-92.

6. The participation of Mexican political leaders in Web 2.0 in 2011

German Espino Sanchez
Autonomous University of Querétaro, México

Abstract: In spite of the fairly large number of authors who have claimed Web 2.0 is the fuel of a revolution in conventional politics, empirical reports from different parts of the world prove that political leaders are not using social media resources to interact and collaborate with Internet users. This article is based on a case analysis made to evaluate the behavior of Mexican political leaders on the Internet; the most important results come from a content analysis of the Facebook and Twitter accounts of Mexican politicians. The results show that in Mexico politicians do not have an active participation in social media. Instead of using social networks to dialogue, politicians use these resources just to spread propaganda.

Keywords: Internet, Web 2.0, Social Network System, politicians, case analysis.

Introduction

Every day, the increasing number of new users' accounts that break records in social networks compel politicians to jump on the bandwagon of Web 2.0. However, a paradox has emerged in our investigation: on the one hand, politicians access social media (i.e. social networks, wikis, blogs) more frequently than they did in the past, but on the other, they do not actively participate in such social media. In most of the cases, politicians use these resources to disseminate their propaganda at the expense of the dialogue with the users' communities. In other words, they handle Web 2.0 resources as if they belonged to the preceding Web 1.0.

This paper aims to show the results of a study intended to evaluate the use that the main Mexican political leaders make of Web 2.0. From these we endeavor to understand if politicians truly assume the appropriate mindset to exploit the potential offered by Web 2.0, which includes a willingness for peer dialogue, collaboration with other users, participation in social networking sites, and the creation of content to be exchanged on the web.

The conclusions of our empirical investigation show that Mexican politicians are not assuming the challenges posed by Web 2.0; that is, they are not participating actively in the social network system.

Theoretical framework

New technologies are transforming media systems

Many authors suggest a media revolution implies a radical change in our perception of the world and how we relate to social reality (Debrays, 1994; Lowe, 1998) In every age media culture rebuilds the act of perceiving; the individual is limited by a different hierarchical organization of senses and the concepts of what is perceived are offered by a group of epistemic rules. As a result, any perceptual field formed by such factors is a historical formation that changes from one period to another.

According to Castells (2009), the media revolution we are witnessing is rooted in the development of three different interdependent social processes observed in the last two decades: 1) a generalized commercialization of media almost everywhere in the world; 2) the globalization and concentration of media companies through conglomerates and networks; 3) the diversification, personalization and segmentation of media markets with a special focus on cultural identification of the audience (Castells, 2009: 89). The same author believes social actors and citizens around the world are using social networking to organize themselves in order to defend their common interests, to push their projects forward and to reaffirm their values (Castells, 2009: 91).

For many authors the center of the revolution generated by the new technologies is the transformation of the consumers into producers, hence their new definition as "prosumers". Web users choose their consumption in the Internet, create their own contents and transmit them through a network. Communication among individuals is unfiltered. Politicians see media 2.0 as a rich vein to be mined: such communication does not depend on the interpretation of journalists and its use as a source of information reduces time and space costs:

> "I call this new historical form of communication mass self-communication. It is mass communication since it can potentially reach a global audience. At the same time, it is self-communication because one can generate their own message, define the possible receivers and select specific messages or Web and electronic communication networks contents to be recovered. The three forms of communication (interpersonal, massive and mass self-communication, coexist and interact; rather than substitute each other they are complementary." (Castells, 2009: 88)

All these processes revolutionize the old mass regime implemented by television. In the old regime the audiences were mostly passive, far different from the prosumers currently interacting in the Internet.

Web 2.0

Rather than proposing a new version of the World Wide Web, Web 2.0 takes advantage of the improvements made by software developers to modify the interaction between the users and the networks. Web 2.0 refers to a series of applications and websites that use collective intelligence to offer interactive services on line and to allow users to control their own information. (O' Reilly, 2005)

The concept Web 2.0 refers not only to a social phenomenon, but also to the interaction allowed in the Web by different applications designed to facilitate information sharing, interoperability, user-centered design and collaboration. Some examples of these applications are social networks (e.g. Facebook, Twitter, MySpace, LinkedIn); wikis (e.g. Wikipedia); blogs; mashups (i.e. hybrid web applications); video, photo, or audio sharing websites (e.g. YouTube, Flickr); and peer-to-peer file sharing Internet services (e.g. Napster, Bit Torrent) among others.

In the age of Web 1.0 the Internet was basically unidirectional, used by people to look for information but rarely to interact directly with other users. In Web 2.0 relationships are bidirectional and allow the exchange of all kinds of contents (documents, audio, video, and images) and the uploading and editing of online files in real time. Web 2.0 users can interact or change websites contents. The interaction of Web 2.0 users generates a new social fabric interwoven with the new social networks. Web 2.0 websites work as meeting points that depend on their users.

Is Web 2.0 another neoliberal social control device?

In the current research about Internet campaigning, there are two major trends: 1) technological determinism, in which technology is intended to represent a powerful force that profoundly influences social change; and 2) social determinism, according to which technologies are merely tools for certain political and social forces. (Vaccari, 2010)

Coming from the point of view of technological determinism, many intellectuals and business gurus (see Tapscott and Williams, 2010) suggest dialogical relations developed through social networks promoting the construction of communities and a digital deliberative democracy. According to this idea, communicative interactions developed multidirectionally among multiple participants dissolving power relations among users. These ideas lead many researchers to suggest that these new forms of participation generated in online social networks could serve as impulses for the establishment of a digital deliberative democracy.

There are at least two major criticisms of these optimistic interpretations of Web 2.0. In the first place, participative models have not been successfully implanted in conventional politics. Secondly, and more importantly, this new public arena belongs neither to people nor to governments, but to marketers; that is, such a public arena does not serve democracy but the market.

A review of the criticisms made of the new public digital arena leads us to acknowledge that from the latter part of the 20th century to the beginning of the new century, a consumer society has dominated the sociopolitical panorama. Cornelius Castoriadis (1997) claims the capitalist system has reached its peak by learning to institutionalize the dissident tendencies of social groups. According to this author no important alternative to the market economy has been raised in the last decades.

New business intellectuals and gurus try to argue that the universal benefits of a democratized digital arena are based on the fact that collective work is perfectly functional within commercial culture (see Tapscott and Williams, 2010).

In opposition to this optimistic view, an important group of critical researchers point out that Web 2.0 technologies pose risks for the political and social development of some individuals. Examples include: 1) the immense flow of personal information created through social networks that can be exploited by anybody; 2) the emergence of tools to keep users and workers under surveillance; 3) the capacity of companies to exploit unpaid labor for purposes strictly related to marketing and thereby corporatize spaces and social resources (Zimmer, 2008; Dahlberg, 2010; Fuchs, 2011).

From this critical perspective, many researchers argue that instead of promoting democracy, the political economy of new media is closely related to neoliberal control as well as to corporate controls and the exploitation of users' creative practices (Dalhlberg, 2010; Zimer, 2008; Scholz, 2008). Thus, the optimistic conception of Web 2.0 would represent a powerful ideology that helps legitimize capitalism, not the formation of a digital public arena.

Users' exploitation

Trebor Scholz (2008) holds that online social life is always linked to market relations no matter whether users participate for profit or not. In the first place, the current generation, made up of Internet users by definition, develops deep identity links with the Internet. Social networks determine a great part of individuals' psychological lives, so the formation of users' identities is reflected in the building of profiles in social networks. According to Scholz (2008), Internet social networks represent an ideal social psychology lab for marketers and spy agencies in modern states. Nowadays marketers can learn from the stories we tell each other in our more intimate circles, thanks to social network profiles and chats. In this manner, the social network system would work as a fantastic panopticon for governments and companies. In order to study the population of a country, economical and political elites just have to sign in to Facebook, Twitter, or MySpace. All the personal information veins can be used to make qualitative or quantitative studies of what we are, do, think or dream. Creating sophisticated users' profiles from their browsing history is an easy task. This kind of espionage is easy to put into practice since many companies in the international market sell software to hack social network systems and people's browsing histories, as proved and reported by the creator of Wikileaks, Julian Assange, at the end of 2011 (Chatterjee, 2011). This kind of political control would leave Internet users at the mercy of governments and business people and the huge machinery of social networks would be a control device of the neoliberal capitalist system rather than a space for democratization.

Web 2.0 companies collect large amounts of information to build users' profiles and use them to develop aggressive personalized marketing campaigns; these data banks have become gold mines for Internet companies, but they have also been used to develop more strict control over populations by some authoritarian governments. The Chinese state, for instance, has used data collected by companies like Yahoo and Google to pursue the opponents of the regime (O' Brien, 2011).

In addition, Scholz (2008) points out that business people are taking advantage of masses of Internet users as unpaid global labor. Internet companies are worth a fortune thanks to the millions of people who participate and improve their systems: in this way prosumers work and make companies' owners even richer. Innovations are actively or passively developed by prosumers but in the end the owners of Web 2.0 companies commercially exploit such innovations.

Is a deliberative democracy possible in cyberspace?

Dahlberg (2010) strongly criticizes the most propagandistic version of the liberties offered by the new digital public arena. In his opinion, the supposed freedom of Web 2.0 is limited in two main aspects: the prosumer's subjectivity and practices are framed by consumer society and of online sources of personal information are used for surveillance and control.

The critical political economy, according to this author, suggests that prosumers' practices that are based on the technology of the Web 2.0 are part of the dominant trends of the consumer society: entertainment, show and the demobilization of people. The political economy of media criticizes the mainstream trends of consumer society such as entertainment, show business or demobilization structure prosumers' practices based on Web 2.0 technology. Dahlberg insists: the formats of participation that reproduce the system and that are provided companies have made these trends possible. Company services and even everyday work force of communities have been adapted to the production system of consumer society (Dahlberg, 2010).

This author argues that entertainment and cyber show business sponsored through Web 2.0 provide an illusion of freedom and empowerment that is very useful to demobilize the population.

These critical authors point out that in spite of egalitarian tendencies promoted in social media, profound inequities still exist. One of them is that the World Wide Web is oriented to lead users towards corporation contents and not to independent websites that provide free resources. Again, mainstream, entertaining sites connected to the consumer society get the largest benefits through all kinds of tricks like the manipulation of web browsers or the investing millions of dollars in the production of contents and technological innovations (Dahlberg, 2010).

Barabasi's (2002) research shows that webs follow two different patterns: growth, in which new nodes are added to the Web; and preferential attachment, in which, in an election of two nodes, the node most frequently linked to will be chosen. Accordingly, famous celebrities, large media corporations, well-known TV or radio presenters, and relevant economical, social or political leaders are privileged as the center of the Web. These kind of celebrities work as hubs, centers of control from which the Internet relations are ordered. Therefore, from the viewpoint of these critical authors (such as Dahlberg, 2010), a democracy 2.0 as proposed by the Internet propagandists would mean the exclusion of large segments of the population (those not connected to the Web) and the empowerment of a few: the elite of digital citizens who have financial resources, or have been well educated.

Dalhberg (2010) believes that, since the target of social networks and Web 2.0 companies is entertainment, the secondary role played by the issue of politics in these platforms is not coincidental. Communities are not used to having a political compromise. Any other compromise lasts only as long as individuals satisfy their wishes and necessities. They are free to log in or out with a single mouse click, as opposed to citizens in traditional democratic theories, where they are expected to be civically virtuous. In virtual communities, concepts as "collective identity", "solidarity", "public sovereignty" or "communal values" are out of fashion. These notions were associated either with paternalism or with a state-centered social system, which is exactly the enemy of the cyberlibertarian demos. Dahlberg (2010) concludes that cyberlibertarian ideologists have changed their enemy: they do not target global capitalism but the old nation-state.

Participative democracy without a real basis

Christian Fuchs (2011), among others, cautions against the use of concepts like "participative culture", which comes from political science and is strongly linked to theory of "participative democracy". However, this last concept is far more profound than the concept conceived by cyberevangelists. The public sphere referred to by Habermas is another concept that is frequently simplified.

Fuchs (2011) reminds us that Habermas himself had pointed out the limits and handicaps of the bourgeois public sphere. For instance, cultural and economic asymmetries in a population are a clear limit to freedom of thought; a democratic public arena can hardly coexist with asymmetries in education and economic resources. In this respect the domination of the public sphere by great economic or political corporations is a clear limit to freedom of association. This reflects a problem that can be observed nowadays: not every user of the Internet attracts the same attention.

Some authors argue that not even well developed countries have reached a massive use of social media and question the level of Web 2.0 activity developed by most of its users. For instance, in Sweden, one of the most economically advanced countries in the age of information, only 6% of the population have their own blog; of all the Internet users only 8% post in their blogs occasionally; and only 16% ever upload videos occasionally (Findahl, 2010).

According to Fuchs (2011), for many Web 2.0 propagandists participation means only that people meet at networks, form groups and share self-made contents. This concept omits the fact that people's participation is framed by large companies whose owners make the big decisions on the development of the Internet. Decision-making is only shared by the owners, the companies' CEO's, while the common people or the average employee in these companies are not taken into account.

In the end, online participation depends on the network effect, which works in this way: the more people are connected, the higher the participation will be and the better the network will work. Consequently, since their business depends on the amount of people involved, network marketers will always be advertising the marvels of an online life.

As a result, and based on the quoted authors, my conclusion is that as long as large corporations dominate the Internet, a digital participative democracy does not seem to be possible. As a matter of fact, most companies representative of Web 2.0 do not support the idea of a participative democracy, Dahlberg (2010) insists.

The only signs of a participative Internet are based on those areas that are resisting the domination of corporations, where users participate and build non-commercial models, which do not expect any profits. Wikipedia, Diaspora and Torrent are exceptions, not the rule.

Political leaders from all around the world are not participating in Web 2.0

In reports from empirical research in different European countries and the U.S.A, and in several international congresses devoted to this issue I have attended, researchers have warned that politicians are adopting Web 2.0 resources very slowly.

A fairly comprehensive report on the situation in Germany (Schweitzer, 2012) shows that politicians only use new technologies for traditional-style politics; that means, on the Internet they just are doing campaign 1.0.

The *Report on politics and social networks* (Intelligence Compass, 2011), in the context of Spain, shows that most of the politicians (94%) assess social networks as a remarkable tool for keeping in touch with citizens, but when asked whether Obama's campaign could be implemented in their country, 70% of them answers negatively.

One of the conclusions of another study (Tuñez and Sixto, 2011) made to evaluate the "compromise 2.0" of Spanish deputies is that "Congress people's attitude towards the network with a level of compromise 2.0 is globally very low or non-existent. For an 83.7% of them it is either null and void or very low, as opposed to a 7.42% of them with a high or excellent level of compromise 2.0."

A discovery in a British report (Lilleker and Jackson, 2009) is that keeping control of the power in dialogic relations is one of the basic worries of politicians who dare use Web 2.0 applications. Debates on government decisions, profound criticisms to parties and politicians are very difficult to handle in social networks and very easy to publish in the mass media. In this context, politicians wonder if they would win or lose by participating in social networks (Lilleker and Jackson, 2009).

This study concludes that politicians prefer not to get involved in online discussions and choose to use social networks mostly to disseminate their image; that is, they employ Web 1.0 strategies to use Web 2.0 applications. These authors writing empirical reports in England (Lilleker and Jackson, 2009) confirm that politicians actually care what citizens might say to them in a social network but are afraid of losing control of the discussions that might arise in such platforms and benefit their adversaries.

Empirical report on Mexican politicians' participation

The research was developed as a case study, but most of the collected data were processed in a content analysis. In my research I endeavored to evaluate whether Mexican politicians are committed to participating in social media. As anybody knows practically all of them have accounts in the main social networks, but the question is if they actually participate and what kind of participation they have. Do they use the networks only to disseminate their propaganda and not to establish a dialogue? Do they use them in the old fashion of Internet 1.0 or fully develop the potential offered by Web 2.0 as Barack Obama did in his campaign in 2008?

Authors of political marketing have stipulated that in order to be successful in the field of social marketing, opening an account is not enough (Edelman, 2009). They used to say that using these resources, posting comments, debating with other users or answering information requests are necessary. In this research I endeavored to evaluate the typical variables of Web 2.0 by investigating whether political leaders:

1. Have created the typical resources of the social Web, or at least the most common: a personal blog, an institutional e-mail account, a profile in Wikipedia, a channel on YouTube, or an account on Facebook, Twitter or LinkedIn.
2. Have created websites 2.0 or only websites 1.0; websites 2.0 are those where links to the politician's social network accounts (e.g. Facebook, Twitter) are posted in order to establish a dialogue.
3. Post comments and dialogue through any of the main social networks: Facebook and Twitter.
4. Answer information request in any possible form, from e-mails to social networks.

To evaluate politicians I carried out three exercises: 1) counted the resources of the social media used by the politicians, such as social networks, blogs or video channels; then 2) I sent them an e-mail to ask for information and by doing so evaluated if they answered e-mails sent by citizens and finally; 3) I analyzed their participation in Twitter and Facebook.

Politicians' behavior changes every day, but the most important moment for them are campaigning time. For this exercise I gathered the sample out of a campaign period to find out if they use social networks when they are not campaigning. In the upcoming presidential election most of the politicians will surely have a growing social activity on the Internet.

The 81 politicians analyzed had the following positions: The president of the Republic (1), secretaries of state (22); state governors (32); the candidates for the governorship of the State of Mexico (3); the presidents of the national political parties (14); the presidents of the Chamber of deputies and Chamber of Senators (3); the leaders of the political parties' parliamentary groups at the Chamber of Deputies (4); two political parties' informal leaders (Andres Manuel Lopez Obrador and Margarita Zavala). It is worth stressing that we searched for all the accounts of the politicians to be evaluated but not all of them had accounts or their accounts were not active at the time.

Web 2.0 resources used by the politicians evaluated

The first exercise I made was to analyze the number of social web resources used by every politician. The investigation was made in May 2011. Accounts in Wikipedia (80), Facebook (80) and Twitter (72) represent the resources most frequently used. The next resource that politicians use more often is the e-mail (56 cases). Third place is for a personal channel in YouTube (29 cases). As we will see in the analysis of Twitter and Facebook, most of the politicians' accounts are classified as inactive since most of their owners hardly ever use them. Inactive accounts were not included in the analysis of politicians' participation in Facebook and Twitter, since they do not account for politicians' use of the social web resources.

Many state governors were ranked in the first places (9 cases). In this group, where the head of the government of the Federal District is included (in order to have 10 cases), together all of them comprise 50% of the cases. Since most of them belong to PRI, their party is predominant in this table (7 cases). On the contrary, the president's secretaries, who used fewer resources, got some of the lowest rates. This makes me think that the fact that governors are subject to the popular vote leads them to have more motivation to use social media than senior officials, who are appointed only by the president.

The answers to the e-mail

My research assistant searched for the institutional electronic mail addresses of the national political leaders and found out 56 accounts. She sent an information request to all of them in June 2011, in which she asked them: which media did they review every day? By using this procedure we expected to ascertain how politicians respond to citizens' very basic information requests.

Only five politicians answered the message we sent to make contact with them; the rest of them (51) did not reply. Five of the electronic mail accounts that did not answer were bounced automatically. Two months later we resent the same mail to the five blocked accounts but our message was bounced again.

This makes us think these five politicians have an overloaded e-mail account and never clean it out. For all practical purposes they have abandoned their e-mail accounts.

From the five e-mails answered, only the Minister of Economy provided the information requested. The rest, including the president Felipe Calderon, asked us to redirect our request to other officials.

My conclusion is that politicians are not used to answering information requests through e-mails, and as a result they do not establish a dialogue with the population using this tool.

Results of the analysis of politicians in Twitter

For every politician in Twitter only the historical backgrounds of each account were evaluated. The main variables taken into account were: 1) the age of the account, 2) the number of followers, 3) the number of accounts followed and 4) the number of tweets the politicians had published. In total the "active accounts" of 72 politicians were analyzed in Twitter. The observation of Twitter was conducted between May and June.

Inactive accounts, such as Governor of the State of Mexico Enrique Peña Nieto's, were not evaluated in the analysis. Peña Nieto reactivated his account some months after our analysis, on the seventh of November, as a result of the beginning of his pre-campaign for the Presidency. In his first day in Twitter his account exceeded 5.000 followers. Even though our work had been done some months before and we did not include this information, we considered how meaningful it could be that the presidential pre candidate leading the polls in 2011 did not have an active Twitter account.

The average of 11 months of politicians' use of Twitter shows the use of this network is recent. However, many cases vary a lot from this average: six of them have used Twitter for more than two years; 29, from 12 to 21 months; 13 of them, between seven and 11 months and; 23 politicians have used Twitter for six or fewer months. The followers' average is 22,322, a high number with respect to the number of common citizens using this social network. Maybe only show business celebrities (journalists included) are above politicians in this variable. Besides, the number of tweets they send is not very high (1,066). When this number is divided into the 11 average months it shows the average of tweets politicians send every month is 96.9.

We made a ranking of politicians combining the two fundamental variables of our analysis: number of followers and amount of tweets sent. In this ranking politicians are rated from 0 to 10 depending on their achievements in both variables.

In the variable "number of followers", the result was that the politicians analyzed have an average of 22,322 followers. President Felipe Calderon is above all the others with 673,176 followers; for this reason he will be given a rating of 10 on a scale of 0 to 10. Through an operation of basic algebra the rest of the politicians will be evaluated. In this case the aim is to consider the other politicians' ratings in order to keep the proportion of Felipe Calderon.

In the variable referring to the number of tweets I did a mathematical operation to account for the number of followers. The basic rule was to comply with the proportion of the large number of Felipe Calderon's followers; in order to do so, ratings are pondered in the tweets variable to comply with this huge difference. The following Table 1 shows the first 28 places of the Twitter ranking.

Participation in Facebook

Since more variables were taken into account for the analysis of politicians' behavior in Facebook than in Twitter analysis, the accounts were monitored only for a week, from the 15th to the 21st of July 2011. The lack of electoral processes in progress that could bias the follow-up was an important reason to choose this week. We must remember there are two kinds of accounts allowed in Facebook: personal profiles and public pages.

To show the results of our studies a table was made in which the data from the different accounts (profiles and pages) held by each politician was collected. For this overview the accounts of every politician's support groups were excluded, and later used for another counting. In that moment the focus of the table was to show politicians' direct participation and not the participation of their support groups.

However, I made an exception in the variable "number of followers": to count the data for this variable I used the numbers obtained on their pages and personal profiles as well as the followers politicians had in the pages of their official support groups. Following this procedure I made a table that concentrates the results of the 28 politicians who had active accounts; we must take into consideration that many politicians have several accounts (of profiles and pages). According to some of the averages achieved by politicians in Facebook it can be said they post few (17 posts a week) but have a great base of followers (64,902).

The ranking of politicians was made according to the two main variables of the analysis: number of followers and number of posts; according to their achievements in both variables, politicians are rated in a scale from 0 to 10. A ranking that combines politicians' rankings in Twitter and Facebook is displayed in Table 1. This ranking tries to analyze how many of them have a good performance in both social networks.

Table 1. Influence ranking in both social networks (Twitter and Facebook)

No	Name	General average on Twitter	General average on Facebook	General average on both social networks	Party
1	Felipe Calderón	5.17	2.09	3.63	PAN
2	Ivonne Ortega	2.79	0.95	1.87	PRI
3	Ney González	0.32	3.03	1.68	PRI
4	Heriberto Félix	0.05	2.91	1.48	PAN
5	Josefina Vázquez Mota	0.31	1.18	0.75	PAN
6	Gabino Cué	0.66	0.8	0.73	Coalition
7	Marcelo Ebrard	1.34	0.08	0.71	PRD
8	Manlio Fabio Beltrones	0.24	0.93	0.59	PRI
9	Roberto Borge	0.08	1.04	0.56	PRI
10	AMLO	0.78	0.26	0.52	PRD
11	Dante Delgado	0.92	0.04	0.48	Convergencia
12	Margarita Zavala	0.64	0.3	0.47	PAN
13	Emilio González	0.21	0.56	0.39	PAN
14	Rafael Moreno Valle	0.02	0.68	0.35	Coalition
15	Alonso Lujambio	0.36	0.28	0.32	PAN
16	César Duarte	0.22	0.4	0.31	PRI
17	José Ángel Córdova Villalobos	0.2	0.39	0.3	PAN
18	Carlos Navarrete	0.48	0.11	0.3	PRD
19	Gustavo Madero	0.45	0.11	0.28	PAN
20	Jorge Carlos Ramírez Marín	0.05	0.46	0.26	PRI
21	Javier Duarte	0.28	0.21	0.25	PRI
22	Santiago Creel	0.37	0.09	0.23	PAN
23	José Calzada	0.17	0.15	0.16	PRI

24	Ernesto Cordero	0.28	0.04	0.16	PAN
25	Miguel Alonso Reyes	0.08	0.21	0.15	PRI
26	Mariano González Zarur	0	0.23	0.12	PRI
27	Francisco Olvera	0.14	0.01	0.08	PRI
28	José Guadalupe Osuna	0.01	0.09	0.05	PAN

Source: Prepared by author

Politicians committed with both networks

Apparently the first ten politicians ranked in Table 1 have a good performance in both networks; however when the details for each politician's participation are evaluated, the result is that most of them give priority to one over the other. The exemplary case is governor Enrique Peña Nieto, who dominates Facebook but does not even have an active account in Twitter (that is why he is not included in this ranking). Another example is Marcelo Ebrard, who was rated second in Twitter and is only 27th in Facebook.

In this manner, if we discard the ones who have a low average in any of the two networks, the list of the first ten places drops to seven. As a result only seven of the 81 politicians monitored could be considered as committed to participating in social networks. Nevertheless, these politicians' commitment is very low, as proved by the null response they give to electronic mail messages and by the fact only three of them have created Web 2.0 pages.

This empirical study was contrasted with other empirical research made by private consulting firms on the same issue: activity by the main Mexican politicians on the Internet. (Dos en social 2011; los30tuiteros.com 2011; Twitter-México.com 2011). Their measurements are basically similar to the results of the present empirical research. However, some of the commercial reports compiled (Los30tuiteros.com 2011; Twitter-México.com 2011) allowed for a different kind of analysis: comparing Mexican political leaders and show business celebrities in terms of popularity. The result of this comparison proves that show business celebrities' popularity is much higher than politicians'. Ranking elaborated by Twitter-méxico.com (2011) in September shows the first three show business celebrities ranked are followed by more than two million people. The first nine of them have more than one million followers, whereas, among politicians, the president Felipe Calderon was the only one to reach the million followers in the time monitored; Marcelo Ebrard, rated second, hardly exceeded 164,000 followers, and the rest of the politicians each had less than 100,000 followers.

Another example of the importance of show business on social networks is given by IBOPE (2010) study; this quantitative investigation points out that in 2010, in México, the most important topic for Television and social networks was the FIFA soccer world cup. The main actor in this topic in Twitter was not even human, but the "Octopus Paul", who predicted the results of the championship.

One obvious conclusion to be drawn after comparing politicians and show-business celebrities is that social networks are co-opted by the dynamics of the show business rather than by conventional politics. As suggested by Dahlberg (2010), from these tendencies it can be deduced that social networks are useful to consumer society; they could hardly be used for the development of a public sphere for debate. No trace is kept from the idea of the benefits of networking for a deliberative democracy defended by the Internet propagandists.

The results of our investigation show that in the case of Mexico, neither are the politicians committed to social networks nor does the population give enough importance to political action through the Internet, and that is why people are linked en masse to show business celebrities through the social networks.

In conclusion: how do Mexican politicians use Web 2.0 resources?

Using the information I have compiled for years while observing politicians' behavior, I have deduced the following pattern: most of the politicians who have significant participation in social networks began their activity with an electoral campaign. As pointed out before, this is the reason governors are very active in using the resources of social media.

However, I have also observed a tendency in which most politicians do not continue their work on social networks after their campaigns. However, this tendency has to be qualified: politicians who win an election keep a moderate activity in social networks, which is never as intense as it is during the campaign; this is the case of the governors. By contrast, defeated politicians abandon their activity in social networks.

Another important element to highlight is that the national political leaders, compared to the generic population, usually have a large number of followers. Only show business celebrities are more popular than politicians.

Another pattern discovered is that most of the national politicians have a more active participation on Twitter than on Facebook (except for Enrique Peña Nieto). I believe the fact that politicians connect with journalists and media in general via Twitter is responsible for this tendency. This means the media usually follow politicians' Twitter accounts to learn what their official responses to any event are. In general terms the use of Twitter to connect to media and to have a major impact in society has been a successful strategy for politicians.

On the contrary, the lesser presence of politicians on Facebook makes me think they do not have a clear strategy to interact with this social network. This lack of strategy is paradoxical, since most Mexican netizens, some 28 million users, participate in Facebook (checkfacebook.com, 2011). It is estimated that in 2011 there were 34 million Internet users in Mexico (Espino, 2012: 189). It is hard to understand why most of the politicians do not interact sufficiently on Facebook, where most of the Mexican netizens participate.

In general, the fact that Mexican politicians have little or no interest in Facebook, and that many of them are absent from Twitter, leads me to conclude that most of the politicians analyzed are not committed to having a distinctive participation in Web 2.0. Since this report was made out of the campaign time, this lack of interest might change in electoral seasons. In 2012 we will analyze the other side of the coin: politicians' behavior in social media during the time of campaigns; this will surely modify politicians' attitudes, but I do not think the campaign effervescence will last on the Internet once the elections are concluded.

References

Barabasi, A-L. (2002). *Linked. The new science of networks. How everything is connected to everything else and what it means for science, business and everyday life.* Perseus Publishing. Cambridge.

Castells, M.l (2009). *Communication power.* New York: Oxford University Press

Castoriadis, C. (1997). *El avance de la insignificancia,* Buenos Aires: Anagrama.

Chatterjee, Pr. (2011). The new cyber-industrial complex spying on us. *The Guardian.* 2 December 2011. London.

Dahlberg, L. (2010) Cyber-libertarianism 2.0: a discourse theory/critical economy examination. *Cultural politics.* Volume 6, Issue 3, 331-356.

Debray, R. (1994) *Vida y muerte de la imagen. Historia de la mirada en Occidente,* , Barcelona: Paidós.

Dos en social (2011). *Rumbo al 2012: Los presidenciables de México y l#RedesSociales [Infografía*].marzo de 2011, en www.dosensocial.com, Downloaded 30 July, 2011.

Edelman-Digital public affairs (2009). *The social pulpit Barack Obama's Social Media toolkit.* Downloaded 23 april 2011.

http://cyber.law.harvard.edu/sites/cyber.law.harvard.edu/files/Social%20Pulpit%20-%20Barack%20Obamas%20Social%20Media%20Toolkit%201.09.pdf

Espino Sánchez, G. (2012) *¿Cyberrevolución en la política? Mitos y verdades sobre la ciberpolítica 2.0 en México.* México: Fontamara.

Findahl, O. (2010). *Swedes and the Internet.* Stockholm. SE.

Fuchs, C. (2011). The contemporary world wide web: social medium or new space of accumulation? In *The political economies of media. The transformation of the global media industries*, eds. Dwayne Winseck and Dal Yong Jin, 201-220. London: Bloomsbury. http://fuchs.uti.at/wp-content/uploads/PEI.pdf.

IBOPE (2010) *2010, Anuario Media Performance, Highlights*, IBOPE AGB México, Downloaded November 27, 2011, https://www.ibopeagb.com.mx/biblioteca/anuario.php.

Compass (2011). *Informe sobre política y Redes Sociales*. Downloaded 27 April, 2011, www.intelligencecompass.com.

Lilleker, D. G. and Ni.Jackson (2009), *Politicians and Web 2.0: the current bandwagon or changing the mindset?* Paper presented at the Politics: Web 2.0: an International Conference. London, U.K.

Lowe, Do. M. (1986) *Historia de la percepción burguesa.*, México: Fondo de Cultura Económica

Los30tuiteros.com (2011).*Top 30 políticos nacionales en Twitter: Junio 2011*.Downloaded 21 July 2011, http://www.los30tuiteros.com.

O´Brien, D *Ataques a la prensa en 2010: Análisis de Internet*. Committee to Protect Journalists, 2010. Downloaded December 14, 2011. http://www.cpj.org/es/2011/02/ataques-a-la-prensa-en-2010-analisis-de-internet.php.

O' Reilly, T. (2005).*What Is Web 2.0.*, Downloaded 23 April, 2011. http://oreilly.com/lpt/a/6228

Scholz, T. (2009) Market ideology and the myths of Web 2.0., *First Monday*, Vol. 13 and Number 3. Downloaded October 28, 2011. http://firstmonday.org/htbin/cgiwrap/bin/ojs/index.php/fm/issue/view/263/showToc.

Schweitzer, E.J. (2012) The Mediatization of E-Campaigning: Evidence From German Party Websites in State, National, and European Parliamentary Elections 2002-2009. *Journal of computer-mediated communication.* Downloaded June 3, 2012. http://onlinelibrary.wiley.com/doi/10.1111/j.1083-6101.2012.01574.x/full.

Tapscott, Don and A D. Williams (2010), *Wikinomiks. How mass collaboration changes everything*, Portfolio-Penguin, United States of America.

Túñez, M. y Sixto, J. (2011): "Redes sociales, política y Compromiso 2.0: La comunicación de los diputados españoles en Facebook", *Revista Latina de Comunicación Social*, 66. La Laguna (Tenerife): Universidad de La Laguna, Downloaded April 4, 2011, http://www.revistalatinacs.org/11/art/930_Santiago/09_Tunez.html.

Twitter-México.com (2011) "*20 tuiteros más populares en México*", Twitter-México.com, la página de inicio de Twitter en México, Downloaded July 21, 2011, http://www.twitter-mexico.com/.

Vaccari, C. (2010) Technology is a Commodity: The Internet in the 2008 United States Presidential Election, *Journal of Information Technology and Politics,* London, Downloaded November 15, 2011. http://www.tandfonline.com/loi/witp20.

Zimmer, M. (2008) The externalities of Search 2.0: The emergency privacy threats when the drive for the perfect search engine meets Web 2.0, *First Monday*, Vol. 13 and Number 3. Downloaded October 28, 2011. http://firstmonday.org/htbin/cgiwrap/bin/ojs/index.php/fm/issue/view/263/showToc.

7. Municipalities Mastering Social Networks. But For What?

Ewa Krzątała-Jaworska
University of Paris 1 Panthéon-Sorbonne in Paris, France

Abstract: French municipalities have been increasingly present on social networks, as confirmed both by empirical examples and a review of the literature. However, the research remains relatively silent on the reasons underlying this strategy, which in the majority of cases is not very successful. This chapter aims to demonstrate the challenges and the limits of the municipalities' presence on social networks, studying the case of municipal project promotion on Facebook and Twitter. I argue that social networks represent diverse challenges for municipalities but that their use is limited by the lack of strategic adaptation. Firstly, I distinguish the socio-political and communicational issues of the phenomenon. Secondly, I identify the limits of this new form of political communication in promoting public policy.

Keywords: social networks, political communication, municipalities, digital communication, Facebook, Twitter

Introduction

Local governments have been using digital communication increasingly. In the 1990s, French municipalities launched web sites that have become more and more interactive through the opportunity to contact elected officials via email, blog or forum (Loiseau, 2000). Today, many municipalities mark their presence on social networks or even invest in the creation of local social networks on their own territory (i.e. Issy-les-Moulineaux and its local social network i-Folio). In brief, authorities seem to share the belief that today, social networks play an important role in political communication.

Municipalities on Social Networks: a General Trend

This observation is confirmed by literature that is prolific in the field of territorial marketing and information and communication science. Researchers point out the presence of local authorities on Facebook as a general trend in France, especially in regions and departments. Michel Barabel (2010) argues that "the local governments in every area of France are on Facebook and this phenomenon is not marginal as it concerns also the less known departments." Also, according to the most recent study by the website blogterritorial.expertpublic.fr, in 2012 almost 80% of large French cities (over 100,000 inhabitants) have an official page on

Facebook. The same trend is true for municipalities. Their presence on social networks is seen by scholars as part of the much more general phenomenon of digital political communication amplification initiated by the development of telematics in the 80's, fuelled by the development of the Internet and supported by the arrival of "participatory web," also called "Web 2.0" (Loiseau, 2011). From this large perspective the use of social networks by local authorities should be interpreted as proof of Internet trivialization in social practices and as an element in the strategy of diversifying communication (Bouquillion and Palliart, 2006). The popularity of social networks among local governments has been also increasing because of the emergence of resources local communities can use to choose the best strategy for mastering social networks. Specialized consulting agencies, community managers, multiplication of web sites offering tips and guiding the municipalities through social networks are just few examples of this phenomenon. Gérard Loiseau, who has been studying digital political communication within French municipalities since the 80's, reports that now in France 14 large cities out of 43 use social networks: 13 use Facebook, 12 use Twitter and 11 use both (Loiseau, 2011).

The review of the literature and the trends observed on the web confirm the presence of local governments on social networks. The questions most frequently asked by professionals and scholars concern the promotion of the territory (Marketing), the proliferation of institutional communication (Communication Sciences) and the relationship between elected officials and citizens in this new communicational context (Political Science). Moreover, existing research focuses on the consequences of social networks' use but is relatively silent about the reasons for this choice. In consequence some questions remain unanswered, such as why the local authorities wish to be present on social networks or why users do not follow a large number of municipal social network projects.

This chapter aims to identify issues and limitations connected to local authorities' use of social networks. Equally important, it contributes to the ongoing debate concerning political institutions' presence on social networks. Despite the scholarship mentioned above, this subject is still largely undeveloped in contrast to the research on the role of social networks for social movements (i.e. Arab spring), for political parties (*Coopol, Créateurs du possible*) or for political campaigns (i.e. Barack Obama).

General Estates of the Digital City

In order to address the problems reported above, the chapter is based on fieldwork conducted in Fontenay-sous-Bois, where I studied the case of the General

Estates of the Digital City, a public offline and online consultation held from April 2009 to May 2010 on the role of digital technology in four areas: local democracy, solidarity, education and sustainable development. The process consisted of several steps. First, an informational seminar for local councilors was organized. Then, it was followed by 16 public meetings (4 for each topic) and a seminar entitled “Internet for All”, which brought together specialists in these subjects and representatives of other interested cities.

The project leaders adopted the participatory approach following local government’s political program, which states that: “The City attached to the development of participatory democracy wishes to involve citizens, elected officials and public officials.”

The consultation of citizens was organized in two ways: face-to-face, through the 16 meetings held during the week between 18:30 and 20:30, and remotely, via the website dedicated to the project (www.fontenaynumerique.net). In addition to the web site created ad hoc, the municipal project was promoted on social networks. According to the project leaders, digital communication tools were supposed to facilitate discussion and bring together stakeholders interested in this problem.

Methodology

To study this case, I combined quantitative and qualitative methods. I analyzed the entire content concerning the project published on its Facebook and Twitter accounts. The study of digital communication (data concerning the website dedicated to the project www.fontenaynumerique.net as well as the project’s Facebook and Twitter accounts) was supplemented by semi-structured interviews with the Webmaster of the website, who is also one of the Facebook and Twitter accounts administrators. The political and administrative context of the project was traced through the archives of the town hall.

This chapter aims to determine the extent to which social networks can become a tool of political communication around a city. Initially, I will present the political and communicative issues linked to the presence of municipalities on social networks and we will finish our discussion by demonstrating the limits of this strategy.

Social Networks and Political Communication

Following the general trend, the project leaders of the General Estates of Digital City decided to be present on the two most popular social networks: Facebook and Twitter. In the following section, I will demonstrate the socio-political and communicational issues of this strategy.

Sociopolitical Issues

The challenges of using social networks to promote a municipal project will first be presented from sociopolitical point of view. To what extent does the use of social networks contribute to the image of the city? Does the use of social networks to facilitate political communication allow the city both to reach a wide audience and to target a population usually not interested in politics? According to some scholars, public authorities use Facebook because some of its characteristics facilitate political communication (Westling, 2007). Firstly, it allows the creation of "real" public space, because there is no other network that brings together so many people despite geographical distances. Secondly, this network combines the best qualities of traditional channels of political communication like the municipal newsletter, public meetings and newspapers. Contrary to public meetings, the topics on Facebook seem to be proposed by Internet users and not imposed by authorities. In addition, the message is communicated to those who want to receive it. Finally, thanks to Facebook, politicians get the public's reactions to what they say.

The main purpose of the General Estates of the Digital City as highlighted by the stakeholders of the project was to organize a public debate within different social groups concerning Information and Communications Technology (ICT) issues. In particular, it was supposed to establish links between associations, landlords of public housing units, professionals, teachers and social workers. The project manager, head of the municipal Department of Information and Telecommunication Systems formulated this objective as follows:

> "We managed to bring together many people seeking a dialogue. Often they lead projects related in some way to the digital, but these projects, although very closely-related, are disconnected. As an example there are teachers and associations of parents, social workers or organizations that help the disadvantaged population. We also succeeded in building relationships with various state agencies that would enable us to conduct our digital policy in the future."

From this perspective, social networks were seen as an important tool for linking individuals and groups that could work together to lead their projects *pro publico bono.* Firstly, before physical meetings at the town hall, they might already become familiar with other people involved in the project by visiting their Facebook pages and reading the statements posted on the project's Facebook wall. On the other hand, after the physical meetings, the Facebook account was supposed to be transformed into a remote debate space with already established and strong relationships. In brief, the presence of the municipal project on social networks was supposed to foster the local social capital.

Similarly, social networks were seen as a solution to another political issue, which was not specific to Fontenay-sous-Bois: the lack of interest in politics among young people. Indeed, no one under 40 years old has participated in meetings organized within the project:

> "We wanted to reach more young people because local democracy is usually not a topic of interest to them, so we tried to attract them by the meeting in a modern bar in Fontenay. It did not work. It was one of the less crowded meetings, but we still managed to have two people, and the discussion, even if it was not what we expected, was interesting."

Since young people are avid users of social media, new technologies are often presented as possible means to make them interested in politics (Clarke, 2010). According to the most recent study of the Observatory of Social Networks from IFOP, 2009 was marked in France by an important growth of social networks. 77% of surveyed Internet users declared that they used at least one social network and this percentage reached 96% for the 18-24 year old group. The analysis of this score by the sub-age groups shows that social network use is highest among young people and is inversely proportional to the age of the Internet users. Thus, high school and college students are most likely to have a Facebook account (69%). That is why so many scientists consider new media as an efficient means of political communication, arguing that youths need immediacy and rapid exchange, while traditional democratic procedures are not sufficiently reactive. In addition, young people are likely to benefit from new forms of political participation as shown in the example of Canadians cited by Amanda Clarke (2010). This study of Canadian youths conducted in 2009 shows that 52% of respondents have created a Facebook group or joined such a group among others in order to defend a cause. 47% have participated in a debate online and 39% have forwarded an email regarding causes to defend. However, other studies show that some young people feel harassed when individuals and public institutions seek to join their social networks.

In addition, the presence of municipal authorities on social networks is also seen as a factor of the city's competitiveness among others. From this perspective, it is important to note that Fontenay-sous-Bois is highly ranked in the annual classification of municipalities of all sizes that implement significant policy in democratization of ICTs and their use by citizens. Since November 2009, the association Villes Internet (Digital Cities) has awarded Fontenay-sous-Bois "@@@@@", a sign of ICT involvement; it has been among the best cities rewarded. This label, although it does not bring any direct material gains, may contribute to the prestige of the city and may increase its competitiveness with others. The voluntary nature of all investments in ICT is clearly highlighted in the municipal public communication (i.e. the municipal website and the Acts of the General Estates of the Digital City). Information and communication technologies are introduced in various municipal institutions such as schools or digital public spaces. The local government also emphasizes the promotion of the Internet within disadvantaged social groups to reduce the digital divide.

Moreover, the city, like a large majority of French cities, has a municipal website (SIM) (www.fontenay-sous-bois.fr). The site is seen as a strategy for diversifying communication tools, replacing the usual centralization of public communication. Also, the municipal site includes elements of interactivity. There is an integrated forum, several administrative services are available online and the Internet users have the opportunity to contact elected officials.

However, it should be emphasized that these new media are in fact primarily the reproduction of existing information, such as the municipal newsletter and municipal archives. Therefore, the device increases public access to information but does not modify its content. Indeed, the use of ICT in communication does not replace traditional procedures of information. Rather, it complements them.

The Challenges of Communication

The promotion of events related to the General Estates of the Digital City is an important issue from a communications point of view. Social networks were also used for this purpose. That is why, after considering the socio-political issues in the use of social networks by the city, it is essential to focus on political communication via social networks.

First, one of Facebook's functionalities—"events"—was often used during the General Estates. Fifteen events were announced this way. The original purpose was to inform members of the dates of public meetings. However, it was equally important to have a return on the level of participation in public meetings, as mentioned by one of the Facebook community managers in an interview:

> "We also invite people for the public meetings via Facebook. And this way we can see if there was any response. People clearly say: I'm coming, I'm not coming, I do not know yet."

Even if this return was only declarative, it helped the organizers to estimate the number of participants and to prepare logistics. It also helps to prevent the omission of invitation for potential participants. Interestingly, the most important officials in city hall always confirm their presence in order to attract more people and to get them involved in the project. This is the case of the mayor who was present only at the launch meeting of the General Estates, which gathered the majority of the public. Afterwards, even if he confirmed his presence on each and every public meeting via Facebook, he never came.

Twitter was also used to recall evening meetings held with the participation of the public. The aim was clear: to create a buzz and stimulate word-of-mouth around the project. This means of communication improved attendance because it reminded people of meetings they may have forgotten. The tweets, short messages, served as announcements and reminders of events but they did not provide any content that would encourage a discussion. Also, these messages were sent only to those who had already shown their interest in the project by subscribing to the Twitter account of General Estates, so it could not be used as a means of enlarging the public involved.

The communicational use of social networks was also based on the hyperlinks used to keep the public informed and to mobilize it to speak in public meetings. This is obvious from an analysis of the contents of the Facebook account of the General Estates, where a large number of links embedded in posts were published. They are present in the notes posted on the wall, in advertisements of events, and in the presentation of the account. At first glance, the Facebook account of the project is very open and leads the user to other websites. However, most of these links lead in fact to the website dedicated to the project. The municipality follows the strategy of companies to keep Internet users within their own network as long as possible.

Table 1. How do the visitors access the website?

Position	Origin	Visits	Percentage
1	direct access	3515	57.34%
2	search engines	1313	21.42%
3	links	1302	21.24%
Total			100%

Source: data from site access statistics, collected with Analog, a standard tool for monitoring Apache web server statistics.

Consequently, even if a few links on the Facebook account do not lead to the website dedicated to project, they still keep users focused on the same subject. Indeed, these links lead to the municipal website or to the websites of some project partners such as the previously mentioned association Digital Cities or ARTESI.

While in the economic sector such a closed network of the websites helps to retain the users and lead them to make a purchase, in the analyzed case it rather makes them familiar with the project and convinces them to join it. Also, this strategy can generate the online traffic of the website dedicated to municipal project, which can then be used by leaders of the project as an argument to convince policy makers of local citizens' interest in the project. Data concerning the website dedicated to the project clearly show that in some cases the links indeed provided some audience to the General Estates website. The site's administrator said in an interview that only 38% of users passed through the home page to browse the site, meaning that the rest reached the website through a direct link. What is even more striking, some visitors came from websites where the project was not formally or voluntarily advertised. For instance, there were some entries to the project website from the URL www.linkedin.com where the project was not directly advertised. Obviously, this is only because one of the project stakeholders put the link to the website on his LinkedIn profile and some Internet users clicked on the link. This example shows the importance of social networks today. An effective use of social networks includes not only the release of information and links on multiple websites, but also the control of information published outside the corporate campaign.

However, according to data provided by the Webmaster, social networks generated minimal traffic to the project.

Figure 1. The website traffic sources (%).

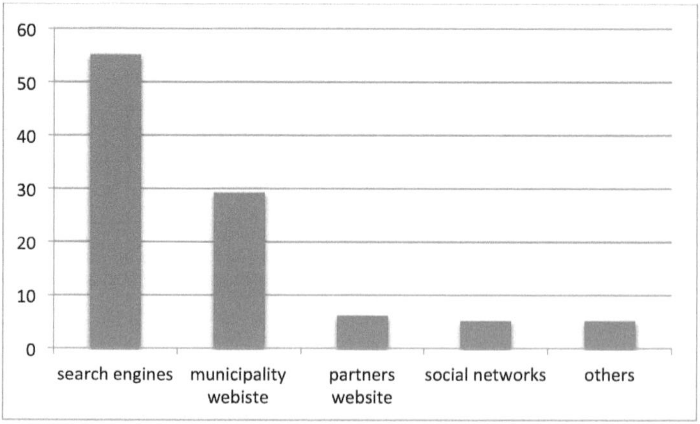

Source: data from site access statistics, collected with Analog, a standard tool for monitoring Apache web server statistics.

As the graph shows, only 5% of Internet users who reached the website from other websites were led there by social networks. In comparison with the rate of visits from search engines and the main municipal website, it is clear that the expectations of the project leaders concerning the social networks were not met.

What Limits to This Conquest?

The objective of this section is to show why there is such a discrepancy between the expectations of the project promoters concerning social networks and the observed reality. Why is there a gap between real Twitter and Facebook use and project leaders' expectations?

Low Level of Public Investment

The first difficulty that I identified is the low participation of Internet users. The project director admits that it is difficult to attract people and to make them navigate a municipal website. In this case, in order to increase the number of members of the project's Facebook account, the stakeholders relied on some existing virtual communities by mobilizing the official Facebook page of the city as well as the official Facebook page of the mayor. Despite this strategy, neither the Facebook friends (176) nor the Twitter followers of the project (22) were numerous. However, the real value of these numbers cannot be simply evaluated; it is crucial to refer to a standard like Metcalfe's or Reed's laws, under which the value of a social network depends heavily on the number of users of this network. According to Metcalfe, the value of a network is proportional to the square of the number of nodes connected to it. According to Reed, the networks that encourage the construction of communicating groups create value that grows exponentially with network size (Lefebvre, 2005).

Of course, if the number of network members is considered as the only variable, the value of these accounts must be estimated as very low. The number of members of the Facebook group of the General Estates, or the number of subscribers to tweets of the project leaders is visibly lower than the average over the Internet. By comparison, the Facebook page of Issy-les-Moulineaux, another town in the Paris suburbs, attracts more than 2000 fans.

However, this calculation has its limits and seems to be too simplistic. A comparable value is assigned to each social network while they are not used with the same intensity. To refine the analysis it is important to study the profiles of Facebook group members and the intensity of exchanges between the network nodes.

In brief, a large majority of Facebook project group members work at the town hall or are actively involved in local public life and evidently are in contact with local government agents. Also among the members are relatives of some project stakeholders. Even though it is impossible to analyze the profiles of all the Facebook group members because of the limited amount of information revealed by some users, some interesting observations can be formulated. To analyze the data available, I will rely on Mark Granovetter's theory of weak ties and strong ties (Granovetter, 1973). According to this theory, strong ties are those that connect us with members of our family, close friends and regular colleagues. In other words, strong ties are developed within a direct and long-term relationship, characterized by a high reciprocity. In contrast, weak ties are related to short-term relationships or casual context.

Since the majority of Facebook account members work together at the town hall, their relationship can be characterized by strong ties. Paradoxically, the strength of these bonds decreases the value of the analyzed networks. As individuals belong to the same online and offline networks, the information about the project is not likely to be largely disseminated. Also, since strong ties link these individuals, they have similar points of view on the ICT and the project itself. This makes the Facebook group too homogeneous and prevents a real discussion defined as an exchange of opposing arguments.

Not only is the Facebook group small and linked by strong ties, but also the rate of participation in the discussion launched by the community manager is very low. This observation is contradictory to the leitmotif of the Web 2.0 enthusiasts who consider Web 2.0 as a factor of higher involvement of Internet users compared to their prior passivity (Rebillard, 2005).

Indeed, analyzing the Facebook account of the project, at first glance it seems that many users get involved in the debate by posting on the Facebook wall. However, after examining the profiles of these people, it becomes obvious that the contributors are only the administrators or moderators of the Facebook group. The few contributions of other users come from representatives of organizations that are trying to forge a partnership with the municipality and to get the project leader interested in their services.

The analysis of messages posted on the wall shows that the project leaders tried in vain to make Internet users discuss issues on the Internet. Not only did the members of Facebook group not take the initiative to launch a debate, but they also did not even respond to questions the community managers asked.

However, the debate between Facebook group administrators and Internet users is not the only missing element. The analyzed virtual space also lacks any sign of users' commitment. The fact of joining the Facebook page of the project is the only indicator that confirms a sort of link between users and the project page. However, it is not enough to indicate commitment. The act of joining a Facebook group is quite easy, instant and free of charge, so users often subscribe to many groups in which they do not get involved. In addition, in the case of this project Facebook page, many users joined because they felt obliged to do so since they worked at the town hall. However, membership itself is for them a sufficient bond; they do not want to go further and contribute to anything on the Facebook page.

Also, even the less demanding Facebook functionalities such as clicking on the button to "like" or "unlike" a post were not utilized. In the few comments found on the wall of the page there are no emoticons. Finally, people do not publish pictures or images and do not comment on those already published.

The Lack of a Community Manager

Apart from the described attitude of users, I also observed some limitations on the communication strategy, particularly related to lack of community management. These limits are manifested in the form of messages posted, as well as in the way the Facebook group was animated. First, the contents of Facebook and Twitter accounts of the project were not always adapted to the devices used, a foresight more visible on Facebook than on Twitter. As for Twitter, the content is fairly well adapted to the tool because the posts are short and they announce and advertise upcoming events. This adaptation could be explained both by the message length dictated by the formal limits of Twitter (maximum characters: 140) and by peoples' habit of using mobile phones and SMS.

On the contrary, the use of Facebook is much more complicated and innovative. It is a tool that allows administrators a lot of freedom on the size and shape of posts. At first glance, looking especially at the events section, the content seems to suit the medium. Announcements of public meetings are short and written like advertisements. However, after clicking on the event for more information, the user accesses a traditional institutional message, very formal, which looks like an official letter sent by the administration via traditional mail. This clearly shows that even if they use new media, municipal officials remain committed to traditional forms of communication.

Also, both Facebook and Twitter accounts are very irregularly updated. Very often many posts are published at the same time and afterwards no other messages are posted in the weeks that follow. This lack of regularity discourages the users, who have no incentive to return to the project page in order to follow the discussion or to keep updated on the project. Users can also get the impression that if the Facebook page of the project does not change, the project itself is not so dynamic or interesting.

Moreover, communication on the project via social networks is still vertical and does not differ from the city's "corporate" communication that you can find on the municipal website or on the website dedicated to the project. Facebook becomes an arena within which messages are disseminated. The community managers publish invitations to meetings and information about meetings that have already occurred. They also post messages to describe the municipal project in detail even if the simple act of providing information does not start debate. In consequence, users do not feel involved in the Facebook community and do not express their point of view within this virtual space just as they are unlikely to do so through a more institutional channel.

In addition, the virtual communities created around the Twitter account and Facebook project are not animated by one person responsible for this mission. On the contrary, several people share this position and perform community manager tasks in addition to their daily professional activities. The Webmaster of the municipal website who is also one of Facebook and Twitter community managers said in an interview:

> "I did my best, but I could not really dedicate my working hours to site management and to dialogue with users. This task was additional for me."

This statement shows that the lack of manpower may impede communication via social networks. Limited human resources resulted in a proliferation of community managers who are four in total. As each of them has a different vision for managing the virtual community, their presence on Facebook does not have the unifying function often attributed to community managers. It is not possible to find a coherent shared strategy on the project's Facebook page.

Moreover, a local web map has not been identified. The project managers did not use blogs or Facebook accounts linked to the city or those created by individuals and groups outside city hall (associations, inhabitants). The project's website administrators and community managers did not use partnerships either, even if they could have provided free publicity for the project.

Finally, weak communication via social media is also caused by a lack of cooperation between the project leaders and the city's media institutions. In the interview one of the Facebook and Twitter community managers admitted that it was mainly the official city site and other media in the city that had not really communicated that there was a site of the States General. The result? Very few subscribers to the Facebook and Twitter accounts.

Conclusion

In this chapter, the role of social networks in promoting a municipal project is analyzed using the example of digital communication on the project called General Estates of the Digital City. The analysis reveals that social networks are both a challenge and an unwieldy tool for local communities.

First, as the stakes of the General Estates of the Digital City were closely related to new technologies, the use of digital communication tools to promote the project seems natural. In addition, it had its origins in previous actions of the municipality in the field of new technologies that had already highlighted the elected and administrative functionality of these new tools. It also corresponds to a more general trend of the growing use of new technologies highlighted by scholars observing local governments such as Philippe Bouquillion and Isabelle Pailliart, Michel Barabel or Gerard Loiseau. However, while such tools as the municipal site or mailing list have been used by the city for a long time, and although a proactive policy in the ICT field was conducted, the promotion of a municipal project via social networks is still relatively new to the local institutions.

Second, the presence of the project on social networks represented many challenges for the municipality. I distinguished three goals of this presence: informational (to inform Internet users about the project or call meetings), political (to bring various actors together and to involve both the people and elected officials in the consultation) and communicational (to increase traffic of the website dedicated to the project in order to create a buzz and to catch and to retain the user).

Third, despite the identification of these issues, the strategy carried out in Fontenay-sous-Bois did not prove successful. This could be explained by lack of human capital (no community manager or many community managers), as well as lack of prior experience analysis (presence of inhabitants on social networks). This observation converges with a larger study by the website blogterritorial.expertpublic.fr, which observes that while 80% of cities have a Facebook page, only 28% of them have an internal or external Community Manager. Municipalities' use of social networks can be seen as a form of local institutions' response to changes in the dominant media public space. As shown on the example of Fontenay-sous-Bois, social networks are perceived not only as an issue of communication and information flow, but also as mobilization and political participation tool. However, it is essential to understand through empirical research the effective range of these alternative arenas for political communication and participation. The case analysis points out that social networks can be seen as a catalyst of political practices but do not constitute their cause.

Admittedly, the results of this analysis focused on a specific case, and thus cannot be generalized. Without further research, it is difficult to draw definite conclusions about the role that social media can play in promoting a municipal project. In order to be able to judge, we should study the cases of other municipalities with differing socio-demographic structures and Internet use patterns. However, the contribution of this study is a different perspective on the role of social networks by local government that complements existing analyses which focus on heterogeneous representative samples, but do not capture the particularities of studied cases. Besides, looking at other cities where digital communication strategy is developed (e.g. Issy-les-Moulineaux's presence on Facebook and its launch of its own local social network, i-Folio), we can see that the dynamics of their accounts is not different from the dynamic that I have described in case of the General Estates of the Digital City.

References

Barabel M. et al. (2010). Les médias sociaux au service du marketing territorial: une approche exploratoire [Social media in the service of territorial marketing: an exploratory approach]. *Revue Management & Avenir,* 2, 32, 233-253.

Bouquillion P., Pailliart I. (2006). *Déploiement des Tic dans les territoires. Le rôle des collectivités.* (*ICT deployment in the territories. The role of local governments*). Grenoble: Presses Universitaires de Grenoble.

Clarke A. (2010). *Les médias sociaux. Utilisations politiques et conséquences pour la démocratie représentative. (Social media. Political uses and implications for representative democracy).* Retrieved June 15, 2010, from http://www2.parl.gc.ca/Content/LOP/ResearchPublications/2010-10-f.pdf.

http://www.slideshare.net/azizhaddad/ifop-observatoire-rseaux-sociaux-janvier-2010

Granovetter, M. (1973). *The Strength of Weak Ties. The American Journal of Sociology*, 78, 6, 1360-1380.

Lefebvre A. (2005). *Les réseaux sociaux. Pivot de l'Internet 2.0.* (*Social networks. Backbone of the Internet 2.0*) Paris: MM2 Editions.

Loiseau, G. (2011). Les sites internet des municipalités, les blogs et les réseaux sociaux: vers une multiplication des modalités participatives dans l'espace public local? *(Municipalities' websites, blogs and social networks: towards a proliferation of participatory methods in local public space?)* In E. Forey and C. Geslot, *Internet, machines à voter et démocratie*, Paris: Harmattan, 209-235

Loiseau, G. (2000). *La démocratie numérique municipale française : au-delà des parangons de vertu.* (French municipal digital democracy: beyond the paragons of virtue). *Hermès*, 26-27, 2000, 213-232.

Rebillard F. (2007). *Le web 2.0 en perspective.* (*Web 2.0 in perspective*) Paris: L'Harmattan.

Westling M. (2007). *Expanding the Public Sphere: The Impact of Facebook on the Political Communication, Society*, vol. 28, 835-860.

8. Political Communication, Social Media and Popular Culture: The *Adisucks* Facebook Protest Case Study

Jakub Nowak
University of Maria Curie-Sklodowska in Lublin, Poland

Abstract: This paper focuses on the question of how new (social) media work as tools of political messages' distribution within converged media systems. Using a case study of the *adisucks* Facebook protest organized in Polish social media in March 2011, the author demonstrates how the internet may work as a space of symbolic and participatory engagement in the collaborative creation and dissemination of grassroots political messages. The analysis is framed by a theoretical consideration of recent transformations in political communication patterns caused by changes within the sphere of civic engagement and the transformations of 21-century digital media. The author discusses: narrative or mythical and performative levels of users' contribution to the protest profile and considers possible changes in the status of modern online activism by recalling the concept of "communicative capitalism".

Key words: political communication, citizen engagement, social media, popular culture, social semiotics

Introduction

Theoretical explorations of the changes in political communication in the 21st century emphasize shifts in two areas: 1) the sphere of (post)modern civic engagement and 2) the changing patterns of political messages' circulation enabled by the development of new (increasingly social) media. This perspective helps to describe postmodern politics by focusing on the shifts in political participation towards more informal and more popular culture-oriented activities. Such a shift can be perceived as related to changes in patterns of the circulation of political messages. Because social media quickly gained an important political role, they have become a system of densely connected semi-public communication spheres in which political symbols are being (re)defined.

This paper focuses on the *adisucks* Facebook protest organized in Polish social media in March 2011. Drawing upon the analysis of the collective input to the profile, I demonstrate how the internet (especially social media) may work as a space of symbolic and participatory engagement in the collaborative creation and dissemination of grassroots political messages. I set my theoretical consideration in the context of the recent transformations in political communication patterns: 1) changes within the sphere of civic engagement and 2) the development of new media in the 21st century. In the *Discussion* section I analyze narrative or mythical and performative levels of users' contribution to the protest profile. I also discuss possible changes in the status of modern online activism by recalling the concept of "communicative capitalism".

Theoretical context

Shifts in citizen engagement

The last decades of the 20th century and the beginning of the third millennium are perceived as a time of important shifts in citizen engagement in liberal (often called "late modern") democracies (Giddens, 1991, 2006; Bennett, 2003; Dahlgren, 2001, 2003; Axford, 2001; Beck 1998, 2005). The transformations consist of a broad array of interwoven phenomena including shifts in citizen roles, new modalities of political communication, weakening social and political affinities, increasing choice concerning social (lifestyle) identities, the development of new and increasingly popular sets of citizen actions' repertoires labeled by Ulrich Beck as sub- and (in his latter works; see: 2005) transnational politics.

In these new conditions one can observe an additional status in the very nature of citizenship: the citizen has been more and more often perceived as a political consumer. As Rose (1999: 166) points out, citizenship at the close of the 20th century has been primarily realized not by relations with the state within the uniform public sphere, but through active engagement in variety of private, corporate and quasi-public practices like labor or consumption. In other words, the power of individuals who constitute the society shifts from strictly electoral roles to new non-institutional forms of new political culture. The real (*actual* and actually *used*) power of individuals, as Bennett (2003: 145) argues, transfers from the electoral roles to the capacity of consumers to discipline the centers of corporate power in the economic realm. Whereas these new citizen engagement modalities are obviously not the *only* sphere of actions by which modern citizens can formulate and accomplish their goals, this market-driven domain of consumer engagement has been important enough to gain analytical attention.

These fresh hybrid forms of political-economic engagement are increasingly based on symbolic and representational activities; the mediated visibility of particular sets of actions increases their performative potential. Symbolic power (understood as the *power of symbols*), the ability to effectively construct and proliferate symbolic representations of particular meaning(s), is one of the most important resources for such "citizen-consumers" and is conducive to growing the status of media (perceived here as technological and social systems of messages' dissemination).

The new media ecosystem

Digital media have been traditionally perceived as an important factor in the process of symbolic empowerment and activation of media audiences. New media modalities, in contrast with traditional mass-media communication, make the act of contributing through symbolic representations in (at least initially) digital communication spaces profoundly easier. Moreover, the 21st-century internet is very different from the late 20th-century web. It is more participatory (hence strongly based on user-generated content) and more oriented toward social networks. These two mutually related features are the most important constituents of social media (Kaplan and Haenlein, 2010), web applications that play the key role in communication flows in today's digital media. Social media—blogs, collaborative projects (Wikipedia), social network sites (Facebook), content communities (YouTube), and virtual game worlds—create and consist of spheres of different forms of both symbolic and performative representation[1].

Several internet attributes gain importance in an era of increasingly meditated and consumer-oriented politics: multimodality of communication, visualization of social networks, and immense users' horizontal connection and content diffusion (Rheingold, 2002; Shirky, 2008), all of which lead to the formation of a more and more dense media network consisting of mainstream and non-mainstream, traditional and new, media. Such a highly complicated entity is sometimes called "the new media ecosystem" (Bowman and Willis, 2003; Gillmor, 2004) and has become a technological and symbolic environment for *all* messages published offline and online by both non-professional and established media operators.

General research questions

For the reasons listed above, one cannot miss the questions of new citizen engagement modalities and of the social media impact on the process when analyzing 21st-century political messages' flows. Therefore, the main question here is this: what are the changes of political message flows enabled by the recent development of new media (social media in particular)?

This is a very broad field of transformation, encompassing a wide range of changes in the social practices of all kinds of political actors and media audienc-

1 Such performative potential of the internet cannot be, however, mistaken with its potential for becoming a new digital public sphere (in terms of the Habermasian normative point of view)—see Papacharissi 2002.

es. In this paper I focus on a more detailed aspect of these systemic changes. The question above can be addressed differently: how new (social) media work as tools for political messages' production and distribution within the 21st century media system (Q1)?

To answer it the *adisucks* Facebook protest case study is examined. Drawing upon the findings thereof, I demonstrate how the internet may work as a space of symbolic and participatory engagement in the collaborative creation and dissemination of grassroots political messages (Q2).

The *adisucks* protest case study

In late March 2011 the Adidas company started painting over the wall that surrounds a horse racing track in Warsaw, Poland. The nearly 1.5 km-long wall is covered with graffiti and has been considered a legendary space for Polish graffiti artists. Adidas intended to paint over the graffiti with a huge advertisement. On Friday, the 25th of March, the wall was surrounded with barriers and began to be painted black.

On the same day a grassroots boycott group was set up on Facebook. The *adisucks* profile was created in order to "announce a general boycott of Adidas products" and to make Adidas "know they are doing wrong"[2]. During the following weekend it quickly gained popularity among Facebook users and the attention of the mainstream Polish media. Soon Adidas decided to publish a statement in which it announced a decision to "withdraw the project".

Table 1. Protest timeline

	25th of March (Friday)	26th of March (Saturday)	27th of March (Sunday)	28th of March (Monday)
The Służewiec Wall	The wall is surrounded with barriers, the graffiti is being painted over with black paint	The wall is still being painted over	Painting is stopped	Adidas company publishes statement of withdrawal from the project
The *adisucks* profile	evening: the profile is created	morning: 300 likes; 11.30pm: 10.000 likes	2pm: 13.000 likes	12pm: 21.000 likes

2 Taken from the boycott profile (*Adisucks,* 2011).

Mainstream media coverage	none	Online publications on several Polish news websites: - citizen journalism website Alert24.pl, - regional mainstream media websites: zyciewarszawy.pl, warszawa.gazeta.pl	The information about the protest is published online on the main page of one of the largest mainstream media websites gazeta.pl (it is repeated a few times with the latest news)	The news about the protest is published on a two-page of *Gazeta Wyborcza* (second largest Polish daily newspaper)

Source: author's elaboration (the analysis of media content and screenshots and links posted within *adisucks* profile)

The issue of the *adisucks* protest can be explored through several theoretical approaches. This analysis is set in the context of Facebook usage as a communication space for expressing opinions and reinforcing attitudes towards a particular (political) case. From this point of view the profile works as a tool for organizing a media protest by which political messages are published and distributed in order to accomplish particular goals:

- express objection towards actions of the Adidas company;
- mobilize support and organize advocacy on an informal, grassroots level;
- mobilize mainstream media interest in order to…
- … "win" the case and force the corporation to stop painting over the wall.

This perspective emphasizes users' social practices within the profile. It also takes under consideration mainstream media interest in the case, but the case study mainly involves users' activity within the *adisucks* profile. The first important variable is the number of people *liking* the *adisucks* profile. When one clicks the *like* button to express that he or she *likes* the *adisucks* profile (or any content published within it) not only does he or she express support for "the cause" but also contributes to the dissemination of information about the protest. This is because one of the most important features of modern social media systems is that the simplest act of evaluating web content (like the act of "liking" something in Facebook) is also the act of distributing the content within a subnetwork of particular social medium users: clicking the *like* button makes this act visible on other users' Facebook walls[3].

3 The Facebook wall is a part of the user's profile visible to anyone who is permitted by the profile user. The wall works as a space for posting messages, links, and other content.

The second and most important subject of the study is one kind of users' activity within the profile: the act of publishing images.

I also take into consideration media coverage of the protest, which can be perceived as a partial outcome of the users' activities within the profile. While this provides important background to the research (how does mainstream media framing copy the narratives collectively created within the profile?), it is not the main research focus in the article. While the *adisucks* case study could be examined from the point of view of agenda setting and building and media framing theories, this article will not do so due to volume limitations.

Method

As stressed above, the most important part of this research is the analysis of images posted in the protest profile. There are several reasons to analyze images:

Firstly, I assume they are popular content on the Facebook website and its users are more likely to view one's galleries in full than to read all the posts on one's wall. I base my assumption on one of the general statements of the uses and gratifications theory (Katz, Blumler and Gurevitch, 1973), according to which media users want to minimize the effort and time spent on the medium and maximize the particular outcome they seek (here: information about the issue). Moreover, in this case people could prefer viewing images because the images offered specific gratifications (the pleasure of decoding culture texts and the reinforcement of citizen-consumer identities—as analyzed below).

Secondly, images can be perceived as multimodal communicative acts. User-generated images (created and posted online) can have a very specific form and content that combine various possible readings—in short: they can potentially connote much.

Thirdly, an image (containing graphic and verbal elements) is a natural form of communication for members of the graffiti culture. Graffiti art has a high level of symbolization for those who have specific communicative competencies.

For these reasons, I set the subject of the analysis as all images posted within the *adisucks* profile between 25 and 31 March (I extended the analyzed period until the end of March because I perceive the profile as a communication space

---

This mechanism raises an interesting methodological problem: the exact rules of such content distribution within the Facebook site are restricted by the Facebook corporation. Therefore, when analyzing content distribution within the Facebook site, the researcher knows that the range of content distribution is directly proportional to the number of *likes*, but he or she cannot get precise data of the process.

that reinforces the users' shared identities—from this perspective the profile *worked* also after the Adidas' withdrawal)[4].

I assume that the best method to analyze the graphic content of the profile are social semiotic tools for image analysis (van Leeuwen, 2005; Kress and van Leeuwen, 2006; Barthes, 1973, 1977). From this perspective the analyzed images are perceived as multimodal communicative acts—multimodal compositions combining verbal or typographical and pictorial elements. Therefore, three key questions of the analysis drawn from the social semiotics theoretical tradition are:

1) What people, places and things are represented in the images?
2) What kind of connotative or symbolic meanings are associated with these representations?
3) What was the role (function) of these images as messages used to distribute information about the boycott?

While the last question is about the performative aspect of images posted online, the first two represent two layers of meanings associated with particular communicative acts: denotation and connotation (van Leeuwen, 2005: 37-39). Barthes (1977: 23) perceives visual denotation as referring to concrete people, places and things, and visual connotation as referring to abstract concepts, culturally shared meanings, or "culturally accepted inducers of ideas". Simply put, denotation is literal and concrete; connotation is an abstract mixture of concepts.

More than one hundred images were posted on the *adisucks* profile in the period from 25-31 March: 33 images posted by the founder of the profile (the user's name is Adisucks) and 77 images posted by the other 64 users (N=110 of total objects analyzed). The images were divided into three basic categories:

- *screenshots* (21 images) that capture parts of several websites, mainly to evince online content (like the number of people supporting *adisucks* profile, Adidas company statements, and mainstream media coverage of the issue).
- *photographs* (59) functioning in their most basic meaning as visual representations of reality (mostly pictures of the wall).
- *graphic projects* (40)—multimodal acts (some of them combining different visual and textual modalities) with a relatively high level of symbolization (this category includes the protest logo shown in Fig. 1, visual remixes of the Adidas logo, and desktop wallpaper projects).

4 In fact, the profile was active in this role to the end of September 2012: it worked as a communication space for people interested in graffiti culture.

As the figures show, several images were put into two categories because some of the graphic projects (like desktop wallpapers) are strongly based on photographs (of graffiti walls). Moreover, a few photographs capture new graphic projects painted on the Służewiec wall (see Fig. 2); their function is to introduce both a particular piece of reality (the re-painted Służewiec wall) and a new graffiti project, so they are assigned to both categories.

Findings and discussion

The narrative or mythical level of users' contribution

The analysis has shown that almost all contributions to the *adisucks* profile utilize visual symbolism to promote the concept of general yet fundamental division on two sides of the conflict. While the denotations of the graphical contribution—understood as the list of people, places and things represented in the images—are easy to recall[5], connotative and symbolic meanings associated with analyzed representations are wide and multilayered.

The photographs of the Służewiec wall compose the narrative of *winning* the fight with the Adidas company; the Facebook profile worked as communication space to which people contributed to make Adidas stop covering the wall with advertisements.

The narrative contains strong normative evaluations. The pejorative ones are focused around the Adidas company, the obvious villain in the story. The negative connotations can be decoded from the objects graphically connected to Adidas logos and products in the *graphic projects* category: e.g. a toilet, urine, feces, mercenary-looking soldiers, male genitals, a middle finger raised in an offensive gesture, and unattractive women (according to the media-driven aesthetic canon). Even some *screenshots* connote the cynicism and hypocrisy of the Adidas company that seeks to be perceived as supporting street-art culture.

Some of the images posted are graphic remixes of the Adidas logo. They refer to the tradition of culture jamming and subvertizing, anti-consumerist tactics of subverting meanings imposed by mainstream corporate, media or political institutions in order to, as Lasn (2000: xi) argues in a bombastic yet straightforward manner, "topple existing [symbolic] power structures (…) and change the way in which meaning is produced in the society". In this tradition the symbolic

5 Most of denotations can be divided into several groups: various representations of the Służewiec wall, particular Adidas products, screenshots denoting information on the protest published online, graffiti works, various remixes of the Adidas company logo, and more complicated digitally altered images. See: *Adisucks,* 2011.

attack on the Adidas logo reinforces the wider goal of reclaiming the street-art tradition endangered by company's corporate purposes. The protest symbol (Fig. 1) is a meaningful example: the Adidas logo is subverted not only by being filled with pieces of graffiti art but also by the horizontal rotation of the brand symbol. This transformation can be seen as degrading for the rotated object (as it is, for example, with horizontally reversed football scarves according to football fan culture).

Figure 1. The adisucks protest logo

Source: *Adisucks*, 2011.

The connotations present in the images are based on symbols from the most fundamental (post) modern symbols' repository: media-driven popular culture—as Barthes (1977: 22) states, "there is unwritten dictionary of poses which is known to everyone who is at all exposed to the mass media". Some of them are more or less obvious poses and objects (a smiling boy urinating on the Adidas logo; an offensive gesture of a middle finger). Some of them, though, are less straightforward, like the image in Figure 2. It shows a segment of the Służewiec wall with the new artwork placed on a segment freshly painted black and is an interesting example of a highly symbolic communicative act deeply rooted in popular culture. The image contains graphical elements referring to Adidas logos and the Palace of Culture and Science (one of the strongest symbols of the city of Warsaw). The overall graffiti composition refers to Space Invaders, a classic arcade video game from the late 70s and the 80s. The general aim of the game is to defeat waves of aliens with a laser cannon: the player is shooting the aliens in order not to let them reach the bottom of the screen. When it happens, the alien invasion is successful and the game ends.

Picture 2. Image posted in the profile on 31 of March

Source: Adisucks, 2011.

Picture 3. The screenshot from the original Space Invaders video game

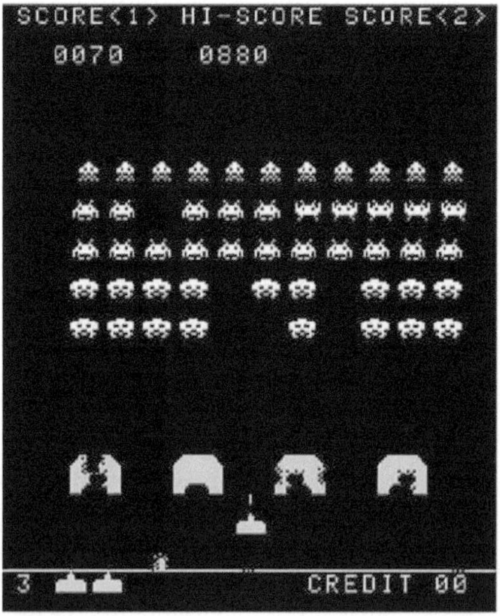

Source: Space Invaders, 2013.

The graphical reference to the video game reinforces the division into two sides of the conflict and the company's logos in place of cohorts of aliens, transforming the Adidas company into the invading aliens: Adidas is trying to invade the city, they are from the outside and they are numerous (countless aliens that keep on and keep on appearing). But Warsaw is fighting back (The Palace at the bottom as the shooting laser canon), therefore the message can be decoded as: *We, the people of the streets of Warsaw, are the good guys; they—the people from Adidas—are villains who invade our territory. We are winning and are not going to let Adidas take over our city* (because the wall is covered with graffiti again). This metaphor, though, if taken consistently, cannot connote a happy ending: the player cannot *win* (finish) the Space Invaders video game because shooting down all the aliens brings another wave of them, more and more difficult to defeat.

This last interpretation takes the image to a more universal, complex and (therefore) elusive level in which the users' contributions to the *adisucks* profile signify a much broader set of meanings that can be described in terms of myth, understood as a broad and diffuse concept which condenses everything associated with the represented people, places and things into a single entity (van Leeuwen, 2005: 37-40) and which, according to Barthes (1973: 124), is defined by its intention much more than by its literal sense.

From this perspective, the overall online contribution has two separate yet mutually connected functions: the analyzed contribution reveals and simultaneously supports the myth of a great fight between street-art culture and the market-driven profit-oriented corporation. In other words, the *adisucks* imagery adds another story into this mythical narrative, in which harmful corporate activity is stopped by the spontaneous rising of those who express their outrage towards cynical commercial plans.

A broad set of connotations has been used to create this system of coherent meanings and evaluations. Some of the images (barriers surrounding the wall, the car of a private security company) contain negative connotations not only in this issue's particular context but also from a wider perspective in the tradition of the graffiti culture in which they represent the system's (understood as the power of the state or corporations) unauthorized hegemonic resistance to free artistic transformations of the city's objects and places.

On the other hand, many of the online pictorial contributions connote the general apotheosis of street art or graffiti culture. On the obvious level pictures with graffiti art are posted to express respect to the Służewiec wall as one of the most important symbols of the street-art culture in Poland. The other art works posted within the profile (like Banksy's iconic remix of the image from the movie *Pulp Fiction*[6]) and spray cans serve the same function. Of course, *all* us-

6 The image, depicting two men dressed in suits with bananas in their hands, is a remix of the *Pulp Fiction* movie scene. Banksy, the author of the remix, is a pseudonym of

ers' activities within the profile (images, commentaries, links, *likes*) connote on a more general level the strength and vitality of Polish street art culture (*We're active and visible*). Even the *screenshots* connote this message: the images with the number of protest supporters and screenshots with mainstream media websites signify the power of the protest and the community gathered around the *adisucks* profile.

Moreover, the general point of view (the myth about the spontaneous versus a harmful corporation, "rage against the machine") seems to be even more important after analysis of both mainstream and non-mainstream media coverage of the protest[7]. One of the most important framings of the news on the *adisucks* case was in fact the repetition of this binary division made collectively by profile visitors. This repetition of evaluations, firstly, comes from the fact that mainstream media tend to picture activism in frames that help win audiences' attention, and the mythical narrative described here is one such example. Secondly, it is caused by journalistic routines, like the simple copying of sentences from the description of the protest posted by its founder without marking them as quotes (creating the impression that such sentences are parts of the narrative produced by a professional news medium, and incidentally providing it with credibility). In other words, the mainstream media not only effectively disseminated information about the protest but also involuntarily legitimated discourses in opposition to the protest (Nowak, 2013).

On the other hand, it has to be acknowledged that the collaborative input is strongly based on multiplication of the imagery produced by neoliberal culture industries. The main goal of the protest was to stop the devastation of the Służewiec wall. Though it was successful, the *adisucks* protest has also resulted in a very high media visibility (in all, traditional and new, mainstream and grassroots media) for the Adidas company. The problem was reflected also in the conversations between the profile's Facebook users. In the comments below one of the images (Figure 2) one of the users wrote: "It's bad that such things appear on the wall. People don't understand anything. [...] Duplicating the logo is always duplicating the logo, no matter if it is reversed or not".

---

a legendary street-art artist, one of the most important icons of the street-art culture as a whole.

7 The mainstream media framing is included in the forthcoming article about media agenda and mediatized public agenda aspect of the case—see footnote 4.

The performative level of users' contribution

Connotation can be an effect of the style of artwork or techniques used in creating visual images, a feature described by Barthes (1977) as "photogenia". This strongly connotative combination of form and content is an attribute of digital images in 2.0 internet, in which images posted online comprise an important performative aspect: the natural possibility of their remixing and (re)distribution by other users. Of course this has been one of the features of digital media in general (Lister and other, 2003: 14-23), but social media and applications based on user-generated content have made this kind of contribution easier than ever before.

This effect is evident when considering connotations embedded in an image posted on 26 March (see Fig. 4). The image is deeply rooted in popular culture as it is a graphical remix of two images: the head is one of King Leonidas (played by Gerald Butler), a character of the fantasy action movie *300*, the cartoon corpse is from the Japanese TV anime series *Dragon Ball Z*. Yet the sentence "It's over nine thousaaaand!!!" most likely refers to the number of *likes* of the *adisucks* profile, creating another level of connotation from the image.

The form refers to the new popular culture tradition of the meme, understood here as culture object (an image that combines pictorial and verbal elements), that has become *popular* in Fiske's (1989: 99-121) terms and that spreads via the internet mainly by horizontal distribution outside the culture industries[8]. This image *is* in fact a meme: the combination of the *This is Sparta* meme (based on *300*) and *It's over 9000* (referring to the *Dragon Ball Z* series). Its usage within the profile also refers to the culture of online cultural participation: it is the message encoded by the digital form of the image (meme) itself and is connected to its performative function of possible distribution (every digital image connotes its easy copying and online dissemination).

8 The primary meaning of the term "meme" refers to the unit of cultural evolution and the field of study called "memetics"—see: Dawkins (1989); Blackmore (1999).

Picture 4. Image posted on the 26th of March

Source: *Adisucks*, 2011.

Clay Shirky (2010, p. 15), writing on 'lolcats' (a popular kind of internet memes having cats in visual denotation), calls the process of making a lolcat (meme) the stupidest possible creative act, but these nevertheless connote a very important message: *You can play this game too*. This message is embedded in digital modality and the simple form of a meme offers a crucial change in patterns of traditional (mass) media usage, for two reasons. Firstly, it is creative ("The stupidest possible creative act is still a creative act"). Secondly, it is social:

> "The pleasure in *You can play this game too* isn't just in the making, it's also in the sharing. The phrase 'user-generated content', the current label for creative acts by amateurs, really describes not just personal but also social acts. [...] The sharing, in fact, is what makes the making fun—no one would create a lolcat to keep for themselves." (Shirky, 2010: 15)

And this increasingly collective nature of participation in popular culture is perceived as an important feature of today's popular culture in general (Jenkins, 2006).

Returning to the performative aspect of the images analyzed, some of them are in fact designed to be *used* in a literal sense, e.g. as wallpapers or as graphic projects to be placed on do-it-yourself T-shirts. But from the performative point of view, all images published online (like those within the profile) connote the opportunity (therefore also the possibility) of their further online use due to the ease of copying or remixing and distributing them across the media (notably, *not* only across the internet). This high level of images' potential transformation and distribution intensifies their status as components of messages covering the issue of *adisucks* protest. This status of digital images is tightly connected to technological and market transformations of 21st-century media: the development and evolution of the new media ecosystem is conducive to spreading information about events and issues like *adisucks*.

Of course one cannot assume that all members of the *adisucks* profile audience can decode the full connotation of the *It's over 9000* image, but they do not have to. Many of the messages published within the profile, especially those from the *graphic projects* category—in their performative role—are created, published and distributed in order to have an effect on various audiences. For people interested in street-art culture, *adisucks* users' contribution most likely works as another tool that reinforces their lifestyle identities (shared languages and meanings have a community-building function) and their cultural status is an important factor that influences their reading of profile contents; they can be perceived as Fish's (1982) interpretative community. Accidental users get a less developed version of the narrative collaboratively created in the profile. Of course they are also an active part of the protest, simply by clicking the *like* button by which they distribute information about the boycott.

Symbolic (consumer) activism in "communicative capitalism"

Moreover, all the contribution within the *adisucks* profile in fact has additional meaning: collectively elaborated output is a political message (self-aimed firstly to those who produce it) because the sum of all contributions can be described in Tatarchevskiy's (2011) term as visual labor. The internet as a site for visual representation utilizes easily accessed visual symbolism to promote the image of community and to help the protest gain legitimacy, public recognition, and support. When *liking* the profile and posting online content, the users operate within the infrastructure of symbolic exchange that enables them to easily reinforce shared identities and legitimate particular choices that are both lifestyle- and consumer-related in their nature. Visual labor, as Tatarchevskiy (2011: 306) argues, is something one can easily do—the pleasure of posting, remixing, commenting and redistributing the images (and fantasies behind them) makes this kind of contribution fun and entertaining—even though it is done *for the cause*.

This raises questions about the reformulation of online activism. One of the most important features of the users' online engagement in modern online activism is such engagement's higher possible visibility. Tatarchevskiy (2011: 307), in her analysis of the online ONE campaign, argues that "lay activists are summoned to participate in the performative labor" within "organizational culture that equates success in activism to the extent that it is *visualized*. In other words, one is 'active' if her actions are visible through certain collective symbolic representations".

Such skepticism is not, however, new. The question whether activist engagement online counts as *real* activism has been raised since the very beginning of digital media (McCaughey and Ayers, 2003: 5). Here, the more important question seems to be whether the diagnosis made by Tatarchevskiy can be applied to users' involvement in the *adisucks* protest. The symbolic and performative contribution to the Adidas boycott in fact *was* visual labor from this perspective. More importantly, the protest could not have been organized in any other manner, the media strategy of *adisucks* supporters (though often elaborated and performed unconsciously) seems to be the best possible method of managing (and participating in) political-consumer boycotts like this.

This is because of another, more systemic, reason for the protest's success. Advocacy was performed in ways that perfectly match postmodern politics and market driven media logic. Jodi Dean (2009) labels such systems as "communicative capitalism" and argues that in democratic, consumer societies, political goals cannot be achieved without the employment of systems of media and entertainment, so communication becomes the main commodity to be exchanged to accomplish political goals. In such a political-economic formation, Dean (2009: 24-26) argues, under conditions of extensive proliferation of media, the intense circulation of media content divides political antagonism into a myriad of irrelevant issues and events; the messages' success is defined by their longevity because their exchange value overtakes their use value. The only relevant thing about media content is its circulation and recognizability. In such conditions social media turn out to be effective tools of symbolic politics within "communicative capitalism": the visual collective output of *adisucks* supporters perfectly matched the media (and market) environment conditions. We can therefore perceive the protest as an example of effective adaptation of political-consumer protest to changing economic and media conditions.

It can be, however, perceived also as both elaborated by and reinforcing the structure described by Dean. The online symbolic exchange is realized within a system designed to generate profits from all kinds of social engagement. Moreover, the crucial part of the system (Facebook as the social networking service) is an online communication sphere that cannot be perceived as democratic or public from a normative point of view (its users are allowed to perform only within a closed and strictly guarded set of activities; the algorithms that regulate all the interactions within the system are not open to the public; the system's architecture is designed according to profit-oriented motivations).

Conclusion

The *adisucks* protest profile on the Facebook website turned out to be an effective space for collective (communicative) action and, at the same time, representation. These strictly connected functions contributed to reinforcing the identities of profile users who performed at several levels of online engagement: expressing approval (by *liking* the profile); contributing to its content (posting comments and images); and, what was the immediate effect of those activities, disseminating information about the protest within sub-networks of their Facebook *friends*.

Therefore, the 2.0 internet can work as a space of engagement in the collaborative creation of grassroots (political or consumer) messages (this is the answer to Q2): it provides tools for easy, comfortable and enjoyable contribution, a contribution that is by definition social (collective) and based on symbols from the popular culture repository. In other words, the engagement in the online protest was, among other things, the act of participation in popular culture: the intersection of sets (spheres) of popular culture, citizen engagement, consumer action and politics is becoming larger and the borders between them are blurring.

Moreover, the Facebook website worked as an effective tool for the messages' distribution within a converged media system (answer to Q1). The main prerequisites of success were fulfilled: new media were a natural communication environment for the protesters and the story of the conflict was attractive for mainstream media (the "rage against the machine" narrative told by the protesters' online contribution was copied in media coverage). From this perspective, social media are symbolic spaces full of multimodal communicative acts which can be, in particular conditions, easily incorporated into mainstream media agendas (yet under conditions set by the mainstream media operators).

While this issue fits the optimistic scenario well from a critical political economy approach, optimism should be tempered. The collaborative engagement in the protest against the market-oriented corporation has been performed within a communicative environment manufactured by another market-oriented corporate agent and with the usage of digitally altered culture industries' products. And while the *adisucks* protest was effective (the Adidas corporation stopped and withdrew their efforts to deface the Służewiec wall), it is difficult to tell to what extent such online collective contribution is *real* social engagement: whether it is simply a formal adjustment to changing (media and market) conditions, or whether it should be labeled with the lowering term "visual labor", in which, as Tatarchevskiy (2011: 310) argues, "passivity is (…) celebrated through the symbols that interpret it as active involvement". Perhaps it is both, in which case this kind of engagement becomes one of most natural forms of political and consumer modalities of today.

References

Adisucks. (2011). Facebook profile page. Retrieved May 20, 2013, from http://www.facebook.com/pages/adisucks/134728066598497.

Axford, B. (2001). The Transformation of Politics or Anti-Politics? In B. Axford and R. Huggins (Eds.), *New Media and Politics*. London: Sage, 1-29

Barthes, R. (1973). *Mythologies*. London: Paladin.

Barthes, R. (1977). *Image, Music, Text*. London: Fontana.

Blackmore, S. (1999). *The meme machine*. Oxford: Oxford University Press.

Beck, U. (1998) *World Risk Society*. Cambridge: Polity Press.

Beck, U. (2005) *Power in the Global Age*. Cambridge: Polity Press.

Bennett, L. (2003). Lifestyle Politics and Citizen-Consumers. Identity, Communication and Political Action in Late Modern Society. In J. Corner and D. Pels (Eds.), *Media and the Restyling of Politics*. London: Sage, 137-150

Bowman, S. and Willis, C. (2003). *We Media. How audiences are shaping the future of news and information. The Media Center at The American Press Institute.* Retrieved December 20, 2011, from http://www.hypergene.net/wemedia/weblog.php.

Dahlgren, P. (2001). The Transformation of Democracy? In B. Axford and R. Huggins (Eds.), *New Media and Politics*. London: Sage, 64-88

Dahlgren, P. (2003). Reconfiguring Civic Culture in the New Media Milieu. In: J. Cornerand D. Pels (Eds.), *Media and the Restyling of Politics*. London: Sage, 151-170.

Dawkins, R. (1989). *The Selfish Gene.* Oxford: Oxford University Press.

Dean, J. (2009). *Democracy and Other Neoliberal Fantasies: Communicative Capitalism and Left Politics.* New York: State University Press.

Fish, S. (1982). *Is There a Text in This Class? The Authority of Interpretive Communities.* Harvard: University Press.

Fiske, J. (1989). *Understanding popular culture*. London: Routledge.

Giddens, A. (1991). *Modernity and Self-Identity*. Cambridge: Polity Press.

Giddens, A. (2006). *Europe In The Global Age*. Cambridge: Polity Press.

Gillmor, D. (2004). *We the Media. Grassroots Journalism by the People, for the People.* Sebastopol: O'Reilly Media. Retrieved December 20, 2011, from http://oreilly.com/catalog/wemedia/book/index.csp.

Jenkins, H. (2006). *Convergence Culture: Where Old and New Media Collide*. New York: NYU Press.

Kaplan, A. M., and Haenlein, M. (2010). Users of the world, unite! The challenges and opportunities of Social Media. *Business Horizons*, 53, 59-68.

Katz, E. and Blumler, J., Gurevitch, M. (1973) Uses and gratifications research. *The Public Opinion Quarterly*. 37 (4), 509-523.

Kress, G. and van Leeuwen, T. (2006) *Reading images. The grammar of visual design.* London: Routledge.

Lasn, K. (2000). *Culture Jam.* Ney York: Quill.

Lister, M. and colleagues (2003). *New Media: A Critical Introduction*. London: Routledge.

McCaughey, M. and Ayers M. (2003). Introduction. In M. McCaughey and M. Ayers (Eds.), *Cyberactivism. Online Activism in Theory and Practice*. New York: Routledge, 1-21

Papacharissi, Z. (2002). The Virtual sphere. The internet as a public sphere. *New media & society*. 4 (1), 9-27.

Rheingold, H. (2002). *Smart Mobs: The Next Social Revolution*. Cambridge: Basic Books.

Rose, N. (1999). *Powers of Freedom. Reframing Political Thought*. New York: Cambridge University Press.

Shirky, C. (2008). *Here Comes Everybody: The Power of Organizing Without Organizations*. London: Penguin Books.

Shirky, C. (2010). *Cognitive surplus. Creativity and Generosity in a Connected Age*. London: Penguin Books.

Space Invaders. (2013) Wikipedia. Retrieved May 20, 2013, from http://upload.wikimedia.org/wikipedia/en/2/20/SpaceInvaders-Gameplay.gif.

Tatarchevskiy, T. (2011) The 'popular' culture of internet activism. *New media and society*. 13 (2), 297-313.

van Leeuwen, T. (2005) *Introducing Social Semiotics*. London: Routledge.

Part III
Election Campaigns in New Media

9. Between tradition and innovation: Election campaigns for the European Parliament in Germany (1999–2009)

Jürgen Wilke
Johannes Gutenberg-Universität in Mainz, Germany

Abstract: The chapter is based on three comparable studies of campaigns for the European Parliament in Germany (1999, 2004, 2009). After basic definitions and distinctions, seven framework conditions are identified (voter turnout, budget, extent of media coverage, personalization, national focus, transnationality, and position in the election cycle). Then four types of campaigns are described. The main question is how campaigning changed particularly through the use of technologies and media that have been developed only recently. Nevertheless there still exists continuity, deriving from the relatively constant amount of money invested in the campaigns. But particularly the use of the Internet increased. In 1999 this medium was primarily used for information. Interactive elements were not available and were not used. In 2004 the Internet served already as a central instrument within the campaign, but the target groups were still primarily the party members. The European election campaign in 2009 was then shaped by the Web 2.0 in its promotion of the interaction between parties, members and potential voters. The parties' websites have been opened for interactive elements. Direct communication has been extended furthermore through SMS, E-Mail or Twitter, being added to traditional channels as letters, posters and street ads.

Key words: European Parliament, Election Campaigning, Germany, Internet, Web 2.0

Introduction

If we are concerned with political communication in the era of new technologies, this topic can in principle be understood through an examination of the different areas and types of political communication. One obvious possibility is to focus on election campaigns. In the following analysis, this issue will be examined by looking into the elections to the European Parliament. In order to detect any changes that have occurred, the analysis will include the last three elections, namely those in 1999, 2004, and 2009. Ten years lie between the first (actually fifth) and third (actually seventh) elections. Historically speaking, that is only a short time span, but considerable innovation in the field of communication technology and media formats has taken place in the course of this decade.

The basis for my analysis is three studies which were conducted at the Institute for Communication Studies at the University of Mainz (Germany) in 1999, 2004, and 2009 (Tangemann, 2000; Thib, 2005; Wagner, 2010). They will be evaluated here. Their purpose was a general inventory of the campaigns run by the relevant German parties during the European elections. Therefore, extensive research was conducted and large amounts of material and data were collected. In addition, interviews took place with those in charge of the political campaigns. Based on these endeavors, it is now possible to assess how far these campaigns were dominated by continuity and tradition or by innovation and change.

Significance and Types of Campaigns

Originating in military terminology, the word "campaign" was already adopted in the realm of politics in the 17th century when it was used in connection with the British Parliament's terms of office. In the course of democratization it obtained its current meaning, which relates to the candidacy for a political office or mandate (Leggewie, 1997: 153). When connected to political campaigns, the term is defined as follows:

> "Election campaigning is the process by which a campaign organization (be it a party, candidate, or special interest organization) seeks to maximize electoral gains. It consists of all those efforts (promotional or financial) made by the campaign organization to meet that goal." (Farrell, 1996: 161)

Election campaigns have the distinct purpose of informing the electorate about the parties' goals in order to influence them in a positive manner and mobilize them against adversaries. Numerous tools are employed for this. Basically, every campaign consists of several parts, and it is possible to identify different campaign components. Radunski has identified the three following components (1980: 44):

1. The campaign in the mass media
2. The publicity campaign
3. The party or mobilization campaign

The first is the "decisive part of every campaign" (Radunski, 1980: 44) and is mirrored by continuing media coverage. The second, which uses posters and pamphlets as well as television and print advertisements comprises the campaign in a "stricter sense" (Radunski, 1980: 45). In the third, the central element is the mobilization of the party members and supporters. Of course, all three levels are interconnected.

The three types of campaigning have advantages as well as disadvantages for the political parties. Although campaigns are mainly focused on the media and journalists, the journalistic coverage itself is out of the parties' control. On the other hand, the journalistic and media coverage is free of cost ("free media"), and it is less likely that voters will be conscious of the potential effects of such coverage, and thus they are more susceptible to its possible influence. The publicity campaign is based on "paid media"; the parties have to pay for the advertising, and therefore they can control its contents. Nevertheless, the voters are likely to grow immune to this form of campaigning. While the campaign advertisements in the media target the general public, the party and mobilization campaigns are directed internally, towards the party members. More direct means of communication are used for this.

Radunski made this classification more than 30 years ago, and assigned the pivotal role in mass media to television. However, with the advent of the internet in the 1990s, a new communication technology has surfaced affecting, in addition to many other aspects of social life, political campaigns. Despite these facts, assigning the internet to the media campaign underestimates that medium's potential because the internet can be employed for the publicity campaign as well as for the party and mobilization campaign. The multifunctional character of the internet, and especially its potential for innovation, are good reasons for talking about the internet campaign in the following analysis, and thus adding it as a fourth component of the campaign typology.

European Elections and their Framework Conditions

The first direct elections of the European parliament were held in 1979 comprising the then 9 member states of the European Community (the European Union since 1993). The goal was to include citizens more directly in European policymaking and to offer them more political access to the European Union; or, at the very least, it was intended to convey the impression that this was the case. Since then, these elections have taken place every five years, the most recent of which (the seventh) was held on 17 June 2009 (Tenscher, 2011). Over the course of time, the framework conditions for these elections have changed decisively. Firstly, the number of European member states has increased to the current 27, which has also led to an enlargement of the European Parliament. Secondly, the functions and the role of the European Parliament have altered with time. The national legislation of member states has increasingly been influenced by decisions taken at the European level, which are in turn increasingly dependent on consent by the European Parliament. At the same time, the parliament has taken control of more tasks and has to make decisions on appointments, especially in the case of the European Commission. Nevertheless, the turnout in the European elections has decreased in most European countries. While 65.7% of Germans voted in 1979, only 43% did so in 2004, and this record low was only slightly improved in 2009 (43.3%).

The peculiarities of European elections have a number of consequences for the election campaigns by which parties are attempting to gain voter support.

Turnout

The number of citizens participating in European elections is smaller than that for national parliamentary elections. This is evident for all elections of this kind since 1979. Obviously, many citizens feel less motivated to participate. This could be explained by a general lack of knowledge and a widespread underestimation of the significance of European policies. The lower turnout is one of the reasons why it has become common to describe the European elections as a "second-order election" (Reif and Schmitt, 1980). Parties are thus facing a severe problem when it comes to the mobilization of voters in European campaigns.

Budget

The difference between parliamentary campaigns and European campaigns in Germany becomes rather obvious when taking a look at the different budgets assigned by the political parties (see Table 1).

Table 1: Campaign budgets for European Parliament Elections 1999-2009 and National Parliament Elections for 2009 in Germany (in million Euros)

	SPD (Social Democrats)	CDU (Christian Democrats)	Die Grünen (The Greens)	FDP (Liberals)	PDS/ DIE LINKE (The Left)
EPE 1999	12.3	10.0	0.25	1.0	3.0
EPE 2004	12.5	8.0	1.2	1.0	3.0
EPE 2009	11.0	10.0	1.5	1.4	3.5
NPE 2009	30.0	20.0	3.4	5.5	5.0

EPE: European Parliament Elections, NPE: National Parliament (Bundestag) Elections

According to the available data (provided by the political parties themselves) the parties (without the CSU, CDU's Bavarian sister-party) spent in total about €25 million on each of the European campaigns in 1999, 2004, and 2009 or, to be precise, €26.55 million in 1999, €25.7 million in 2004, and €27.4 million in 2009. The expenditure on the European elections was thus distinctly smaller than that for national parliamentary elections. In 2009 the political parties spent a total of more than €63.9 million on parliamentary elections, which was almost 60 per cent more than expenditure on the European elections in the same year. The budget for European elections is thus much smaller than for parliamentary elections.

Extent of Media Coverage

Research in communication science has shown that the mass media covered the European elections less extensively than the parliamentary elections. Thus the term "second rate coverage" has been introduced (de Vreese, Lauf and Peter, 2007). This is true for print media in Germany as well as German television. The four leading German dailies (*Frankfurter Rundschau, Süddeutsche Zeitung, Frankfurter Allgemeine Zeitung* and *Die Welt*) covered the parliamentary elections in 2002 with 1,188 articles, while they covered the European elections in 2004 with 167 articles (from four weeks prior to elections' day in both cases). The difference was smaller in 2009 when the four papers covered the parliamentary elections with 604 articles whilst 195 contributions were dedicated to the European elections (Wilke, Schäfer and Leidecker, 2010). The balance of television coverage also shifted towards the parliamentary elections in 2009, when it came to the primary newscasts on German television. In the three weeks prior to elections' day, 15 per cent of all news clips focused on the German parliamentary elections while only 5 per cent featured the European elections (Boomgaarden, de Vreese and Semetko, 2011). These findings underpin the fact that the European media campaigns require special compensation and attention.

Personalization

In the European elections, the voters decide on the composition of the European Parliament. This procedure also applies to the German parliamentary elections, which determine the composition of the Bundestag. However, the parliamentary elections in Germany at the same time determine who will hold the office of Chancellor (Prime Minister) in the future. As a result, the political parties also present their candidates for the position of Chancellor. The candidates for the Chancellor's office have been the centerpiece of election campaigns for a long time. This has added an element of intense personalization to the parliamentary campaigns in Germany, so these are not simply about a decision on governmental functions. However, this element is generally missing in the European elections (Wiorkowski and Holtz-Bacha, 2005; Dörner and Vogt, 2011). This lack of personalization has an undeniable effect on the campaigns and may be in part responsible for the low turnout.

National Focus

Since the first European elections, the primary campaign focus of most of the political parties (not only in Germany) has been on national topics. They have been dominated by a more domestic, national focus than by a European agenda. This can be attributed to the voters' general lack of knowledge of and interest in European matters. Repeatedly, the European elections in Germany have been exploited by the opposition parties in order to attack the parties in power and "teach them a lesson". This national focus, which has pushed back the European component, has of course also affected campaign management.

Transnationality

Nonetheless, the elections for the European Parliament are held simultaneously in all member states of the European Union. In 1999 there were 15 states, in 2004 there were 27, and in 2009, 27. Thus, it can be said that campaigns are happening at the same time in all these countries, all of which retain their own national character. On the other hand, these campaigns also possess a somewhat transnational element because they are a Europe-wide phenomenon. This can also be explained with the fact that the large, ideologically compatible political parties unite in the following factions in the European Parliament (Niedermayer, 1983; Poguntke and Pütz, 2006; wwweuroparl.europa.eu): the European People's Party (EPP), the Progressive Alliance of Socialists and Democrats (S and D), the Alliance of Liberals and Democrats for Europe (ALDE), the Greens/European Free Alliance (EFA), the European Conservatives and Reformist Group (ECR), the Confederation Group of the United Left-Nordic Left and the European Freedom and Democracy Group (plus some non attached members). Therefore, the campaigns can also be coordinated in a transnational manner. How far the German parties are availing themselves of this possibility needs to be considered.

Position in the Electoral Cycle

Apart from the general framework conditions, there is at least one other aspect to be stressed, namely the position in the electoral cycle. In 1999 municipal elections were held in seven German states on the day of the European elections (13 June). In 2004, there were seven more elections at the state and municipal level on the same date as the European elections (also 13 June); and in 2009, five elections to the German regional parliaments (Landtag) took place at around the time of the European elections, three of them four weeks in advance, and two on the date of the European elections (17 June). Furthermore, in that year the national parliamentary elections (Bundestag) followed only three months later (27 September). Such close proximity of European and parliamentary elections can lead to both campaigns interacting with each other.

Campaign Organization

For their respective (European) campaigns the political parties have to undertake organizational preparations well in advance. This necessarily starts quite a few months before election day. The already existing party apparatus can be used, but it is still necessary to mobilize and utilize forces in ways that go beyond this. The political parties have adopted different strategies for this, depending on their financial means and other basic considerations.

In the national parliamentary elections of 1998, the SPD (Social Democrats) established a campaign organization independent from party headquarters, the so-called *Kampa* (von Webel, 1998). The party's success in the elections was later attributed to its effectiveness. Thus, it is not at all surprising that for the European elections one year later a *Europa-Kampa* was created. In 2004 (as with the parliamentary elections in 2002) the SPD oriented their organizational campaign structure according to the *Kampa* model. For the entire 2009 election year, the SPD created a unified campaign headquarters, but this time all the employees of the party headquarters were included.

The other German parties did not separate their European campaign organizations from their respective organizational structure; instead they leaned on their party headquarters. This is what the CDU (Christian Democrats) did, with its division into the three major sections: policy, public relations, and organization. The first section worked out political content, the second took care of pamphlets and internet presence, while the third organized campaign appearances and events. In 2004 the CDU did not create an individual campaign headquarter for the European elections.

During the 1999 European election campaign, the FDP (Liberals) created a division between everyday political business and a special campaign organization. The everyday included the public relations section as well as the sections for organization, policy, and strategy (the latter was in charge of argumentation aids, speeches and support for members). Alongside these, there were two special sections: a project team which began planning the European campaign in 2004 programmatically and strategically, which was later replaced by the campaign commission, which combined the work of several areas under the supervision of the secretary general.

The European campaign put forth by the Green Party was still lacking professionalism in 1999. For financial reasons alone, it had to be conducted at the same time as the everyday political business, thus relying heavily on the permanent staff. Topics and strategies were agreed upon in sessions held by a coalition committee, which also included a member of the European division of *Bündnis90/Die Grünen* (Alliance '90/The Greens). The campaign staff was in charge of organizational matters. In 2003 the European Greens decided to conduct a joint campaign. This decision led to the creation of a European control group, and the campaign's milestones were decided upon by this committee. In 2009 the Greens led a European campaign characterized strongly by transnational coordination.

The European campaign of DIE LINKE (The Left; formerly known as PDS, until unified with WASG in 2007) has only been analyzed since the 2000 elections. The campaign headquarters were the party's head offices in Berlin, whose staff were mainly involved in campaign planning and implementation; however, an individual team was assigned to the European campaign. The *WahlQuartier (Election Quarter)*, a subunit below the politically relevant level, was in charge of the campaign's practical realization.

Apart from their own structures and staff, the German parties increasingly relied on external advisors and service providers for their European campaigns, as is typical for professionalized campaigns nowadays. Basically, there are three areas for external involvement: (1) the creative delivery of political messages by advertising agencies, (2) the provision of data from opinion research, and (3) the layout of internet presences by specialist agencies. The SPD had already employed the services of such an agency by 1999, and the need for such services has increased for all parties ever since.

The organization of European campaigns poses similar problems and challenges for the parties involved. These problems were resolved in different ways. The strategies depend on the campaign budgets, but also reveal different political and organizational styles. Since the same tasks principally need to be tackled in every new election, there is an element of continuity. This continuity of course is justified and reinforced by election successes. If the opposite is the case, changes become necessary or at least advisable.

Areas and Types of Campaigning

In the following analysis, the four areas or types of campaigning in the European elections in 1999, 2004, and 2009 will be examined more closely. The primary focus will be on the internet campaign, since it is most likely to reveal how innovative and new media techniques affect political communication.

Publicity Campaigns

Publicity campaigns are used by the parties to address the voters directly and convince them to vote for a certain party. Traditionally, a number of advertising materials are used for this purpose, including, most commonly, posters. Posters have still been of pivotal importance in the last three European elections. They were put up in different waves and displayed different layouts. Posters with text and motives were dominant, given the lesser degree of personalization in European elections. However, this depersonalized approach can only be maintained to a lesser extent today. A perfect example for this is the FDP which prominently featured its top candidate Silvana Koch-Mehrin on campaign posters. The Greens did the same, albeit less extensively, with their top candidates. The SPD followed with their top candidate Martin Schulz. The CDU advertised their top candidate only marginally, because he was little known. By contrast, the parties employed the popularity of their respective national party leaders. The FDP is the only party which can truly be said to have led a personalized campaign so far.

Despite the fact that European topics are mostly uncontroversial, the posters were used for attacks on political opponents ("negative campaigning"). The Greens did so in 2004, using a poster which displayed CDU leader Angela Merkel with Silvio Berlusconi in the background ("There is not always wisdom behind it"). In 2009 the SPD used very aggressive posters targeted at the CDU/CSU, FDP and DIE LINKE. In 2009 the FDP used posters to link the online with the offline campaign.

Another classic advertising resource is the printed media. Because of cost and strategic considerations, political parties employ advertising in differing degrees. The SPD used advertisements in 1999 primarily in national newspapers and magazines. The CDU concentrated their advertisements in daily newspapers in Eastern Germany. In 2004 such advertisements only played a marginal role. In 2009, the party only began to use such advertisements in popular national newspapers shortly before the European elections. The FDP left the use of advertisements for the European elections to their regional organizations. The Greens focused their use of advertisements on rather leftist newspapers (*tageszeitung*, *Frankfurter Rundschau*) as well as urban magazines.

Television advertisements are the parties' most common audio-visual advertising resource. All German parties have employed these in the course of their campaigns, albeit in differing degrees. This can be explained by the fact that these (self-produced) slots are aired free of cost by the public service broadcasters. The frequency of the slots is determined by the party's political strength, which is why the SPD and CDU/CSU have been able to employ more television advertisements than the FDP, the Greens, or DIE LINKE. Advertisements on private television stations have to be paid for, and could therefore be afforded in the largest number by the CDU and SPD.

The Media Campaign

Despite the fact that the publicity campaign has to rely on the media, it differs from the parties' media campaigns in that the goal of the latter is to ensure that their political messages and content are included in the journalistic and media coverage. This is quite difficult to achieve, especially from the parties' perspective. Firstly, the media campaign depends on journalists who are (at least officially) independent; and secondly, according to all interviewees, European topics are hard to include, and they are even viewed as "ratings killers". Still, the political parties are not dissuaded from attempting to exercise influence via the use of media campaigns. In order to achieve this, they have conducted daily media work which includes press releases, press conferences, visits to editorial rooms, and events which attract media attention. Classic press releases pertaining to European topics were used rather seldom, however.

It was more important to the parties to include their candidates in television formats (e.g. on talk shows). The FDP was especially successful in this with their top candidate Silvana Koch-Mehrin. Not only was she quite attractive, but she also fit the stereotype "woman with child". The FDP even went as far as to create a position called "boulevard representative" for the European campaign, for which they appointed an experienced yellow press journalist. The Greens relied on presenting their top candidate, Daniel Cohn-Bendit, in 2004. His appearance in Maybrit Illner's popular talk show was viewed as a major success.

The Party- and Mobilization Campaigns

The parties' mobilization campaigns are aimed at the party members but at the same time are supposed to radiate into the wider public's attention. It is crucial for any campaign to intensify the continuing internal care for the parties' own members. Conventional forms of communication which are used for that purpose are assemblies, phone calls, internal magazines and newsletters. These have been used by the parties in 1999, 2004, and 2009, but their importance has decreased since the internet offers new and multifunctional technology which surpasses the capabilities of "old" media.

The Internet Campaign

Since the 1990s the spectrum of communications employed in election campaigns in Germany (as in many other democracies) has widened considerably. The new communications technology provided by the internet was a crucial factor in this development. The convergence of the classic media occurring on the internet caused this spectrum of internet campaigning to develop. Furthermore, the internet is a very cost-effective medium and thus very advantageous when budgets are limited.

The parties in Germany began to establish internet presences in 1995/96 (Bieber, 2001). These were party-focused websites, whose goal was to serve internal as well as external communication. The first campaign in Germany which relied heavily on the use of computer networks was the national parliamentary election campaign of 1998 (Clemens, 1998; Kuhlen, 1998). The experience thus gained by the political parties could be put to use a year later in the European elections (Tangemann, 1999: 116ff). This was particularly true for the SPD, since it had been very successful in the national parliamentary election one year before, and Gerhard Schröder had been elected chancellor. Special Europe pages on the internet announced the European candidates. In addition to that, there was information on certain topics as well as the SPD's election manifesto. Hyperlinks led to campaign initiatives and supporter groups. The television advertisements were also available on the SPD's website. The CDU offered a special European campaign website, which in turn linked to several pages with different functions: welcome, events, press releases, election manifesto, and key topics. Links led to the candidates as well as to the European institutions and partners, and the television advertisements could also be accessed.

The FDP also presented its own European page within the party's existing online presence. This was also true in the case of the Greens, where the European campaign page was included in the regular online service. The information was subdivided into four sections comprising topics, candidates, program, and posters and others. In addition, the possibility of contacting the party via email was offered. Topics relevant to the European campaign could be discussed on the website with the help of a webboard.

With regard to the 1999 European elections, Tangemann called the internet a "treasure trove for all questions related to the elections" (2000: 126). CDU and SPD offered a wide selection of online information. The FDP used the web in order to address their members and enlist their support. In comparison, the Green Party's online presence was still very quaint. One element which was still widely missing at this point was interactive features. The features were almost exclusively limited to information, and the voter's inclusion was virtually nonexistent.

Five years later, in the course of the 2004 European elections, the German parties placed a stronger emphasis on internet campaigns without neglecting the classic means of communication (Thib, 2005: 68ff.). The SPD started early with the online part of its European campaign underway as early as 13 November 2003. This was supposed to signify the election's great importance. For the

CDU, the internet was also an important medium for communicating with its subdivisions and party members. The internet was mostly used in this respect for mailing lists which reached down to the municipal level. Traditional mail could be avoided completely this way. The intranet offered the members additional services and information. An additional electoral platform was used for services devoted to outside communication. According to the FDP, the internet was the most important internal and external medium during the European campaign in 2004 (Thib, 2005: 110). The internet campaign took place on two platforms. There was the federal party's platform, and the platform of top candidate Silvana Koch-Mehrin. The feature "SMS by Silvana" was updated daily, comprising a short message of approximately 160 characters offering information about the candidate's current activities. In the case of the Greens, it is remarkable that the party conducted its European internet campaign in 2004 not at a national level, but through a European network. The German website offered only a few clues and advertisements. Predominantly, communication was run by the website of the European Greens. The idea behind this was to interconnect the union's member parties. The internet enabled the parties to upload and regularly update all important documents in 15 languages on www.eurogreens.org.

The internet campaign attained a widely different character in the course of the European elections in 2009. This can mostly be attributed to the fact that the internet itself had undergone a transformation, caused by the introduction of the Web 2.0 and its interactive possibilities. The SPD modernized its website in early 2009 in order to further establish its "role as a modern internet party" (Wagner, 2010: 57). The website was updated mostly with respect to elements of the Web 2.0. The visitors were encouraged "to participate, to support the party and engage in dialogue with it" (ibid.). The party's regular internet presence was used for information and an additional campaign platform was provided for the interconnection and recruitment of campaign supporters as well as the connection to social networks. The SPD presented itself extensively on Twitter, Facebook, YouTube and Flickr. Apart from the social networks the party's member network was also available.

The CDU also revised its website in 2009 quite radically, aiming to transform a "classic information and mobilization portal [...] into a 'landing strip and runway'" (Wagner, 2010: 70). In addition to that, the website was constantly updated with current information on the campaign and on political topics. The CDU was present on the Web 2.0 platforms StudiVZ, MeinVZ, Facebook, YouTube, and Twitter. The users were supposed to be connected not only with each other, but also with the party and its candidates. Another innovation was the party's own YouTube channel "CDU-TV" which offered current videos and interviews related to the European elections, as well as contributions from the

CDU-feature "We in Europe". The central platform for communication and information for the members was the member-network. The support network *teAM* Germany's website was also closely connected to the party's website.

The internet also played a pivotal role in the Greens' European campaign in 2009, since they felt that it offered possibilities to be active "without a budget worth millions" (Wagner, 2010: 82). In addition, the Greens could boast a voter segment largely composed of young members who were open to the internet and its possibilities. The party had decided against a campaign website in 2009 and used its party website as the central internet presence. This website was to be used as a news platform and dialogue center at the same time. As an example of this, the Greens started a fundraising campaign for posters in May 2008, in which the sympathizers could essentially fund a large campaign poster and in turn determine where it would be installed. The homepage offered the possibility of registering for the newly created interactive platform "my campaign". This enabled the users to actively participate in the Greens' campaign via petitions and protest activities. Members could create their individual profiles on the member platform, *Wurzelwerk*. The Greens were also quite active in the Web 2.0 services like Facebook and StudiVZ. They also featured a channel on the video hosting platform YouTube, called "Channel Green". The two top candidates were featured with their own profiles on Facebook. Apart from the national activities in 2009, the European internet platform (www.europagreens.eu) played an important role again.

The FDP also created a special website designated exclusively to the European campaign. It featured the party program, news updates, and current videos. In addition to that, it was possible for members and sympathizers to interact and exchange information on the communication platform "my.fdp". This website also offered current information about the campaign via newsletters and SMS subscriptions. In addition to being present on the social networks like StudiVZ and Facebook, XING was essential to the FDP's internet campaign. "Tvliberal" was the FDP's exclusive channel on the video hosting service YouTube. The designated center for the different online activities was the supporter platform *MitMachArena.*

The central internet presence for DIE LINKE (The Left) during the European campaign was the party's website. It was updated in January 2009 for the election year, and the most important information for the campaign was highlighted. Since January 2009 DIE LINKE was also present in several online services, in Facebook as well as the so-called VZ-group, Myspace, Flickr and a channel on YouTube. The support network (www.linksaktiv.de) was created in April 2009 as another component of the internet campaign. DIE LINKE also counted on its own online community, in which the members and sympathizers could exchange information and interact.

Conclusion

When the European campaigns for 1999, 2004, and 2009 are compared, there are continuities (and traditions) but also changes (and innovations) (Wagner, 2010: 118ff). To state that traditional means of communication have become obsolete would be a harsh exaggeration. Posters are still a very important publicity element of any campaign given their high degree of visibility. Media presence, especially on television, is still considered to be very important. Yet, the European campaign in 2009 differed clearly from campaigns in the past. Direct communication—personal as well as web-based—played a central role for the parties. This was true for addressing both potential voters as well as campaign supporters. In 1999 the internet was mostly understood as a means of providing information services. Interactive possibilities which exceeded the sending of email were almost non-existent, probably on account of the technical standards of the time (Wilke and Tangemann, 2004: 34ff).

In 2004, the internet was already used more intensively and acknowledged as an important campaigning tool by the parties. The main focus was not on direct communication with voters. The internet in this respect was more of a "means for communication and the mobilization of members and interests" (Thib, 2005: 14). Five years later, in 2009, the European campaigns were characterized by Web 2.0 sites, allowing communication between party members, sympathizers, and potential voters; and this also included the cross-party supporter networks. In addition to that, the respective party websites were altered in order to adapt to the possibilities of the internet and now contained numerous interactive elements. In this context, several social networks (StudiVZ, Facebook, Flickr, Myspace) as well as other new communication and information channels the parties used extensively have to be considered.

Questions which remain unanswered include how extensively the innovations were really used by the voters and how they affected the results of the European elections. A coherent analysis is yet to be accomplished and data (probably) gathered by the political parties has not been made available. The turnout in Germany (which was 45.2% in 1999, 43.0% in 2004, and 43.3% in 2009) does not indicate that the online campaign had an especially mobilizing effect. However, without it the turnout may have even been lower. The findings on the use of the internet in the course of the 2009 national parliamentary elections could easily be transferred to the European election campaigns, although the motivation might have been less. Von Pape and Quandt mentioned the "sobering" (2010: 39) findings: "The heavily debated Web 2.0 services hardly played any role in the German campaign of 2009" (Von Pape and Quandt: 397). Similarly, Kepplinger and Podschuweit attest that the internet presences of German parties had a "hardly measurable effect on the decision of whether or not to vote for or against one of the political parties" (2011: 141). This does not render the online services useless, but puts the relevance of the presented innovations into a realistic perspective in comparison with the traditional forms of campaigning.

References

Bieber, C. (2001). *Internet, Parteienkommunikation, Multimediapolitiker. Eine Einführung. In: ParteiPolitik 2.0. Der Einfluss des Internet auf parteiinterne Kommunikations- und Organisationsprozesse*. Studie für die Friedrich Ebert-Stiftung. Konzeption: Dr. Christoph Bieber. Bonn: Friedrich Ebert-Stiftung, 6-27.

Boomgarden, H. G., de Vreese, C. H. and Semetko, H. A. (2011). Hast es nicht gesehen?! Haupt- und Nebenwahlkämpfe in deutschen Fernsehnachrichten. In Tenscher, J. (Ed.) *Superwahljahr 2009. Vergleichende Analysen aus Anlass der Wahlen zum Deutschen Bundestag und zum Europäischen Parlament.* Wiesbaden: VS-Verlag, 181-197.

Clemens, D. (1998). Wahlkampf im Internet. In: Gellner, W. and von Korff, F. (eds.) *Demokratie und Internet*. Baden-Baden: Nomos, 143-156.

Dörner, A. and Vogt, L. (2011). Wahlkampf auf dem Boulevard: Personality-Talkshows, Personalisierung und Prominenzkapital zwischen Haupt- und Nebenwahl. ITenscher, J. (Ed.) *Superwahljahr 2009. Vergleichende Analysen aus Anlass der Wahlen zum Deutschen Bundestag und zum Europäischen Parlament.* Wiesbaden: VS-Verlag, 199-222.

Farrell, D. M. (1996). Campaign Strategies and Tactics. In LeDuc, L., Niemi, R. and Norris, P. (Eds.). *Comparing Democracies. Elections and Voting in Global Perspective.* Thousand Oaks, CA: Sage, 160-183.

Kepplinger, H. M. and Podschuweit N. (2011). Der Online-Wahlkampf der Parteien. Alternative oder Ergänzung? In Oberreuter, H. (Ed.) *Das Ende der Gewissheiten. Wähler, Parteien und Koalitionen in Bewegung*. München: Olzog, 111-145

Kuhlen, R. (1998). *Die Mondlandung des Internet. Die Bundestagswahl 1998 in den elektronischen Kommunikationsforen.* Konstanz: UVK.

Leggewie, C. (1997) Kampagnenpolitik—eine nicht ganz neue Form politischer Mobilisierung. In Röttger, U. (Ed.) *PR-Kampagnen. Über die Inszenierung von Öffentlichkeit* Opladen: Westdeutscher Verlag. Second edition Wiesbaden: VS-Verlag 2009, 119–134.

Niedermayer, O. (1983). *Europäische Parteien? Zur grenzüberschreitenden Interaktion politischer Parteien im Rahmen der Europäischen Gemeinschaft.* Frankfurt/M.: Campus.

Norris, P. (2002) Campaign Communications. In LeDuc, L., Niemi, R. G. and Norris, P (Eds.) *Comparing Democracies 2: New Challenges in the Study of Elections and Voting.* Thousand Oaks, CA and London: Sage, 127–146.

Von Pape, T. and Quandt, T. (2010). Wen erreicht der Wahlkampf? Eine Repräsentativstudie zum Informationsverhalten im Bundestagswahlkampf 2009. *Media Perspektiven,* 9, 390-398.

Poguntke, T. and Pütz, C. (2006). Parteien in der Europäischen Union. Zu den Entwicklungschancen der Europaparteien. *Zeitschrift für Parlamentsfragen* 37, 334-353

Radunski, P. (1980). *Wahlkämpfe. Moderne Wahlkampfführung als politische Kommunikation.* München, Wien: Olzog.
Reif, K. and Schmitt, H. (1980). Nine national second-order-elections: A conceptual framework for the analysis of European election results. *European Journal of Political Research,* 8, 3-44.
Tangemann, J. (2000). D*ie Europawahl 1999 als Kommunikationsereignis. Akteure, Strukturen, Medien.* MA-Thesis Johannes Gutenberg Universität Mainz.
Tenscher, J. (Ed.) (2011). *Superwahljahr 2009. Vergleichende Analysen aus Anlass der Wahlen zum Deutschen Bundestag und zum Europäischen Parlament.* Wiesbaden: VS Verlag.
Thib, S. (2005). *Die Kommunikationsstrategien der deutschen Parteien im Europawahlkampf 2004. Eine Fallstudie zur Wahlkampfführung von SPD, CDU, FDP und Bündnis 90/Die Grünen.* MA-Thesis Johannes Gutenberg-Universität Mainz.
Wagner, M. (2010). *Europawahlkampf 2009. Die Kommunikationsstrategien der deutschen Parteien. Eine Analyse der Europawahlkämpfe von SPD, CDU, Bündnis90/Die Grünen, FDP und LINKE.* MA-Thesis Johannes Gutenberg Universität Mainz.
Von Webel, D. (1999). Der Wahlkampf der SPD. In Noelle-Neumann, E., Kepplinger, H. M. and Donsbach, W. (Eds.) *Kampa. Meinungsklima und Medienwirkung im Bundestagswahlkampf 1998.* Freiburg i.Br., München: Alber, 13-39.
De Vreese, C. H., Lauf, E. and Peter, J. (2007). The Media and European Parliament Elections: Second-rate Coverage of a Second-order Event? In W.van der Brug, C. van der Eijk (Eds.) *European Elections and Domestic Politics. Lessons from the Past and Scenarios for the Future* (. Notre Dame (IN.): University of Notre Dame Press,. 129-147.
Wilke, J. J. Tangemann (2004) (Visuelle) Wahlkampfkommunikation zur Europawahl 1999. In Knieper, T. and Müller, M. G. (Eds.) *Visuelle Wahlkampfkommunikation.* Köln: Herbert von Halem, 13-44
Wilke, J., C. Schäfer, C. M. Leidecker (2011). Mit kleinen Schritten aus dem Schatten: haupt- und Nebenwahlkämpfe in Tageszeitungen am Beispiel der Bundestags- und Europawahlen 1979-2009. In J. Tenscher (Ed.) *Superwahljahr 2009. Vergleichende Analysen aus Anlass der Wahlen zum Deutschen Bundestag und zum Europäischen Parlament.* Wiesbaden: VS Verlag, 155-179
Wiorkowski, A. ,Ch. Holtz-Bacha (2005). Und es lohnt sich doch. Personalisierungsstrategien im Europawahlkampf. In Ch. Holtz-Bacha (Ed.) *Europawahl 2004. Die Massenmedien im Europawahlkampf.* Wiesbaden: VS, 174-196

10. The use of new media in election campaigns in Poland

Jan Garlicki
Daniel Mider
University of Warsaw, Poland

Abstract: This chapter analyzes the ways and the extent to which the Internet has been used in election campaigns in Poland. The analysis was done from the perspective of the emergence of the phenomenon of the permanent campaign. Polish election campaigns were compared to those in the US. The model for analysis was also enriched by the classification of various channels of political communication on the Internet. The chapter criticizes the thesis about the communicational revolution in election campaigns in Poland. An important dimension of the analysis was the comparison of traditional media (television, radio, press) with the Internet in terms of their credibility, attractiveness and effectiveness in the public opinion. The analysis identified a number of shortcomings related to the development of the use of new media in Polish election campaigns. These include: lack of proficiency in the online cultural code, abandonment of Internet communication projects, and posting derivative and undeveloped content.

Key words: political marketing, permanent campaign, online marketing, political culture

Introduction. Internet—the medium of the permanent campaign

Political marketing researchers and specialists in the field of political communication agree that we can observe the phenomenon of the emergence and development of the permanent campaign in many European countries as well as in the US (Garlicki, 2010: 26-27). The main objective of the permanent campaign is to create a positive image of the political party, especially the ruling one, and to maintain its popularity. Due to the intensity of marketing activities and continuous striving for efficiency in the process of political communication the distinction between the election campaign and a political campaign carried out during the term of office fades away. According to Norman J. Ornstein and Thomas E. Mann (2000: 231), a campaign merges with the very process of governance. Phenomena such as the development of public relations' activities or the growing role of media in political communication are determining the nature of the permanent campaign. It is the development of new media, especially the Internet, that created an almost unlimited number of possibilities for the permanent campaign and introduced political communication in the era of the postmodern campaign (Dobek-Ostrowska, 2006: 247-248). However, communication actions, including those in new media, are intensified in the period preceding the elections, namely during the proper election campaign. The new media have been used on an unprecedented scale by Barack Obama's staff during the 2008 presidential election (Grzywińska, 2010: 136-137). The Internet and its capabilities were used not only for political communication. With the help of new media it was possible to create a social movement made up of volunteers working for the election of Barack Obama. The Internet has also become a tool enabling the collection of a record amount of funds for the election campaign. Undoubtedly the characteristic of political communication via the Internet is greater interactivity and personalization of the message. This makes its role become increasingly important. There is a dispute among political communication researchers about whether the new media broke the monopoly of traditional media, especially the impact of television. The Internet provides such opportunities that the current recipient of the message can also become a creator of the message or information on political content. Such opportunities already existed in the Web 1.0. Nevertheless, a development of the Web 2.0 created completely new conditions. The terms Web 1.0 and Web 2.0 were first used by Tim O'Reilly (2005) during a conference organized by O'Reilly Media and MediaLive International in October 2004. It is commonly accepted that the Web 1.0 was created in 1993 when the first specification of HTML allowing the creation of the World Wide Web was published. On the other hand, the Web 2.0 was created as a result of the economic crisis of the Web 1.0 caused by the collapse of the information technology market in 2001, the event called also the *burst of the dot-com bubble*. In general, the Web 2.0 builds on the Web 1.0 by developing its technical and social features. The development of the Web 2.0 started in late 2003 (Cormode and Krishnamurthy, 2008). However, now the Web 1.0 and the Web 2.0 coexist on the Internet.

On the one hand, the opportunities given by the Web 2.0 have resulted in the development of social networking sites like Facebook. On the other hand, they have allowed the creation of independent media and blogs or microblogs on the Internet.

All these phenomena significantly affect the processes of political communication. They create not only new possibilities but also new challenges for political elites. It becomes much more complicated to control communication processes. Moreover, it requires professionalism to use new media intelligently. Are politicians able to cope with new tasks in the sphere of communication? Refashioning the opinions of Ornstein and Mann, the following hypothesis can be stated: "a greater interactivity in political communication enabled by the use of the Internet is just a mask covering the growth of political elites' influence on voters achieved through professional management and the use of new media". It seems that such a trend can be observed in campaigns in the US. Therefore, it should be asked what these processes look like in Poland.

Polish politicians, candidates for president, candidates in parliamentary elections, and their staffs have begun to use new media in political communication. It is, however, worthwhile to ask whether the Internet has actually led to a revolution in marketing communication in Poland. In order to answer this question it is important to analyze the following issues: to what extent are new media used professionally by political elites, and to what extent is the Internet a credible and effective medium? The second question needs further explanation. The credibility of the Internet is understood as the degree to which citizens recognize this medium as a trustworthy source of full, independent and objective political information. On the other hand, the effectiveness of the Internet refers to its capacity to influence voters and gain their support during the election campaign. Both credibility and effectiveness were measured and interpreted on the basis of the declarations of potential voters who followed the campaign on the Internet. Another important issue which needs to be scrutinized in the course of this chapter is the forms and means of Internet political communication which are used by politicians.

New medium—traditional politics

The use of the Internet in election campaigns has created a paradoxical situation. On the one hand, the development of the medium led to a permanent revolution in the sphere of communication. On the other hand we see many signs of some kind of a "creeping counter-revolution" in the sphere of political communication, where the primary actors are political elites. This phenomenon is global and emerges at various levels. Attempts to limit the freedom of expression on the Internet made by decision makers are the most evident example. We are witnesses to a dynamic and relentless struggle for influence over the Internet between citizens, third sector organizations and social movements on the one side and governments on the other. Most of the actions are taken by governments, while citizens usually only respond to restrictions introduced. Public institutions implement solutions that filter and block content, while citizens create software allowing access to censored information. When limiting the freedom of expression states also make use of legislative solutions such as preventive censorship and other direct and indirect forms of pressure or restrictions. A good exemplification of such struggles is a conflict between states and citizens over the implementation of the *Anti-Counterfeiting Trade Agreement* (ACTA).

Another symptom of this "creeping counter-revolution" is the evident reluctance of the Polish political elites to use the Internet under spontaneously developed, customary and unwritten rules. We are dealing with self-restraint because politicians do not want to use the Internet on the basis of equivalence with the public. They try to adapt the Internet to the activities of one-to-one type of media[1].

To a varying extent this phenomenon is related to the different channels of communication on the Internet. Within each of these channels different subcultures have evolved and diverse rules and patterns of activity were developed. The Internet can be divided into two distinct subcultures: Web 1.0 and Web 2.0. The channels of communication in both networks are characterized by identical parameters, but they are present in varying intensities. Therefore, the division was made on the basis of quantitative rather than qualitative characteristics.

Technological solutions implemented in late 2003 and 2004 have given different characteristics to the channels of communication used in the Web 2.0. The channels that make up the Web 2.0 are characterized by a much stronger potential for creating bonds because the applied technologies allow the creation and operation of inclusive and exclusive social networks. Connections between members of these networks are created on the basis of common views, private or professional interests, and problems, or even social or ethnic identity. Examples of communication channels used in the Web 2.0 are numerous social networking sites such as Facebook, MySpace, or LinkedIn. On the other hand, the possibilities of creating social networks in the Web 1.0 are limited. Usenet newsgroups, mailing lists, newsletters or webrings provide significantly poorer abilities to construct network identity and fewer possibilities to communicate in diverse ways.

The Web 2.0 is also characterized by a way of classifying content on the Internet different from in the Web 1.0. The content in the Web 1.0 is organized hierarchically and centrally by a small number of centers, whereas the structure of information resources within the Web 2.0 has a dispersed, bottom-up and amorphous character. In addition to this, users can use any dictionary to categorize content and classifications made by them do not need to be separable or exhaustive. Users assign the corresponding words or compounds (tags) to the published content. This classification is usually presented in a graphical form, in the so-called tag cloud. The more users have used the specific term to classify the specific content, the more this term is exposed in the tag cloud. At the same time

1 The "creeping counter-revolution" phenomenon was confirmed on the basis of a series of quantitative and qualitative researches carried out under the program (N N 116 280338) *Formy i treść ekspresji kultury politycznej Polaków w Internecie w kampaniach wyborczych 2010 i 2011 roku* funded by the Ministry of Science and Higher Education and directed by Jan Garlicki. Some results of these researches were published in *Political Science Studies*, vol. 21, (*Political Culture of Internauts in Poland*).

the tags are links to the thematically identical content. This method of classification is usually called folksonomy[2].

A significant feature that distinguishes Web 2.0 from Web 1.0 is the massive creation and sharing of content by users. The messages sent in the Web 1.0 are usually of a "one-to-many" or "one-to-one" type, while the Web 2.0 has the high-tech capacity to implement also the "many-to-many" type of messages. Technologies implemented within the Web 2.0 (known as mashups) enable the creation and sharing of content of various types. The opportunities given by the Web 1.0 in this area are much more limited because editing content usually requires certain programming skills. The basic instruments used within the Web 1.0 are the World Wide Web and traditional news services moved to the Internet, whereas the Web 2.0 also uses blogs and citizen (participatory) journalism sites. In this type of journalism "everyone is a reporter, everyone is a witness". The citizen journalism phenomenon is called *we-media* or *grassroots reporting* in the literature.

Another feature differentiating Web 1.0 and Web 2.0 is the individualization of received content and the integration of the communication channels used. Within the Web 1.0 users have to use each channel of communication separately. Channels such as chat, email or web page are not accessible in one place. In contrast, there is a strong tendency to integrate different channels of communication within the Web 2.0. Hence, the user receives the possibility of using all the channels in one place and at the same time. Google Buzz is a good example that illustrates this phenomenon. It allows the integration of other services already used, such as Twitter, Flickr or Picasa. What is more, it also provides services such as email and chat. And all these services are accessible in one place. In communication channels thus integrated, the user has the possibility to decide what content, what kind of issues and what resources are important for him and what messages should be ignored (Mills, 2007: 4).

Another difference between Web 1.0 and Web 2.0 concerns the requirements of user competence. High technical and programming skills, e.g. the ability to create web pages and post them on a server using FTP, are essential for an active use of the Web 1.0. This situation creates a barrier for active participation within the Web 1.0. Of course, it applies only to some channels of communication, but to the most important ones such as having your own web page. In turn, within the Web 2.0 social skills play a greater role than technical skills. Among

---

2 More about folksonomy: T. Hammond, T. Hannay, B. Lund and J. Scott (2005). Social Bookmarking Tools (I). A General Review, *D-Lib Magazine* , Vol. 11 (4), accessible at: http://www.dlib.org/dlib/april05/hammond/04hammond.html

others these include the ability to create and maintain social networks or to establish relationships with other users of the Web. Posting content within the Web 2.0 is much easier and does not demand technical skills because the communication channels are equipped with intuitive interfaces and templates. Therefore, almost everyone can become an active user.

The characteristics of the Web 2.0 listed and described form its key feature, that is a culture of participation and dynamic interaction in which potentially anyone can be a sender and receiver of the message. There lacks a single information center. The Web 1.0 may be described as a huge tank full of information, while the Web 2.0 has become a medium of communication which additionally enables the creation of communities. The classification of internet communication channels based on the features described above, distinguishing both generations of webs, can be found in a table in the appendix.

The technical and social development of the Internet suggests that we are witnessing the formation of foundations of the Web 3.0, which will operate using the mechanisms of artificial intelligence capable of searching and categorizing the information not only on the basis of their lexical meaning, but also on the cultural contexts. This phenomenon is referred to in the literature as the Semantic Web (Berners-Lee, Hendler and Lassila, 2001). Some applications and solutions that are recognized as the first representatives of the Web 3.0 are already running. For example, online games or rather virtual environments such as Entropia Universe or Google Lively.

The origin and development of Internet use in election campaigns in Poland

The Web 1.0 was predominantly used in Poland during the election campaigns in the period 1995-2007. There have been almost no quantitative or qualitative changes in the use of the Internet in the period between elections. In 1995 the first attempts to implement the Internet in political communication during the presidential election campaign took place; they were, however, of accidental character mainly because of the low number of Internet users in Polish society. In this year the candidates created web sites for the first time. The use of the Internet in the 1997 parliamentary elections was a bit larger, but these early attempts were regarded as poor and insufficient. Nevertheless, importantly, politicians had noticed the new medium and started to use it. According to estimations of that time, in early 1997 there were only approximately 900,000 people using the Internet in Poland (Zembrzuski, 1997: 14). Only 14 out of 22 registered electoral committees set up their own web sites, and only a few candidates had their own private web sites (Żurawski, 2010: 124; Nowina Konopka, 2008: 174-175). Electoral staffs of the time used to make such rudimentary mistakes as not providing their contact email address on the web site or making up the domain name without any logical connection with the name of the candidate. A qualitative change in the use of the Internet as a means of political communication was brought about by the local government elections campaign of 1998. Politicians were experimenting with a new channel of political communication, the chat room. Particularly active in this field were politicians of the Electoral Action "Solidarity" and the Democratic Left Alliance (Nowina Konopka, 2008: 178). The presidential election campaign of 2000 resulted in significant technical and aesthetic standardization of web pages. A characteristic pattern of candidates' web sites was established. Each such web page would have consisted of a biography, casual pictures of the politician (often with their family), an electoral program, electoral slogans, and sometimes even ludic elements (such as a caricature of a candidate). The increased bandwidth of Internet connections enabled a greater use of video materials. In spite of declarations, the use of the Internet was of minor importance then. There was no unique content created specifically for the online campaign, and there were many technical and marketing shortcomings (Połowczyk, 2004: 98). What is more, among all the channels of communication provided by the Web 1.0, politicians used web sites almost exclusively. Polish politicians adopted the American custom of asking for financial support on the Internet. Nonetheless, unlike the American politicians, none of the candidates allowed the making of payments online (Nowina Konopka, 2008: 179-182). Also for the first time, candidates sent emails on a mass scale. The parliamentary elections of 2001 and the local government elections of 2002 maintained the technical and communication standards outlined above.

After the presidential election of 2005, the Web 1.0 has become an inherent part of building the image of a political candidate. Moreover, the web site has become a peculiar information center containing news about the current activities of a candidate and providing unique information not accessible anywhere else. Mailing was another important channel of communication commonly used in this campaign (Żurawski, 2010: 156). During the parliamentary elections campaign of 2007, politicians used communication channels classified as a part of the Web 1.0 in a standardized and professionalized way. The vast majority of candidates elected to the Sejm in 2007 treated the Internet as an indispensible element of their election campaigns. Among 460 members of the Sejm, 307 of them (66.7 per cent) had web sites designed specifically for the election campaign. The best in terms of the number of web sites were the members of the Civic Platform, 77 per cent of whom had their own web sites. The members of the Polish Peasant Party (54.8 per cent) and of the Law and Justice party (57.8 per cent) had the least number of web sites.

A new trend in the political communication between elites and voters began to be apparent in subsequent election campaigns—during the elections to the European Parliament in 2009, the 2010 presidential election and the 2011 parliamentary elections. The channels of communication provided by the Web 1.0 started to give way to channels provided by the Web 2.0. In 2010-2011 channels of communication from both generations of Webs were used simultaneously, but the scope of use of channels provided by the Web 2.0 has been gradually increasing. The first of the new channels of communication were political blogs. The idea of using blogs in politics appeared relatively early; the first of them were created in the second half of the nineties. However, it was not until 2001-2002 that they gained popularity. The main reason for this was the fact that the first online services facilitating the creation of blogs were launched that time. The massive use of blogs in political communication started in 2004 in the United States and in 2010 in Poland. The first Polish political blog founded on March 13, 2003 was the blog of a local politician Sławomir Wąs (Kołodziejczyk, 2009: 268).

In 2007 blogs were not very popular among Polish MPs or among journalists from traditional media, who were focused on other channels of political communication. Only 23 Polish politicians of the central level had their blogs on the most popular blogging site *blog.onet.pl*. The most active bloggers, according to the number of posts about the election campaign turned out to be Waldemar Pawlak and Janusz Piechociński (Polish Peasant Party) and Grażyna Ciemniak (Democratic Left Alliance). It is worth noting that the leaders of two major parties, Donald Tusk and Jarosław Kaczyński, did not have blogs. The leaders of coalition parties during the Sejm of the fifth term (2005-2007), Roman Giertych and Andrzej Lepper, also did not use this channel of communication. This may suggest that blogs in Polish politics were treated as a substitute channel of communication used only when a politician had limited access to traditional media. It should be emphasized that this channel, as the only one, has been adopted by politicians as a tool for permanent communication of their thoughts, and its use is not limited to the time of the election campaign. In particular, this applies to microblogs, which have become an important tool of political communication starting from the European Parliament elections in 2009. The favorite microblogging service used by Polish politicians is Twitter; services such as Blip or Identi.ca do not enjoy the same popularity. Messages posted by the politicians in the microblogging service Twitter were carefully monitored and published by traditional media. Sometimes they even became the news of the day. Twitter as a tool of political communication has been propagated by the political adviser and journalist Eryk Mistewicz, who persuaded the Law and Justice politicians to use that channel of communication during the 2009 European Parliament elections campaign. Soon thereafter the service gained great popularity among politicians. Before the 2010 presidential election Twitter was being used by over a hundred Polish politicians of the central level. In addition to this, almost half of the members of the Cabinet of that time were using this microblogging service. However, blogs in Polish politics did not become a standard. This is because blogs demand persistence, regularity and interactivity from their owners. Moreover, the attractiveness of blogs depends not only on the content posted there, but primarily on the way the information is presented. It should be presented eloquently, in a literary manner, and there should be a balance between linguistic correctness and the rules of Internet jargon. Blogs are a supplementary channel of political communication. As it was mentioned before, they are often a substitute means of communication for the politicians marginalized in the traditional media, and the fact of having them is not strongly correlated with electoral success.

Another change in political communication came during the presidential election of 2010 and the parliamentary elections of 2011. For the first time on such a large scale, Polish politicians used social networking sites as means for political communication. Of the dozens of social networking sites available in Poland, politicians focused on the two most popular: Nasza Klasa (which in Polish means 'our class') and Facebook. These services have gained great popularity in Poland, especially among young people. The social networking site Nasza Klasa has been visited at least once by 92 per cent of Polish Internet users. Moreover, it has the highest number of real users of all social networking sites in Poland, which is 12,057,100 (67.6 per cent of Polish Internet users). The second place among social networking sites in Poland was taken by Facebook. In 2010 Facebook had 8,074,148 real users in Poland (45.3 per cent of Polish Internet users). The site has been visited by 72 per cent of Polish Internet users and 59 per cent of them had a profile there (Internet Standard, 2010). The most popular politician on Facebook was Janusz Korwin-Mikke. In 2010, 52,000 Facebook users have indicated that they "like" the page, and in December 2011 he had 74,311 "likes". Other politicians have remained far behind Janusz Korwin-Mikke. For instance, the President of Poland Bronisław Komorowski had only 19,413 "likes" in December 2011. At the same time, the Prime Minister Donald Tusk had merely 5,916, and the leader of the biggest opposition party Jarosław Kaczyński had even fewer "likes" at 4,393. One third of the candidates in the parliamentary elections of 2011 who were elected to the Sejm had profiles on Facebook, and 57 of them even had fanpages (Halcewicz-Pieskaczewski, 2011). Nevertheless, these numbers are insignificant (even taking into account the differing absolute numbers of Internet users in Poland) in comparison to the number of members of the Barack Obama Facebook page. His main site has 24,275,207 "likes" and another 355,960 members have "liked" the "Students for Barack Obama" page. The social networking site Nasza Klasa, which was established in November 2006, initially attracted politicians for private reasons. It was not until the European Parliament elections of 2009 when Nasza Klasa became one of the Internet channels of political communication. Among others, Nasza Klasa is used by such politicians as Bronisław Komorowski, Waldemar Pawlak, Grzegorz Napieralski, Radosław Sikorski, Wojciech Olejniczak, and Janusz Korwin-Mikke. Political communication in this social networking site is disrupted by two factors. Firstly, administrators of the site consistently delete the election materials from the profiles of politicians, considering this content as inconsistent with the rules of the site. Secondly, users create many fictitious accounts, containing mocking or even insulting content.

The vanguard of the *internetization* of election campaigns: contribution to the study of election campaigns in the US

The three following dates have particular importance for the use of Internet in the field of political communication: 1996 for the Web 1.0 and 2004 and 2008 for the Web 2.0. In each of the years listed, important qualitative changes related to the conduct of the election campaign on the Internet were made. 1996 was a turning point in the attitude of American politics towards the use of the Internet, precisely towards the use of web sites[3]. Almost 70 per cent of all of the Republican and Democratic candidates to the U.S. Senate and a third of the candidates to the House of Representatives created web sites. Web sites were also commonly used by the candidates for governors; around 95 per cent of candidates from the major parties had their own web sites (Bimber and Davis, 2003). Subsequent years have shown a growing trend in the use of Internet sites in election campaigns. Furthermore, the presidential campaign carried out in the same year led to a breakthrough of another kind: American politicians have begun to use the Internet as a tool for raising funds for election campaigns. The funds collected in that way are commonly referred to as *soft money*. These donations are usually small, but there are lots of them. The reason for this is the regulatory framework concerning payments to the accounts of candidates. According to the federal law each US citizen has the right to support their candidate with a maximum of two thousand and

---

3 The use of web sites in the course of running for elective political office for the first time took place in the presidential campaign in the United States in 1992. Bill Clinton was the first and the only candidate in this campaign who has used this channel of communication.

three hundred dollars in the primaries and the same sum in elections (Kush, 2000: 24-25). In the literature this phenomenon is compared to a revolution in American politics caused by the start of the broadcasting of presidential debates on television (Trippi, 2005: XVI-XVII). Fundraising through the Internet was initiated by the Republican candidate for president Robert (Bob) Dole. His supporters contributed two hundred thousand dollars via the Internet (Rice, 2004: 43). In the presidential election in 2000, George W. Bush collected about two to three hundred thousand dollars in this way after each instance of sending an email. However, the most effective was G. W. Bush's opponent in the Republican Party primaries, John McCain, who made use of this form of political participation on the Internet and collected approximately 25 per cent of all the funds for his campaign in this way (Davis, Elin and Reeher, 2002: 56-57). In the presidential election of 2004 as many as four million Americans made online payments for their candidates (Rainie, Cornfield and Horrigan, 2005). Nevertheless, it was Barack Obama who made a new record in this category. He collected as much as 500 million dollars from donations made through the Internet (Machała, 2010).

Another turning point took place during the presidential election of 2004. Candidates recognized the Internet as the necessary medium of political communication and made use of various online communication channels (especially blogs) provided by the Web 2.0. Scholars call this phenomenon "the internetization of campaign" (Rice, 2004: 5). Another level of "the internetization of campaign" was achieved in 2008 when B. Obama won the presidential election mainly by a consistent, planned and multilevel use of the communication channels offered by the Web 2.0. He made the use of many social networking sites such as Facebook, MySpace, LiveJournal, and YouTube. In this case we are really dealing with a new quality of election campaigns. They are driven centrally, but they are also based on the mass (albeit short-term) participation of supporters, they shorten the distance between politician and voter, they are dynamic and they use word-of-mouth and viral marketing.

The credibility, attractiveness and efficiency of the Internet as a medium for election campaigns in the eyes of Internet users

The new media differ from the traditional ones not only in the technological sense. More important are the differences in their social perception, their use and the scale of users' identification with a particular medium. One important aspect of the perception of the impact of new media is the assessment of their credibility. According to research carried out by a team from the Institute of Political Science at the University of Warsaw, the Internet is more credible than television (table 1)[4]. However, the levels of the credibility of the Internet compared with radio and the press are similar. Most of the respondents, though less than a half, think that both radio and the press are credible to a similar degree as the Internet. However, when you look at the issue through the prism of only strong and unequivocal evaluations, it appears that there are more respondents who consider the Internet as more credible than respondents who think that radio or the press is more credible (Garlicki, 2011: 42-43). On this basis, it can be concluded that the evaluations of the Internet are better because it provides the more credible information. In this respect, the Internet seems to be better than traditional media. Nevertheless, one must admit that this advantage over traditional media is not very high.

Table 1. *Opinions about the credibility of the Internet in comparison to traditional media (N=720)*

	Indications in per cent:			
	Credibility of the Internet and other mass media			
	Medium	the Internet is more credible	the Internet is equally credible	the Internet is less credible
1	the press	40,7	41,8	17,5
2	radio	33,9	42,6	23,5
3	television	44,3	39,8	15,9

Source: *Kultura Polityczna Polaków w Internecie w kampanii wyborów prezydenckich 2010.* INP UW.

4 Data from the study *Kultura polityczna Polaków w Internecie w kampanii wyborów prezydenckich w 2010 roku*, which was carried out between 10 and 14 June 2010. This research was a part of the program (N N 116 280338) *Formy i treść ekspresji kultury politycznej Polaków w Internecie w kampaniach wyborczych 2010 i 2011 roku* funded by the Ministry of Science and Higher Education and carried out under the direction of Professor Jan Garlicki. The quantitative part of the research was conducted on a sample of 720 adult Polish Internet users by using the CAWI (Computer Assisted Web Interviews) method. The respondents were recruited through a mailing done by the Wirtualna Polska portal (wp.pl) and through a custom online panel Inetpanel.pl owned by the Polish market research company CBM Indicator. The sample was weighted according to sociodemographic characteristics such as gender, age, size of place of residence, education, and the time spent on surfing the Internet, which provided its representativeness and the ability to extrapolate the results to the adult population of Polish Internet users. The qualitative part of the research was carried out by using the FGI (Focus Group Interview) method. After the quantitative part was done, two FGIs were conducted with the participants of CAWI research who were intensive Internet users.

More significantly, Internet users appreciated the advantage of the Internet over the other media in terms of attractiveness (table 2). The new medium is perceived as far more attractive than the press and radio, but as attractive as television. Nevertheless in this respect the opinions of Internet users are clearly divided.

Table 2. Opinions on the attractiveness of the Internet in comparison to traditional media (N=720)

	Indications in per cent:			
	Attractiveness of the Internet and other mass media			
	Medium	the Internet is more attractive	the Internet is equally attractive	the Internet is less attractive
1	the press	57,3	27,2	15,5
2	radio	51,8	29,7	18,5
3	television	34,9	37,6	27,5

Source: *Kultura Polityczna Polaków w Internecie w kampanii wyborów prezydenckich 2010.* INP UW.

The perception of the Internet as a credible and attractive medium undoubtedly influences the tendency, revealed in the recent elections in Poland, of politicians to use it ever more in political campaigns. Another issue, however, is an analysis of the extent to which electoral staffs in Poland do it professionally and effectively.

The results of the research carried out during the parliamentary elections of 2011[5] seem to confirm the results of earlier studies (including those conducted during the presidential election campaign) showing that the Internet is not the main source of knowledge about politics for its users (Garlicki, 2011: 19-22). Poles use the Internet for a variety of reasons, but politics is not the most important one. In October of 2011 half of Internet users declared that in order to obtain information about politics they use the Internet as much as traditional media (table 3). More than a quarter obtain knowledge about politics from traditional media, while 23 per cent of Internet users admit that they prefer the new media. At least two conclusions may be drawn from this data. First of all, in Poland too the new media undoubtedly led to changes regarding the acquisition of

5 The data analysed in this paper comes from the study entitled *Kultura polityczna Polaków w Internecie w kampanii wyborów parlamentarnych w 2011 roku.*

information about politics, but the primacy of traditional media, especially television, has not yet been overcome. Secondly, it is clear that transformation processes in the sphere of the influence of the media are dynamic and significant. Twice more Internet users were looking on the Internet for the information about the activities of politicians during the parliamentary elections campaign than it was during the presidential election (90 per cent in comparison to 40 per cent).

Table 3. *Traditional media and the Internet as means of information about politics (N=757)*

	To what extent do you use the Internet to gain information about politics in comparison to the so-called "traditional" media—television, radio and press	Indications in per cent:
1	I gain information about politics mostly through "traditional" media	26,0
2	I use the Internet and "traditional" media to the same extent when gaining information about politics	50,5
3	I gain information about politics mainly on the Internet	23,5

Source: *Kultura Polityczna Polaków w Internecie w kampanii wyborów parlamentarnych 2011*. INP UW.

After analyzing the results of the research one can conclude that looking for information about politics on the Internet requires more time and effort whereas messages communicated by television, radio and newspapers are assimilated or acquired by voters to some extent incidentally while performing other daily activities. Moreover, despite the fact that Internet users are more interested in politics than other citizens, they use the Internet for many different purposes and looking for information about politics is usually not the first priority.

A comparison of the results of the studies of the 2010 and 2011 election campaigns leads to the conclusion that Internet users lost their belief that electoral campaigns and the political communication of elites can effectively influence the choices made by citizens. A poll carried out on the eve of the presidential election in 2010 showed that the majority of citizens using the Internet believed that communication in the media would not affect the behavior of voters or that its influence would be negligible. According to the Internet users the most influential would be the "old" media, namely the press. One third of them believed that the information appearing in the medium would influence the choice of a particular candidate (table 4). Respondents probably had in mind articles on politics rather than electoral advertisements published in newspapers.

After a year, during the study of the 2011 parliamentary election campaigns, the belief of the Internet users in the role of media in shaping the behavior of voters had significantly decreased. The decrease of belief in the influence of the media included practically all types. Only television was considered to be relatively influential. A quarter of the respondents stated that this was a medium that could have influence on voters' decisions. This is a minority group, but the largest among those who thought that campaigns in the media would have an impact on voters' behavior. What is more, the belief in the influence of television increased by several percentage points in comparison to the data from the 2010 presidential election campaign. The majority of Internet users were not convinced that political communication in new media could be effective. In the case of radio and the press a decrease in the number of people convinced about the impact of media on electoral behavior is indeed dramatic. These numbers have decreased several times.

Table 4. The impact of election campaigns in media on electoral behavior (2010—N=720, 2011—N=757)

	To what extent a campaign in a particular medium will affect the choice of a particular candidate	Indications in percents:	
		2010	2011
	A campaign in daily newspapers, weekly newspapers and monthly magazines		
1	It will not affect it	55,2	71,4
2	It will affect it in an ambiguous way	11,0	17,6
3	It will affect it	33,8	11,1
	Total	100	100
	A campaign on the radio		
1	It will not affect it	57,4	67,1
2	It will affect it in an ambiguous way	12,7	21,8
3	It will affect it	29,8	11,1
	Total	100	100
	A campaign on television		
1	It will not affect it	65,1	55,0
2	It will affect it in an ambiguous way	13,3	19,8
3	It will affect it	21,6	25,2
	Total	100	100

A campaign on the Internet			
1	It will not affect it	61,4	54,8
2	It will affect it in an ambiguous way	12,8	23,0
3	It will affect it	25,8	22,2
	Total	100	100

Source: *Kultura Polityczna Polaków w Internecie w kampanii wyborów prezydenckich 2010*. INP UW; *Kultura Polityczna Polaków w Internecie w kampanii wyborów parlamentarnych 2011*. INP UW.

When analyzing the role of the Internet in the political communication of elites with voters it is important to learn about the opinion of Internet users on the use of new media in politics. Nearly two-thirds of Internet users believe that it was a good idea to introduce the ability of voters to contact politicians (not only the other way round) by using new media (table 5). Similar numbers of Internet users consider the introduction of the possibility of holding a referendum via the Internet as a good idea. Over half of the respondents are convinced that the Internet should become the main means of conducting election campaigns instead of television, press, radio and billboards. At the same time slightly more than a quarter of Internet users are concerned that the use of the Internet in politics will cause it to be controlled by journalists and politicians, not by citizens, and that it will enable the manipulation of political information in a fraudulent manner on a large scale.

It can, therefore, be noticed that there is a peculiar duality of opinions among people using new media. On the one hand, they perceive the new opportunities given by the political communication on the Internet. On the other, some of them fear the possibility that politicians would gain control over the Internet. These different attitudes are not necessarily contradictory. They rather show that Internet users are beginning to understand that the development of technological capabilities and solutions is one thing, and the issue of who and how is using them is another thing. Definitely the Internet provides opportunities for symmetrical and personalized communication between the elites and the citizens and, therefore, creates a new quality in conducting election campaigns. However, the temptation of using new media to increase influence on voters' behaviors is enormous. The direction in which these processes will head depends on both sides of the political scene. We should also not forget about the journalists. On the one hand, the journalists from traditional media create Internet portals and web services more and more often. On the other, we are witnessing the development of citizen journalism and the creation of independent media on the Internet. It is also worth noting that even though during the last election Polish Internet users did not consider the new medium as effective, most of them are convinced that the Internet should become the main means of conducting election campaigns instead of television and other traditional media. Hence, it can be said that we are dealing with the view that the use of new media is "the future of politics".

Table 5. Opinions on the use of the Internet in politics

	Indications in percent:					
	Statement	Definitely not/ definitely a bad idea	Rather not/ rather a bad idea	Neither agree nor disagree / neither a good nor a bad idea	Rather yes/ rather a good idea	Definitely yes/ definitely a good idea
1	I consider the possibility of contacting politicians by voters on the Internet as	2,8	5,0	27,5	46,2	18,5
		7,8		27,5	64,7	
2	I consider the possibility of holding referenda on the Internet as	6,5	7,8	21,5	38,0	26,2
		14,3		21,5	64,2	
3	I consider the possibility of holding public debates of voters and politicians on important issues as	5,0	7,4	31,8	41,6	14,1
		12,4		31,8	55,7	
4	The Internet should become the main means of conducting election campaigns instead of television, newspapers, radio and billboards	4,1	10,8	32,5	31,2	21,4
		14,9		32,5	52,6	
5	The Internet is the future of politics	5,7	13,5	28,9	38,2	13,7
		19,2		28,9	51,9	
6	The use of the Internet in politics will make politics more transparent	6,3	18,4	36,9	30,8	7,7
		24,7		36,9	38,5	
7	By using the Internet in politics ordinary people will have a stronger impact on politics	8,7	24,3	30,1	30,9	5,9
		33,0		30,1	36,8	
8	Politicians should make it possible to vote via the Internet	31,3	27,5	12,9	15,3	19,9
		58,8		12,9	28,2	

9	The Internet should become the main means of communication between citizens and politicians	9,2	25,1	37,4	22,3	5,9
		34,3		37,4	28,2	
10	The use of the Internet in politics will make it increasingly controlled by the journalists and politicians, not by citizens	9,1	31,8	32,4	20,2	6,5
		40,9		32,4	26,7	
11	The use of the Internet in politics will enable the manipulation of political information in a fraudulent manner on a large scale	9,0	30,3	34,1	18,6	8,1
		39,3		34,1	26,7	
12	The politics conducted on the Internet will be of a lower quality	11,2	32,2	38,3	11,9	6,3
		43,4		38,3	18,2	
13	The use of the Internet in politics is a threat to democracy	24,4	37,9	26,9	7,1	3,6
		62,3		26,9	10,7	

Source: *Kultura Polityczna Polaków w Internecie w kampanii wyborów parlamentarnych 2011*. INP UW.

Conclusions

The following conclusions arise after analyzing the election campaigns conducted in the new media. First of all, the development of the political communication of elites with voters on the Internet has an only partially cumulative character. In other words, politicians and their staffs abandon or neglect the channels of communication already used in favor of newly emerging tools. In each of the campaigns conducted in the period 1995-2011, politicians have used a different configuration of communication channels on the Internet, but they have done so inconsistently neglecting the task of removing old content. The phenomenon of “abandonment” applies in particular to web sites and online discussion forums, and, to a lesser extent, to blogs and profiles on social networking sites (Cyrkulewski, 2009). The best example is the “abandonment” of channels used in the Web 1.0 in favor of those used in the Web 2.0 during the parliamentary elections of 2011. Candidates and parties became much more active in the area of social networking sites, leaving traditional web sites behind. Many of the web sites of MPs were neither updated nor deleted: they were simply abandoned. Similarly, starting from 2005, MPs use chats in discussions with voters less and less often. Among the worst such cases are traditional online discussion forums created by political parties. Discussion forums poor in posts and entries are abandoned but can still be found on the Internet. This causes the formation of a specific melting pot of information. Current events and news are mixed with out-of-date information. This phenomenon can negatively affect the image of a party or a politician in addition to making it difficult for less skilled Internet users to access the proper information. This kind of behavior can be discrediting for politicians and political parties, the more so because research shows that Internet users think that not only blogs but also traditional web sites, discussion forums and chat rooms should be the primary means of communication in the era of the permanent campaign. Nearly two thirds (65.8 per cent) of respondents indicated the web site as a necessary means of communication for parties and politicians [6].

Secondly, Polish political elites are usually far from proficient in knowing the cultural Internet code. Experts have formulated numerous objections in this regard. These objections or problems are related to both communicational and technological perspectives. Generally, politicians begin to use the new channels of communication with some delay, thereby generating an image as newbies (Wlodkowska, 2011). The lack of vigor, courage and creativity is noticeable in politicians' activities. It is surprising that none of the channels of communication attributed to the emerging Web 3.0 have been used in any election campaign so far, because the use of virtual worlds such as Second Life could be a really good idea. Another problem is related to the collection of money for a campaign on the Internet. The scale of use of this method of financing is insignificant in Poland.

Thirdly, on the level of communication a kind of failure tactic has been developed. This tactic can be summarized in following sentence: "I inform and represent the views, but do not try to convince and do not agitate". Hardly any politician uses the potential of the Internet to mobilize voters. This is particularly evident in the Web 1.0, namely in web sites. They have become in a sense information centers (sometimes even containing out-of-date information) which do not try to convince voters. Furthermore, politicians usually ignore the interactive nature of the Internet and use it mainly to communicate only in a one-way, so-called top-down direction. They prefer the "one to many" type of communication. In the case of the channels based on the two-sided principle of communi-

---

6 Data from the research titled *Kultura polityczna Polaków w Internecie w kampanii wyborów parlamentarnych w 2011 roku*, which was carried out between 27 September and 5 October 2011 on a sample of 757 individual respondents using the CAWI (Computer Assisted Web Interviews) method.

cation politicians try to limit interactivity. For example, they block the possibility of posting comments on their blogs or they provide email addresses to their offices rather than to themselves. What is more, the way politicians shape their messages usually deepens the communication distance. The message is more often expressed in the third person than the first, and it does not address specific groups of citizens. The communicational and mobilization potential of the new medium is definitely not properly used.

Another defect is related to the fact that content presented has derivative character. In other words, most of the content on the Internet is taken from such sources as television, radio or even online press. The practice of posting borrowed content in an unchanged shape, even without a comment, is very common among the Polish political elites.

After an analysis of the results of the study it can be concluded that actors who have the biggest impact on Polish politics treat the Internet primarily as a tool for communicating information, with a special emphasis on one-sided, "one to many" type communication, ignoring its opportunities to mobilize voters or recruit new party members. The observations presented seem to confirm the conclusions drawn by Western researchers who claim that politicians use the Internet in a minimalist way, according to the model of the "elegant shop window" (Porębski, 2001: 127). The hypothesis formulated at the beginning of the chapter, which assumed that the increased interactivity in political communication created by the Internet is only a mask covering the growth of the impact of political elites on voters, turned out to be untrue in the Polish environment. The approach of Polish politicians and their staffs is dictated by a kind of cognitive conservatism and aspiration to maintain the *status quo* of communication. This passive attitude may be described by the concept of *slacktivism*, which is a term formed out of the words slacker and activism. The apathetic attitude of political parties to take a proactive activity is an ideal example of *slacktivism.*

Appendix. Classification of communication channels on the Internet

<table>
<tr><th>Web 1.0</th><th>Web 2.0</th></tr>
<tr><td rowspan="2">Web sites (traditional)</td><td>Social networking sites
(general, professional, thematic, encyclopedic (based on a wiki mechanism))</td></tr>
<tr><td rowspan="3">Blogs
(text blogs, video blogs, photo blogs, audio blogs, link logs)</td></tr>
<tr><td>Discussion groups (USENET)
(national, thematic)</td></tr>
<tr><td>Mailing lists and newsletters</td></tr>
</table>

Discussion forums (forums of news services, independent discussion forums)	
News portals (online press, Internet publishing houses, television, radio)	Citizen journalism / grassroots and independent media (citizen journalism, newsfeeds)
Chats / IRC	Microblogs
Instant messaging clients	

Source: Own elaboration of D. Mider.

References

Berners-Lee, T., Hendler, J. and Lassila, O. (2001). *Sieć semantyczna* [The semantic Web]. Retrieved July 2001 from Świat Nauki41-49.

Bimber, B. and Davis, R. (2003). *Campaigning Online. The Internet in U.S. Elections*. New York: Oxford University Press.

Bratkowski, P. (2011). *Czemu nikt nie lubi polityków na Facebooku?* (*Why nobody likes politicians on Facebook?*). Retrieved 30 June 2011 from Newsweek.

Cormode, G. and Krishnamurthy, B. (2008). *Key Differences between Web 1.0 and Web 2.0*. New York. Retrieved December 2011 from http://citeseerx.ist.psu.edu/viewdoc/download?doi=10.1.1.145.3391&rep=rep1&type=pdf.

Cyrkulewski, A. (2009). *Polscy posłowie a Internet. Raport z badań* [Polish members of Parliament and Internet. Report from research] Retrieved December 2011 from http://www.cyrkulewski.pl/images/Polscy-poslowie-a-Internet-raport-z-badan-Documentum-pl.pdf.

Davis, S., Elin, L. and Reeher, G. (2002). *Click on Democracy. The Internet's Power to Change Political Apathy into Civic Action*. Cambridge: Westview.

Debek, P. and Dębek, P. (2000). *Klikanie na władzę* [Clicking on the power]. Retrieved November 2000 from Chip.

Dobek-Ostrowska, B. (2006). *Komunikowanie polityczne i publiczne* [Political and public Communication]. Warszawa: PWN.

Gajewski, M. (2010). *Być jak Barack Obama, czyli polscy politycy na Twisterze* [To be like Barack Obama—Polish polititicians on Twitter]. Retrieved 21 June 2010 from Chip.

Garlicki, J. (2010). Komunikowanie polityczne—od kampanii wyborczych do kampanii permanentnej [Political Communication—from electoral campaign to permanent campaign], In Strategie i mechanizmy marketingu politycznego [Strategies and mechanisms of political marketing]). *Studia Politologiczne*, vol. 16. Warszawa: Elipsa, 26-45.

Garlicki, J. (2011). Kultura polityczna polskich Internautów [Political culture of Polish Internet users]. In: Kultura polityczna Internautów w Polsce [Political culture of Internet users in Poland]. *Studia Politologiczne,* vol. 21, 13–50.

Grzywińska, I. (2010). Zastosowanie nowych mediów w procesie komunikacji politycznej na przykładzie kampanii prezydenckiej w Stanach Zjednoczonych w 2008 r. [New media in a communication process based on presidential election campaign in United States in 2008]. In Strategie i mechanizmy marketingu politycznego [Strategies and mechanisms of political marketing]. *Studia Politologiczne*, vol. 16, 133-158.

Halcewicz-Pieskaczewski, J. *Kto ma Internet, ten ma władzę*? [Having an Internet, having a power?]. Retrieved 8 July 2011 from Gazeta Wyborcza.

Kołodziejczyk, P. (2009). Blog jako instrument komunikowania politycznego, czyli raport z sejmowej blogosfery [Blog as an instrument of political communication, rapport from parliamentary blogosphere]. In: Kolczyński, M., Mazur, M., Michalczyk, S. (Eds.). *Mediatyzacja kampanii politycznych* [Mediatization of political campaigns]. Katowice: Wydawnictwo Uniwersytetu Śląskiego, 268-284.

Kowalkiewicz, M. (2003). *Glob blogów* [Globe of blogs]. Retrieved from http://gazeta-it.pl/pl/internet/5396.

Kush, C. (2000). *Cybercitizen. How to Use Your Computer to Fight for ALL the Issues You Care About.* New York: Martin's Griffin.

Machała, T. (2011). *Kampania wyborcza w Internecie* [Election campaign on the Internet]. Retrieved 21 January 2010 from http://kampanianazywo.pl/opinie/kampania-wyborcza-w-internecie.

Mider, D. and Borówka, O. (2012). Internet—medium bez cenzury? [Internet—medium without a censorship?]. In: Komunikowanie polityczne. Wybrane zagadnienia [Political communication. Selected issues]. *Studia Politologiczne*, vol. 25, 141-176.

Mider, D. and Marzec, P. (2012). *Zdaniem Internautów: ACTA to zamach na demokrację* [According to surfers: ACTA as an attack on democracy]. Retrieved February 2012 from http://www.indicator.pl/index.php?id=331.

Mills, L.B. (2007). *The Next Wave Now. Web 2.0.* The School Administrator. 64 (8).

Nowina Konopka, M. (2008). *Rola Internetu w rozwoju demokracji w Polsce* [Role of the Internet in the development of democracy]. Kraków - Nowy Sącz: Wyższa Szkoła Biznesu—National-Louis University.

O'Reilly, T. (2005). *What Is Web 2.0. Design Patterns and Business Models for the Next Generation of Software*, Retrieved December 2011 from http://www.oreillynet.com/pub /a/oreilly/tim/news/2005/09/30/what-is-web-20.html.

Ornstein, N.J. and Mann, T.E (Eds.). (2000). *The Permanent Campaign and Its Future.* Waszyngton: AEI and The Brookings Institution.

Połowczyk, Ż. (2004). *Internet—media—edukacja—polityka* [Internet—media—education—politics]. Poznań: Wydawnictwo Forum Naukowe.

Porębski, L. (2001). *Elektroniczne oblicze polityki. Demokracja, państwo, instytucje polityczne w okresie rewolucji informacyjnej* [Electronic face of politics. Democracy, state, political institutions in an informational revolution]. Kraków: Uczelniane Wydawnictwa Naukowo-Dydaktyczne.

Rafa, J. (2011). *Wyborczy Internet* [Electoral Internet]. Retrieved December 2011 from http://www.wsp.krakow.pl/papers/news-wyb.html.

Rainie, L., Cornfield, M., and Horrigan, J. (2005). *The Internet and Campaign 2004.* In *The Pew Research Center*. Retrieved December 2011 from http://www.pewinternet.org/pdfs/ PIP_2004_Campaign.pdf.

Rice, A. (2011). *Campaigns Online: The Profound Impact of the Internet, Blogs, and E-Technologies in Presidential Political Campaigning,* Center for the Study of American Government at Johns Hopkins University, Retrieved January 2004. from http://www.campaignsonline.org/reports/online.pdf.

Social Media 2010. Internet Standard. Retrieved from http://www.internetstandard.pl/whitepapers/1594/Raport.Social.Media.2010.html.

Hammond, T., Hannay, T., Lund, B. and Scott, J. (2005). *Social Bookmarking Tools (I). A General Review*, D-Lib Magazine, 11 (4). Retrieved December 2011 from http://www.dlib.org/dlib/april05/hammond/04hammond.html.

Trippi, J. (2005). *The Revolution Will Not Be Televised. Democracy, The Internet, and The Overthrow of Everything*. New York: ReganBooks.

Twitter i Facebook zablokowane [Twitter and Facebook blocked], Retrieved 6 September 2009 from http://www.tvn24.pl/12692,1613522,0,1,twitter-i-facebook-zablokowane,wiadomosc.html.

Twitter ofiarą wojny na Kaukazie [Twitter as a victim of the war in Kaukaz]. Retrieved from http://www.tvn24.pl/-1,1613610,0,1,twitter-stal-sie-ofiara-wojny-na-kaukazie,wiadomosc.html.

Twitter zaatakowany przez „Irańską Cyberarmię" [Twitter attacked by „Iran Cyber Army"]. Retrieved from http://www.tvn24.pl/-1,1634244,0,1,twitter-zhakowany-przez-iranska-cyberarmie,wiadomosc.html.

Uhlig, D. (2010). *Uwaga, Twitter: „Będą ćwierkać, świstać, kwilić..."* (Attention, Twitter: „They tweet, whistle, wail…"]. Retrieved 11 March 2010 from Gazeta Wyborcza.

Włodkowska, I. *Ćwierkając bez strategii* [Tweeting without the strategy]. Retrieved from http://www.proto.pl/PR/Pdf/cwierki.pdf

Zembrzuski, S. (1997). *Milion Polaków w sieci.* [Milion of Polish on the Web]. Teleinfo 14/97

Żurawski, J. (2010). *Internet jako współczesny środek elektronicznej komunikacji wyborczej i jego zastosowanie w polskich kampaniach parlamentarnych* [Internet as a modern way of electronic election communication and its use in Polish parliamentary campaigns]. Kraków: Księgarnia Akademicka.

11. Political dialogue on Facebook—myth or reality? A case study of the Law and Justice and Civic Platform parties in Poland

Ilona Grzywińska
University of Warsaw, Poland

Abstract: Both political parties and voters have increased their use of Internet, particularly social media. Politicians have adopted social media channels such as social networking sites, blogs and microblogs in order to communicate with voters, engage them in discussions on current problems and sustain or increase their electorate base. Voters use different social media to express their support for politicians and to relate to them but also to present their point of view or ask questions. In this paper the author examines the relationship between voters and political parties within two Facebook pages owned by major parties in Poland—Civic Platform, the ruling party, and Law and Justice, its opposition. The purpose of the study is to investigate whether the mentioned parties build the political dialogue with their voters and therefore whether Facebook can be perceived as an implementation of the public sphere concept developed by Jurgen Habermas.

Key words: Facebook, Law and Justice, Civic Platform, public sphere, Jurgen Habermas, political dialogue

Introduction

For more than a decade scholars and opinion leaders have raised the question of whether the Internet has or will have an impact on political dialogue, the development of democracy and the public sphere (Dahlgren, 2005). This debate has been especially robust since the appearance of discussion groups and social networking sites at the end of the 90s. The last few years have brought rapid growth in online political experiments and Internet democracy projects conducted by governments, political parties or different organizations and citizen groups (Dahlberg, 2001). Scholars who favor the deliberative democracy theory argue that informed discourse leads to rational decision making (Van Mill, 1996). Some "social choice" theorists oppose this position, suggesting that such an unconstrained discourse results in confusion and chaos and may have irrational outcomes (Arrow, 1963). The purpose of this article is to examine whether the political dialogue existing on the Internet is the contemporary form of Habermas' public sphere (Habermas, 1989) and whether it gives the opportunity for rational decision making based on the conversations between political actors and voters. This issue is analyzed using the case study of discussions held on the Facebook pages of two major Polish political parties—Civic Platform and Law and Justice.

The Internet and Polish politics

The Internet became important in political marketing strategies in Poland in 2004 and 2005 when, for the first time, all political parties had websites during the elections. The increased role of the Internet in political communication started with the rapid growth of social media in Poland and the success of U.S. presidential candidate Barack Obama's campaign in 2008. Obama used social networking sites like Facebook or Twitter to communicate with the voters and collect money for the campaign. He also built his own online community, my.barackobama.com, to engage users in political dialogue, facilitate "micropayments" as well as recruit and organize volunteers. The online campaign was also supported by a mobile application. After 2008, many politicians in Poland, such as Janusz Korwin-Mikke, Wojciech Olejniczak and Adam Bielan, started Facebook pages or Twitter accounts to communicate with their voters on a daily basis. These first individual efforts were later continued on a party level. In 2010, Law and Justice, the second strongest political party in Poland, followed the example of Barack Obama and launched its own online community called MyPis.pl. It was the first social networking site started by a political party in Poland and was designed to communicate with Law and Justice's voters. Registered users are encouraged to send law proposals and give feedback on current actions by Law and Justice Parliament members. During the 2011 election campaign, the ruling party, Civic Platform, launched a website, zapytajplatforme.pl, dedicated to voter questions about government reforms, the economy and other issues, including the party's program. The users could also rate other users' questions and comment on them. Later, the prime minister was supposed to address the most important questions in his videoblog. All the major political parties in Poland have Facebook and Twitter pages as well as YouTube channels and profiles on one major local social networking site, Naszaklasa.pl.

According to the survey conducted in 2011 by ARC Rynek i Opinie, the most visible Polish party on the Internet is Civic Platform: 45% of respondents claimed that the actions of this party were the most professional and effective (ARC Rynek i Opinie, 2011). The rest of the parties were ranked for their Internet campaigns by the respondents as follows: Law and Justice (40%), Ruch Palikota (22%) and SLD (17%). This ranking is consistent with the results of the elections (the only other party that received more votes than SLD, PSL, was not selected by the respondents). The survey also showed that political parties used almost all available methods of Internet communication to interact with voters: social networking sites (SNS), websites, blogs and broadcast websites. However, the most noticeable way of reaching the voters was traditional display advertising: 54% of respondents indicated that ads were the most common method for political parties to communicate on the Internet.

There is little academic research on the significance of social media in Poland's political discourse. One of the most complex and conclusive studies on the subject was conducted by the University of Warsaw. The study considered participatory democracy in the Internet (Mider, 2008). The author compared different concepts of plebiscitary democracy and argued that the Internet exacerbates the phenomenon of decision chaos because of the polarization and fragmentation of the traditional social groups. The important factor in this process is the level of political culture in a particular society. Polish democracy can be considered young and still consolidating (Diamond, 1995). What is characteristic for this type of democracy is the constant fluctuation of conflict and consensus. The political culture of Polish Internet users reflects that state through frequent aggression and cyber violence in online discussions as well as high responsiveness to negative content (Mider and Marcinkowska, 2011).

Social networking sites and the concept of the public sphere

The phenomenon of social networking sites and the rapid development of Web 2.0 after 2004 attracted the attention of many scholars. However, there is still confusion among academic researchers on what social media is and what exactly should be included in this term. According to Kaplan and Haenlein, social media is "a group of Internet-based applications that build on the ideological and technological foundations of Web 2.0, and that allow the creation and exchange of user-generated content" (Kaplan and Haenlein, 2010). Another group of scholars argues that "social media employ mobile and web-based technologies to create highly interactive platforms via which individuals and communities share, co-create, discuss, and modify user-generated content" (Kietzmann, Hermkens, McCarthy and Silvestre, 2011). Scholars also disagree about which Internet tools should be included in social media and how to categorize them. Kaplan and Haenlein (2010) differentiate social media categories based on social presence and media richness. The first category is collaborative projects (e.g. Wikipedia), blogs, content communities (e.g. YouTube), social networking sites (e.g. Facebook), virtual game and social worlds (e.g. World of Warcraft and Second Life). Social networking sites, a category of social media, is defined separately as "web-based services that allow individuals to (1) construct a public or semi-public profile within a bounded system, (2) articulate a list of other users with whom they share a connection, and (3) view and traverse their list of connections and those made by others within the system" (Boyd and Ellison, 2007).

Facebook.com is the biggest social networking site in the world. In September 2011, the site exceeded 800 million users, more than population of United States (312 million) and Brazil (190 million) combined. Since Facebook is a relatively new phenomenon (launched in 2004), there is little research available on its use in democratic discourse. The first significant research on the subject appeared after Barack Obama's 2008 campaign in which new media played an important role in collecting funds, disseminating messages and initiating collective activities. It showed that social networking sites such as Facebook and MySpace have a political influence in American society (Robertson, Vatrapu and Medina, 2010). Scholars Williams and Gulati (2008) compared the Facebook presence and participation of candidates in the 2006 and 2008 elections and found that "Facebook support had a significant effect on their final vote shares, particularly in the case of open-seat candidates". The researchers also point out that the most active SNS group in terms of political participation is the youngest age cohort (Williams and Gulati, 2008).

Following the research of Robertson, Vatrapu and Medina (2010) and Westling (2007), this study proposes that SNSs are a form of online "public sphere" that is closer to successful democratic deliberation than other types of Internet forums and discussion groups. The most contemporary conceptualization of the public sphere was developed by Habermas (1962), who defined it as "a domain of our social life in which such a thing as public opinion can be formed" (Habermas, 1989: 31). More importantly, the philosopher described the public sphere as a mediating space between the state and civil society where a given community's significant problems are being discussed. The most important factor of Habermasian conception is equality in the communication process, which is necessary since there are always different perspectives in public discourse (Vatrapu, Robertson and Dissanayake, 2008). This is the reason that rationality, freedom of expression and the sharing of thoughts are prerequisites for creating a properly functioning Habermasian public sphere. Facebook and other social networking sites seem to meet these requirements. Robertson, Vatrapu and Medina (2010) who investigated the subject of the sociological function of SNSs provided a summary of the most important public sphere characteristics of Facebook and other social networking sites (Table 1).

Table 1. Public Sphere characteristics of Facebook in particular and other SNSs in general

Sociological Functions	Technological Features	Public Sphere Characteristics
Dissemination	List of friends	Freedom of expression
Opinion	Linear threaded discussion forum (Wall)	Participation
Activism	Threaded discussion forums	Reaction
Advocacy	Status updates	Rationality
Social relations	News postings	Emotionality
	Information sharing	Authority
	User comments	
	Groups and affiliations	
	Unmoderated vs. moderated	
	Open door vs. registered	

Source: Robertson, Vatrapu, Medina, 2010.

Another scholar investigating the concept of the public sphere within online forums (Dahlberg, 2001) pointed out that the main criteria for Internet groups to meet Habermas' conception are the exchange and critique of rational claims, sincerity, reflexivity, equality, autonomy from the state and economic powers and ideal role taking. This study argues that online forums tend to fail all of these criteria except for the exchanging of opinions. However, Robertson, Vatrapu and Medina (2010) claim that SNSs meet all of the requirements. The authors' main arguments are the verification of the authenticity of the users and their opinions by their networks of friends (sincerity), the ability of everyone to post on political parties' pages (equality) and the lack of anyone dominating the discussion. Another important characteristic of SNSs, especially Facebook, that allows the building of communities by political parties is that it is a space where representatives of state and citizens can meet and debate.

Political parties on Facebook

Political parties and politicians have been allowed to have official fan pages on Facebook since 2007. In Poland, Facebook has been used since 2008 both by individual politicians (e.g. Wojciech Olejniczak, Jerzy Buzek, Agnieszka Pomaska, Przemysław Wipler, Janusz Korwin-Mikke) and political parties (e.g. Law and Justice, Civic Platform, Ruch Palikota, Sojusz Lewicy Demokratycznej, Polskie

Stronnictwo Ludowe). The pages can be divided into official (set up by politicians or parties themselves) and unofficial (usually started by fans of a particular party or politician or the opponents thereof). All of the major political parties in Poland link their official Facebook pages to their websites. Parties claim that they use Facebook to talk to the voters. Civic Platform has a large sign on its Facebook welcome page that says, "Let's discuss". Law and Justice, the second biggest party in Poland, does not promise any discussion. Instead, it informs users of its program and provides a list of politicians. The first major use of Facebook by political parties and politicians took place during the parliamentary campaign in 2011 in which parties explored almost all of Facebook's features (social ads, fan pages, applications). In spite of these efforts, political pages on Facebook did not attract the interest of very many users compared with the population of Polish citizens using Facebook (almost 10 million users). The two major parties, Civic Platform and Law and Justice, engaged around 35,000 users altogether. A party called "Ruch Poparcia Palikota", popular among young voters, had around 40,000 followers during the campaign. The relatively small interest in political parties' pages might be caused by these factors:

1) The reluctance of Polish users to follow politicians on Facebook because Facebook is perceived as a social network used for fun, relaxation and connecting with friends
2) The reluctance of Polish users on Facebook to disclose political beliefs (in order to become a fan of a page, one has to click "like" and the action becomes public to all the user's friends)
3) Insufficient efforts by political parties to engage in dialogue with users on Facebook

The initial goal of this research was to understand the pattern of postings across the fan pages of two major political parties in Poland, Civic Platform and Law and Justice, in terms of (a) the degree of engagement of the users, (b) the frequency and persistence of the party's activity (c) users' responsiveness to different types of content posted by the party and (d) parties' efforts to engage in the discussion. This research asks several research questions:

1) Do political parties in Poland use Facebook to converse with their voters?
2) To what degree are the Facebook pages owned by political parties consistent with Habermas' concept of "public sphere"?
3) Which party was engaging users more efficiently on its Facebook page?

Method and sampling

Content analysis

In order to evaluate the objectives in this study, a quantitative content analysis was conducted. It is a research technique for the "systematic, objective, and quantitative description of the manifest content in communication" (Berelson, 1952, as cited in Kaid and Wadsworth, 1989: 197). This method has proven particularly constructive with samples that have a large amount of data because a percentage can be used for analysis and still provide reliable results. What is more, content analysis has been used in previous research on the impact of social media in communication research (Trammell 2004; Trammell, Tarkowski, Hofmokl and Sapp, 2006).

Sampling

The author of the study examined the wall posts from the official Facebook sites of two major Polish political parties: Civic Platform and Law and Justice. Facebook was selected as it is the biggest social networking site in Poland and is the most common communication platform for organizations and companies in the country. During the selected time frame, 310 posts were collected and analyzed, of which Law and Justice contributed 151 posts and Civic Platform 159. It is necessary to underline that only the posts created by the administrator of the given page and the comments below those posts were taken into consideration in this study. The study does not refer to posts made by the users. The reason for that is that the purpose of the research was to examine the dialogue between the political parties and voters on Facebook and the posts made by users are not addressed by the parties in the discussion.

For the sample period, the author focused on the period between August 1st, 2011 and November 31st, 2011 for several key reasons. The first data point was chosen, as it is a symbolic beginning of political campaign for Parliament elections that took place on October 9th, 2011. The month and a half afterward was included to determine whether there is a difference in activity of the parties after the campaign. These dates created a data collection space encompassing 122 days.

Data Collection

Data was collected from Facebook for the sample period, although it should be noted that the author only took into account posts authored by the administrators of the respective pages. External activities and user postings ("wall comments") were not included in the data set. The final data set included 310 individual "posts" from the two Facebook pages (N=310, M = 2.54 posts per day).

A coding guide was developed to examine factors key to the proposed research questions. The following variables of interest were included:

a. *Date of publication*—Dating was based on the following formula: MM/DD /YYYY
b. *Party*—Civic Platform fan page (https://www.facebook.com/PlatformaObywatelska), Law and Justice fan page (https://www.facebook.com/kppis?sk=app_274245479276896&app_data=dlt)
c. *Type of post*—Determined as "Informational" (emphasizing raw facts), "Opinionated" (emphasizing attitudes or opinions).
d. *Is there a link to an exterior source?*—This data determines whether there was a link to a source outside of the Facebook page in the post.
e. *Is there an answer from the political party in the comments below?*—This data reflects whether the administrator of the page participated in the discussion with users below the post.
f. *Is there a question to the users in the post?*—This data determines whether the administrator of the page addressed a question to the users.
g. *Is there a reference to an issue in the post?*—An issue was understood as a problem connected with economy, politics and social matters (the usual sections of each party political program).
h. *How is the opposition presented?*—This category determined the references to the opposition (understood as other political parties in Poland). The reference could be negative, neutral or positive. If there was no reference the category was found not applicable.

Intercoder reliability was determined via the application of Krippendorff's Alpha to a sample of 102 objects, resulting in an intercoder reliability estimate of .83 utilizing the program ReCal2 0.1 (see www.dfreelon.org).

Results

Political dialogue on Facebook

Research question 1 asked whether political parties in Poland converse with the users who follow their Facebook pages. To address this question, the relationship between the number of posts and the number of responses to the users from the political party was investigated. The analysis showed that none of the parties answered voters' questions under each post. Law and Justice took part in the discussion in 35 percent of the cases (where a case is understood as a post made by a party under which users are commenting and asking questions), while Civic

Platform answered only 11 percent of the discussions under the posts on its website. These results indicate that the two main political parties in Poland do not use Facebook as a tool to build dialogue with their voters.

Table 2: Mean comparison of parties' responsiveness to users comments under the posts (Party 1= Law and Justice, Party 2 = Civic Platform)

Group Statistics

	Party	N	Mean	Std. Deviation	Std. Error Mean
Answer from political party	1	151	.35	.479	.039
	2	159	.11	.310	.025

Source: Author

Additionally, to verify whether political parties on Facebook converse with their voters, the author examined the frequency of questions parties asked users in the posts. The analysis indicated that Civic Platform asked questions in 38 percent of its posts, while Law and Justice asked questions to its followers in 10 percent of the posts. This examination further supports the statement that Facebook pages are not used by these parties to talk to their voters and gather their feedback or opinions.

Table 3: The frequency of questions to users asked by the parties in the posts (Party 1=Law and Justice, Party 2= Civic Platform)

Group Statistics

	Party	N	Mean	Std. Deviation	Std. Error Mean
Q to voters	1	151	.10	.300	.024
	2	159	.38	.488	.039

Source: Author

Facebook as the realization of the Habermasian concept of the public sphere

Research question 2 asked to what degree Facebook pages owned by political parties were consistent with Habermas' concept of "public sphere." To answer this question, the author analyzed the number of posts in which each party referenced an actual issue, and how these references affected the discussion among users. The dependent variable in this test was the number of comments under each post of political party.

The significant majority of posts (71 percent) published by the parties on their fan pages did not refer to any political issues (N=310). What is more, users preferred to comment on posts that did not refer to political issues (N=221, M=47.72).

Table 4: *Mean comparison of comments under the posts that refer and do not refer to the political issue in both parties' posts (dependent variable: comments under the post).*

Group Statistics

Ref to the issue		N	Mean	Std. Deviation	Std. Error Mean
Com ments under		221	47.72	61.849	4.160
		89	29.09	32.815	3.478

Source: Author

Additionally, the author investigated the relationship between the posts that mentioned the opposition and the number of "likes." First, if either party mentioned the opposition, the mention was coded as either negative (N=49) or neutral (N=6). None of the parties made a positive statement about the opposition in the analyzed sample. Although the statistical analysis indicated that users would rather like negative posts about the opposition (M=121.61) than neutral posts (M=42.17), the result was not statistically significant ($p>0.05$).

The consistency of communication by the parties

Research question 3 asked which party was more efficient in engaging its followers. To answer this question, the study investigated the consistency of both parties' communication. An analysis of the evidence collected suggests that none of the parties were consistent in communicating with users on their Facebook pages. Both parties post irregularly and the number of posts per day is connected with the moment in the election cycle. Below, Graph 1 illustrates the frequency of posting by the two parties in the examined time frame.

Graph 1: The frequency of postings on Facebook official fan pages by Law and Justice and Civic Platform between August 1st, 2011 and November 30th, 2011

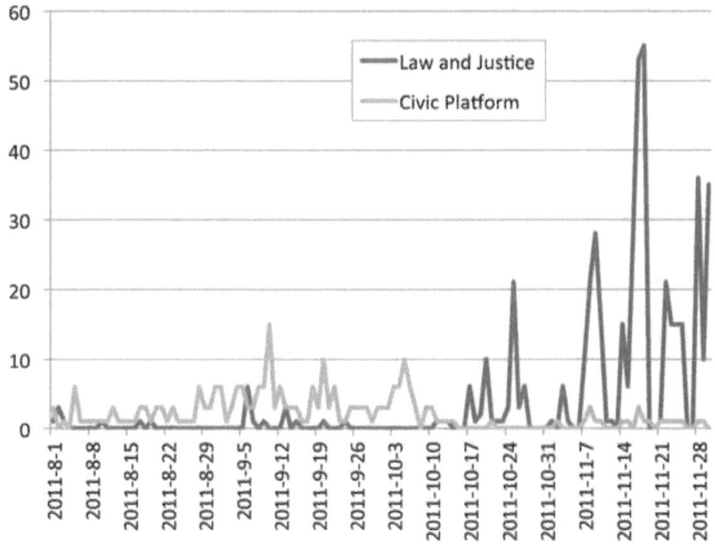

Source: Author

Nonetheless, the graph indicates that Civic Platform is more consistent in its communication—the posts are published almost every day (the time breaks between the posts are smaller), whereas Law and Justice's page administrators have the tendency to post a lot of content on one or two days and then take a break in posting for several days. It is also important to notice that Civic Platform was much more active before the elections date (October 9), while Law and Justice (the opposition party, which lost the election) increased its activity on Facebook after the election, during the formulation of government.

a. Users level of engagement

To address research question 3, the level of users' engagement on both Facebook pages was examined. Engagement is usually measured by the number of interactions on a particular page. Two of the most common interactions are "likes" (a process through which Facebook users signify their approval of the page's content) and "comments" (the user's opinion on the particular piece of content). In both cases, the mean of "likes" and "comments under a post" was bigger for Civic Platform (M=157.16.68) than Law and Justice (M=31.68), which means that users following the page of Civic Platform are more engaged by the content posted by their party. Similarly, the posts published by administrators of Civic Platform page would engage users more often in discussion than those of Law and Justice. Civic Platform's fan page users commented almost four times more on the party's posts (M=65.14) than the users following Law and Justice's page (M=18.4).

Discussion

As with any study, there are some limitations to this research. The first limitation is the data sample—both parties had been using Facebook for more than a year before August 1st, 2011, so there was the potential to collect more observations, allowing for more statistically significant tests. However, before the campaign started the use of Facebook by the two parties was random. Another limitation is the demographics of Facebook users. The small sample of posts mentioning the opposition was also limiting, and caused a lack of statistical significance in the test investigating the relationship between these posts and a number of "likes".

The majority of Facebook users in Poland are young and educated and live in big cities: people who are more likely to vote for Civic Platform than Law and Justice. This might explain why Civic Platform has more followers on Facebook than Law and Justice (25,000 compared to 9,000). What is more, the research investigates only two parties from the Polish political scene, which were chosen based on the criteria of size and representation in Parliament. However, there are other parties in Poland that do not have as many representatives in state organizations but are more successful on Facebook in terms of the number of followers (e.g. Ruch Poparcia Palikota). These parties are worth further investigation for their potential to build dialogue and in consequence create the Habermasian public sphere with the Polish voters. It is also possible that since these additional parties have smaller or non-existent representation in the Polish parliament they put more effort into engaging the voters on Facebook and mobilizing users for future elections.

Finally, although the research confirmed that political parties do not converse with their voters on Facebook, it does not mean they do not try to build dialogue at all. For some reason, the parties prefer to converse with voters within their own channels. Civic Platform encouraged users on Facebook to come and talk to the politicians on the party-owned community (zapytajplatforme.org), while Law and Justice tried to direct traffic from Facebook to its social network (Mypis.pl).

It is also important to acknowledge that the creation of a public sphere depends equally on parties and citizens. This research shows that users on Facebook are not particularly interested in the conversation on issues as much as in laughing at the opposition or discussing other subjects (e.g. the look of a new party t-shirt, visitations in various cities by the prime minister, and information on parties' candidates). Facebook, however, might be a good tool for political parties to create and stimulate emotions about different issues as well as to send a positive message and show "the human face" of politics. This last effect can be especially observed on the Facebook pages devoted to specific political persona like Barack Obama or Mitt Romney. Manuel Castells (2003: 186) defined the role of the Internet in modern politics as the ability of creating cultural codes and spreading information. Existing in the Facebook ecosystem and engaging voters in conversations within the biggest social networking site in the world serves this goal.

References:

ARC Rynek i Opinie. (2011). *Internauci najlepiej ocenili kampanię PO w sieci*. Retrieved November 15, 2012, from http://www.arc.com.pl/newsletter.php?id=12.

Arrow, K. J. (1963). *Social choice and individual values*. New Haven and London: Yale University Press.

Asur, S., Huberman, B., Szabo, G. and Wang, C. (2011, July), *Social media: Persistence and decay*. Paper presented at 5th International AAAI Conference on Weblogs and Social Media, Barcelona.

Castells, M. (2003). *The Internet Galaxy: Reflections on the Internet, Business and Society.* Oxford: Oxford University Press.

Boyd, D. M. and Ellison, N.B. (2007). Social network sites: Definition, History and scholarship. *Journal of Computer-Mediated Communication*, 13(1). Retrieved November 15, 2012, from http://jcmc.indiana.edu/vol13/issue1/boyd.ellison.html.

Dahlberg, L. (2001). Computer-mediated communication and the public sphere: A critical analysis. *Journal of Computer-Mediated Communication*, 7(1). Retrieved November 15, 2012, from http://jcmc.indiana.edu/vol7/issue1/dahlberg.html.

Dahlberg, L. (2001). The internet and democratic discourse: Exploring the prospects of online deliberative forums extending the public sphere. *Information, Communication, and Society*, 4(4), 615–633.

Dahlgren, P. (2005). The Internet, public spheres, and political communication: Dispersion and deliberation. *Political Communication*, 22(2), 147–162.

Habermas, J. (1989). *The structural transformation of the public sphere: An inquiry into a category of bourgeois society*. Cambridge, MA: MIT Press.

Kaplan, A.M. and Haenlein, M. (2010). Users of the world, unite! The challenges and opportunities of social media. *Business Horizons*, 53(3), 59-68.

Kaid, L. and Wadsworth, A. J. (1989). Political television commercials: An experimental study of type and length. *Communication Research*, 5, 55-70.

Kietzmann, J.H., Hermkens, K., McCarthy, I. P., and Silvestre, B. (2011). Social media? Get serious! Understanding the functional building blocks of social media. *Business Horizons*, 54(3), 241-251.

Marcinkowska, A. and Mider, D.(2010). Przemoc w kulturze politycznej polskiego Internetu, *Studia Politologiczne*, 21, 239-297.

Mider, D.(2008). *Partycypacja polityczna w Internecie*. Warszawa: Dom Wydawniczy Elipsa.

Robertson, S.P., Vatrapu, R.K. and Medina, R. (2010). Off the wall political discourse: Facebook use in the 2008 U.S. presidential election, *Information Polity,* 15, 11-31.

Van Mill, D. (1996). The possibility of rational outcomes from democratic discourse and procedures, *The Journal of Politics,* 58(3), 734-752.

Vatrapu, R., Robertson, S. and Dissanayake, W. (2008). Are Political Weblogs Public Spheres or Partisan Spheres?, *International Reports on Socio-Informatics*, 5 (1), 7–26.

Westling, M. (2007). *Expanding the public sphere: The impact of Facebook on political communication.* Retrieved November 15, 2012, from http://www.thenewvernacular.com/projects/facebook_and_political_communication.pdf.

Williams, B. and Gulati, G. (2008). The political impact of Facebook: Evidence from the 2006 midterm elections and 2008 nomination contest, *Politics and Technology Review*, 1, 11–21.

Williams, B. and Gulati, G. (2007) *Social networks in political campaigns: Facebook and the 2006 midterm elections*. Paper presented at the Annual Meeting of the American Political Science Association, Chicago.

12. Populist candidates and social media marketing during the 2009 Romanian presidential campaign

Antonio Momoc
University of Bucharest, Romania

Abstract: The hypothesis of this chapter is that populist candidates display a bigger interest for social media marketing than others. The 2009 online campaign of the Romanian presidential candidates on blogs, social networks and video sharing sites with *user generated content* was monitored to verify the hypothesis that the political candidates with a populist message used new technologies to gain the internet users' votes.

Keywords: populist candidates, social media, electoral campaign, political communication

Introduction

While increasing numbers of Romanians spend time online and on social media, Romanian politicians react mechanically to the changes of the media market. The goal of this research was to observe which politicians have adapted faster to the new technologies, using them more efficiently in their political communication. I have started from the assumption that those who used social media tools to communicate with their audience were the populist candidates.

There is an amount of theoretical optimism regarding social media based on the belief that making the internet and other new technologies accessible for all citizens contributes to the democratization of the society and to increased political participation. I have tried to check this determinist opinion by exploring the hypothesis that the populist and radical Romanian candidates are also able to use these new communication channels successfully. If moderate candidates can use social media as reputation management tools and to create online support communities, why could not the populist candidates also use social media to promote their messages and to build a desirable electoral profile for their target audience?

* This work was supported by the strategic grant POSDRU/89/1.5/S/62259, Project "Socio-human and political applied sciences: post-doctoral training program and post-doctoral research scholarships in the field of the socio-human and political sciences," co-financed by the European Social Fund within the Sectorial Operational Program Human Resources Development 2007-2013.

The hypothesis

The hypothesis is that the Romanian populist parties and their candidates showed a bigger interest in the new technologies than the rest of the politicians. To check this hypothesis the 2009 online campaigns of the 12 candidates have been monitored.

The motivations for choosing this theme derive from the clear lacuna in Romanian political communication research: to our knowledge there are very few published studies about the 2009 Romanian presidential campaign and very few researchers were concerned with the relationship between new technologies and the presidential candidates. Moreover, in Romania there was a lot of debate regarding social media, but the relationship between new technologies and democracy was little explained.

Definitions: Social media and populism

"What is populism?" and "What are the populist politicians' characteristics?" are the questions we ought to answer before any comparative analysis. Can populism be used in the interest of democracy? Do the new technologies serve democracy or do they create a false impression of democratization? To study the relationship between social media and the populist politicians, I have focused on communication via user-generated content websites, which, together with social media, are the newest tools in the online communication arsenal.

The definitions that we operate with when analyzing new technologies are quite vague. Wide scientific consent regarding these definitions does not yet exist within the communications sciences. The notion of social media includes social networks like Facebook, Twitter, and LinkedIn as well as content-oriented networks such as YouTube, Trilulilu, and Flickr. YouTube is not a social network, but it is one of the most popular sources of user-generated content among those who use social networks.

Populism is also an equivocal concept, being one of the "dilemmas of the current political science" (Betea and Dorna, 2008: 257). Although the diversity of populist manifestations makes a general theory on populism difficult, the theoreticians agree on the fact that populism emerges when "the people becomes a target of the political speech", and populists speak in the name of the popular sufferance (Jiglău, 2010: 60).

Reference to the people is constant in populist speech. The populist leader uses it "either with the purpose of proposing a power change or as a means of legitimating a part of the political landscape in order to propel an alternative to the current government" (Betea and Dorna, 2008: 260). Populism is also a political strategy in which a populist leader addresses those who feel excluded and who can be mobilized (Jiglau, 2010).

As I mentioned in another article (Momoc, 2012: 194), "any political speech can be suspected of being populist discourse and any politician can be accused of populism by the rivals. There are some features that can be distinguished in every populist discourse. The various political competitors reach different levels of populism in their speeches."

A speech may be considered populist if it includes at least one of the key features identified by the theoreticians of populism: "Rhetoric from populist leaders always displays an anti-political, anti-parliamentary attitude" (Hermet, 2007: 24-37); it invokes the people very often with consistent references to its personal attachment to the people; it professes an anti-system position criticizing the leading elites: the people versus the corrupt elite.

The research sample

Of the 12 candidates whose online campaigns I have monitored, three Romanian politicians matched the speech and behavior criteria specific to political populism and were classified by different theoreticians and political science specialists as being populist leaders.

The references to "the people" are constant in president Traian Băsescu's speech. In the 2004 presidential campaign, Băsescu stood out on account of his anti-corruption and anti-system speech. The president places himself in the position of leader of the people and counts on partnership with the people to criticize the political elite (Teodorescu, 2006). Băsescu invokes "a return to the people" and blames the government of being incompetent.

Băsescu insists on claims such as a decrease in the Parliament's credibility, the notion that the economic crisis is created by the mass media owners, and the idea that the incompetent parties, state employees or unions are responsible for the bankruptcy of the economy (Jiglău, 2010). Using the same type of speech, Băsescu presented himself in the 2009 presidential campaign as being the voice of the people, positioning himself above the interests of the politicians and of the big business men who made a fortune on the expense of the common people.

George Becali, the New Generation Party candidate (nationalist-orthodox right wing), gave an ultranationalist and populist speech, suggesting his closeness to the people (Dâncu, 2010). Becali's rhetoric was enriched by complex non-verbal cues that created the impression of sincerity. Becali displayed his belief in God and presented himself as a politician who emerged from the common people.

Corneliu Vadim Tudor, the candidate of Big Romania Party (nationalist left wing), justified his entrance in politics as an answer to the request of the *Great Romania* magazine readers, holding as his purpose the restoration of morality in the post-communist era (Gherghina and Mişcoiu, 2010). His speech mixed symbols inspired by national-communist rhetoric and the interwar radical movements. His political style, xenophobic and violent, borrowed elements of anti-Semitic rhetoric. In his message he tried to synthesize the nationalist-ethnic myths of the communist rhetoric of the late '80s.

Research method: Content analysis and image analysis

The content analysis method was used for answering the question of whether the blog or the Facebook accounts were used to promote campaign themes or to denigrate the counter-candidates. The image analysis method was applied to establish what sort of image the candidates displayed in the online environment. Whenever the post was about the candidate himself, his campaign, or his political party, the post attitude has been classified as being self-centered and positive. If the post was about the political competitors, if the candidate criticized his competitors, or if he attacked the government, the presidency or others, his attitude was classified as negative.

The qualitative method of content analysis, as explained by Alex Mucchielli (2002: 38-48), implies the following steps: encoding, categorization and establishing relationships (or data interpretation). Encoding aims to extract the essentials of the testimony posted on the blog by using the blog post key words. Any qualitative analysis condenses continuous and abundant data. This means that the key words or expressions that summarize the phrases of interest must be very accurate and true to the blog testimony. By simply reading the key words, an uninformed reader should be able to reconstitute the blog testimony without having to read it. For encoding, the questions we use are "What do we have here?" and "What is this about?" The answers to these questions become key words or summarizing expressions.

Categorization is illustrated by transposing the key words into concepts. A category is a word that abstractly defines a cultural, social or psychological phenomenon as it is perceived in a data corpus. The category leads to theoretical concepts which establish the relationships between the categories.

The expression "Romanian village" is a code. The expression "agricultural policy", for the same extract, is a category. The first expression is extracted from a post on Mircea Geoana's blog and we may have to return to this essential element later in our analysis. The second expression is richer and more evocative; this is why it is strong.

Establishing the relationship refers to the blogger candidate's attitude (favorable or unfavorable) regarding the theme he is debating ("agricultural policy") and also to the attitude (negative or positive) that he has related to the key words he is using.

The image analysis research method, elaborated by Bogdan Halic and Ion Chiciudean, was used with the purpose of revealing the image strategy that the candidate has built during the presidential campaign. In the case of blog communication, the results of the study will consist in gross data and the offered information will have a small degree of relevance compared to the image that actually reached the public. When I decided to analyze the politicians' blogs, I did not intend to identify the image of the politician as it reached its blog reading audience, but I wanted to discover the type of image that the politicians promote through blogs during the electoral campaign.

As opposed to content analysis, image analysis operates with a set of constantly defined elements called image markers. To be operational, the image markers have to be relevant for the analyzed image, have to be measurable in a binary quantification system (positive/negative), and, when decomposed in a number of image sub-markers, they have to cover the certain dimension of the image that will be analyzed. In order to have a viable image-markers system, each marker has to be decomposed into sub-markers. The image sub-markers are those image elements that compose the image marker and that allow the image to be measured. For the image sub-markers to be operational, they have to be formulated very clearly.

In the image analysis of the presidential candidates' blogs, the recording unit represents the numbering unit. The numbering units represent elements through which the recording units (key words) and the context units (the blog post) are quantitatively expressed. The most frequently used numbering unit is the image sub-marker (key word). The references found in each image sub-marker will be reported to the reference system-image marker in order to discover the share (as a percentage) that each image marker has in the reference system.

An image profile represents the graphic expression of the calculated value of the image elements. The image profile is built by establishing the number of times each image marker or sub-marker was referred to. The image analysis was used in order to establish the type of image promoted by the politicians during presidential election campaigns.

The image analysis was based on the following indicators (image markers): the political dimension (when the post or comment was about the political party, political platform, economical measures, financial crisis, or campaign), the human or personal dimension (posts or comments about his profession, his experience, or his career) and the professional dimension (posts about leisure, family, friends, or hobbies).

Each item (image marker) was subdivided into sub-indicators; for example, the professional dimension was subdivided into transparency, adequate leadership style, and crisis management abilities; the political dimension was subdivided into campaign themes, the party's solutions for the economic crisis, and attacks against the opposing candidates.

Monitoring the campaign blog and the Facebook and YouTube accounts

The results show that the political dimension is the main indicator emphasized by the Romanian presidential candidates in their blog communication, the personal and especially the professional dimensions being scarcely approached.

The 2009 campaign website of the populist candidate Traian Băsescu was deactivated right after the results announcement. Băsescu was the only one of the candidates who never had a blog. He used a website with web 2.0 interactivity elements, but just as in 2004, in 2009 he deactivated the website immediately after finding out the poll results. Although he did not have a blog, Băsescu was present online ever since 2004 through the digital guerrilla (Momoc, 2011) and is also present in the blogosphere due to link references made by others to his campaign.

Dorina Guţu (2007: 167) emphasizes that "Băsescu was the first Romanian politician to exploit the internet as political communication tool". The 2004 elections won by Băsescu constitute the first Romanian campaign in which an SMS guerrilla campaign and an online negative campaign took place.

Of the 12 candidates, Constantin Ninel Potârcă (independent) did not have a campaign blog. Ovidiu Iane (Romanian Ecologist Party) temporarily deactivated his blog. The archives of the presidential campaign blogs of the candidates Sorin Oprescu (independent) and Corneliu Vadim Tudor (Big Romania Party) could not be identified online. Gigi Becali (New Generation Party) had a single post on his blog.

The UDMR (Democratic Union of the Magyars in Romania) candidate, Kelemen Hunor, posted three times on his blog. Crin Antonescu (National Liberal Party) had 13 posts. Constantin Rotaru (Socialist Alliance) made 16 posts on his blog during October-November 2009. Mircea Geoană (Social Democratic Party) posted 29 times. Remus Cernea (Green Party) had 78 posts, being the candidate with the largest number of online articles.

In 2009, the blog did not constitute a fundamental medium for expressing electoral campaign messages. Except for the Green Party candidate, the other candidates (populist or not) showed a minor interest for this platform. The hypothesis of a negative campaign was not confirmed either: although the candidates attacked Băsescu, the general online campaign attitude was rather positive in terms of posts and comments.

Of the 78 posts, Cernea had 60 positive posts and 18 negative. Of a total of 29 articles, Geoană had 16 positive posts and 13 negative. 10 posts out of 16 were positive also in the case of the socialist candidate Rotaru. Of the 13 posts on the liberal Antonescu's blog, in 9 articles the attitude was positive. Becali had a single blog post in which he energized his participation in the elections: the theme was religious and the attitude was positive.

The blogger politicians refused dialogue with their readers. Cernea was the only one who made 39 comments on his readers' posts, of which 25 were political, 12 personal and 2 professional. Geoană answered the readers' comments 17 times: 11 answers were political and 6 professional. Rotaru replied 7 times, with 4 political comments and 3 personal comments. Antonescu only made 2 personal comments. Hunor and Becali posted no comments.

The candidates promoted a political image on their campaign blogs and posted a few mentions about their personal lives. In the case of the Green Party candidate, 76 articles insisted on the political dimension, one article was personal and 1 was professional. Geoană had 21 political posts, five professional and three personal. Rotaru posted 15 political articles, one of which was personal. Antonescu made 11 political posts, one personal and one professional.

The same research methods were used to analyze the Facebook social network. Facebook grew in Romania only after the elections, in 2010-2011. According to the Facebook Pages Monitoring Service in Romania, Facebrands.ro, on January 1st, 2010, there were only 518,140 Facebook users, while on January 1st, 2011, that number had reached 2,405,920. In September 2009, Facebook recorded only 270,540 accounts originating in Romania, while in November 2009 their number had reached 414,000.

In the social media age, having a personal communication platform (such as a personal blog or a Facebook account) becomes a must, especially as not all politicians have access to mass media (traditional media). Social media facilitates permanent communication and direct dialogue with the public audience even during the non-electoral periods. New media are not mediated by gatekeepers, as is the case of television or radio. In online political communication via Facebook or blog, the messages are not filtered by journalists anymore.

The account or Facebook page of the populist candidate Traian Băsescu could not be identified. Nowadays a Traian Băsescu Facebook page exists, but it presents Wikipedia content and an account of the Presidential Administration. Becali and Potârcă did not have Facebook accounts at the 2009 elections. Vadim Tudor did not have a Facebook account in 2009 either, but created one in November 2010. Rotaru did not have an account in November 2009, but opened it in May 2010. Iane had 4 political posts on Facebook during November 2009. Kelemen Hunor posted 130 times during October-November 2009: 110 political posts and 20 personal posts.

The candidates of the big parties had Facebook accounts in 2009: Geoană (Social Democratic Party) had 78 posts on his Wall, of which only 3 were personal, and Antonescu (National Liberal Party) had 115 posts during October-November 2009, all political. The Green Party candidate was active on Facebook during October-November 2009, with 156 posts, of which 37 were on personal topics.

The fact that the campaign blogs and websites of the populists Băsescu and Vadim were deactivated immediately after the elections makes it difficult to supply a firm answer to the question whether populists used the online environment more than other politicians. Why populists hurry to deactivate these platforms, while the other candidates do not do this, also presents a new dilemma. This is the reason why semi-structured interviews with the heads of the campaign teams or with the candidates are necessary.

On the official YouTube channel of president Băsescu, 19 video clips were posted during October-November 2009: 16 have a positive attitude and three a negative one; 7 are electoral videos and 12 show meetings with the voters, mob baths, or press statements. On the official YouTube channel of Geoană, 87 video clips were uploaded (6 electoral videos and 81 campaign videos). The attitude was positive in 76 of them. Antonescu uploaded 54 video clips, of which 15 were electoral videos. Only 5 of these videos display a negative attitude.

Hunor posted 36 video-clips, of which 4 were electoral videos and 4 were negative campaign video materials. On Cernea's channel, 21 video materials were posted, of which just 2 had a negative attitude. Iane uploaded 11 video-clips on YouTube (1 single electoral video), of which 3 were negative. Becali, Vadim Tudor and Potârcă did not have official YouTube channels for posting video materials.

Conclusions

By accessing new technologies, the candidate launches self-promotion messages, attack subjects, mobilizes voters to go to the poll and leaves little room for debate. The blogosphere and the popular Facebook network fragmented virtual space in 2009. The candidates isolated themselves according to their ideologies. The online channel functioned less as a debate platform and more as a political PR tool. The online environment was the reflected image of the Romanian offline political environment.

The absence of the candidates' links towards competitors' posts and the lack of dialogue with their readers show the candidates' preoccupation with their own image and a significant lack of interest for debate between candidates, but also between the voters and politicians. The candidates did not bring ideas or projects into the conversation, and did not answer their readers' questions or comments.

There is an optimistic ideology of web 2.0 participation according to which the internet would democratize society and would turn the user into a responsible citizen by granting him access to information and debate. The optimist ideology of web 2.0 participation claims that the internet offers fast access to information, pluralism of ideas, the freedom to criticize the political power, and that it leads to the citizen-journalism model. Authors like Brăduţ Ulmanu (2011: 69) believe that "the intelligent crowds", born as a consequence of the internet technical revolution, "represent a social evolution."

However, the 2009 Romanian presidential campaign showed that the politician-candidates were not interested in building a space of debate. They were concerned with attracting voters to the poll and promoting their image and political message within their sympathizers. The pessimist ideology criticizes the internet, blaming it for providing a fake power of political influence, which leads to the techno-populism model. An optimistic conviction that information itself can improve the lives of ordinary citizens is widespread (Graham, 2002). The pessimistic vision is reticent when it comes to the intrinsic characteristics that supposedly define the nature of the new technologies.

The 2009 Romanian online presidential campaign showed that the new technologies were used as marketing tactics in a trial to mobilize voters to go to the poll and to promote a political image. Candidates did not support an online electoral debate.

Both populists and the other candidates were interested in transmitting messages through Facebook and their blog, but not in developing a community of dialogue and transparency. The populists showed little interest for the blog and generally promoted a positive online image. This is the reason why one cannot claim that populists had a bigger interest in social media than the rest of the candidates.

Without embracing the pessimistic vision, we can state that for now social media offered the Romanian audience only the illusion of pluralism and of online freedom of expression. Up to the 2009 elections, new technologies did not manage to ensure a more democratic representation of the society's interests, nor did they confer real power to the users who clicked *like* on Facebook. In this respect, the 2014 presidential elections constitute a new opportunity, both for the voters as well as for the candidates.

References:

Betea, L. and Dorna, A. (coord.) (2008). *Psihologia politică, o disciplină societală* [Political psychology, a societal discipline. Bucureşti: Ed. Curtea Veche.

Dâncu, A. (2010). Mitul votului raţional: detonatori emoţionali în comportamentul electoral din România contemporană [The myth of the rational vote: emotional detonators in the electoral behavior of the contemporary Romania]. In Dâncu, V., S. (Ed.) *Mediere. Comunicare. Tranziţie, Anuarul secţiunii Sociologia Comunicării, Cunoaşterii şi Tehnologiei Informaţiei (Mediation. Communication. Transition. The Yearbook of the section on the Sociology of Communication, Knowledge and Information Technology).* Cluj-Napoca: Eikon, 119-153.

Guţu, D. (2007). *New media*. Bucureşti: Tritonic.

Hermet, G. (2007). *Sociologia populismului* [The Sociology of Populism] Bucureşti: Ed. Artemis.

Jiglău, G. (2010). Ştim despre ce vorbim? O perspectivă teoretică asupra populismului [Do we know what we are talking about? A theoretical perspective on populism]. In Gherghina, S., Mişcoiu, S. (Eds.). *Partide şi personalităţi populiste în România postcomunistă* [Populist parties and personalities in post-communist Romania]. Iaşi: Institutul European, pp. 55-83.

Gherghina, S. and Mişcoiu, S. (Eds.) (2010). *Partide şi personalităţi populiste în România postcomunistă* [Populist parties and personalities in post-communist Romania]. Iaşi: Institutul European.

Graham, M. (2002). *Democracy by Disclosure: The Rise of Techno-Populism*. Washington: Brookings Institution Press.

Halic, B.-A. and Chiciudean, I. (2004). *Analiza imaginii organizaţiilor* [The Analysis of the Organizations' Image]. Bucureşti: Comunicare.ro.

Levinson, P. (2009), *New New Media.* Boston: Allyn and Bacon Penguin Academics.

Momoc, A. (2011). The Rising of Romanian President Traian Băsescu and the role of digital guerilla. In E. De Blasio, M. Hibberd, M. Sorice (Eds.), *Leaders and New Trends in Political Communication.* Roma: LUISS, CMCS, 79-95.

Momoc, A., (2012). Religious messages and symbols in the neo-populist speech: the blogs of the 2009 elections candidates. *European Journal of Science and Theology*, 8 (4), 205-214.

Mucchielli, A. (Coord.). (2002). *Dicţionar de metode calitative* [Dictionary of Qualitative Methods]. Iaşi: Polirom.

Teodorescu, B. (2006). Republica Prezidenţială România (The Presidential Republic Romania). In: Teodorescu, Bogdan, Sultănescu, Dan (coord.). *12/XII: Revoluţia portocalie în România* [The orange revolution in Romania]. Bucureşti: Fundaţia PRO'57-71

Ulmanu, A.-B. (2011), *Cartea feţelor, Revoluţia facebook în spaţiul social* [The book of faces, Facebook revolution in social space]. Bucureşti: Humanitas.

Part IV
Traditional Channels of Political Communication

13. The news effect: Shifting salience between media and policy agenda

Ewa Nowak
Maria Curie Skłodowska University in Lublin, Poland

Abstract: Contemporary media and political studies have produced a huge amount of books, articles and analyses about the influence media have upon politics, but there are still very few works devoted to these specific issues: which way, to what extent, and with what result can media coverage influence particular policies and political decision making. There are also very few studies that analyze these questions using empirical data. The proposed study combines the theoretical basis of agenda-setting theory, i.e. the interrelationships between media and policy agendas, with empirical data using statistical and qualitative content analysis. The main assumption is grounded on the opinion that the previous model, in which media agenda generally follows policy agenda, is changing to reflect the growing role of media in making politics.

Key words: policy agenda setting, media effect, television coverage

Introduction

Nowadays, reporting political news is undoubtedly a political process. The role of journalists as political actors in the process is constantly growing. "What they choose to cover, what they ignore, and how they frame political stories influences the perception of elite and mass audiences. In consequence, these perceptions affect political priorities and actions" (Graber, McQuail and Norris, 2008: 1). Reporting the news about politics is a part of making politics, and the media became a kind of political institution. Although studies of media and politics relationships are very popular among scholars, they relatively rarely investigate the topic of media impact on politics and policymaking, with an aim to answer these questions: in what way, to what extent, and with what result can media coverage influence particular policies and political decision making? Papers that treat these questions using and analyzing empirical data are even less common. The conceptual framework of this study is agenda-setting theory. It is used as a theoretical and methodological basis, together with statistical and qualitative content analysis, to investigate the relationships between media and policy agendas. The main hypothesis is based on the notion that previous approaches, in which media agenda generally follows policy agenda, is changing to reflect the growing role of media in making politics. The detailed hypothesis to be proved by the study suggests that media coverage should be considered a significant factor in the political decision-making environment. The impact of media coverage on policy making can be described as the 'news effect', since some political and policy decisions are made in response to news exposure. The need for conducting the study is justified firstly by the progressive mediatization of political life, and secondly by the fact that there are only several studies devoted to shifting salience between media and policy agendas.

Media—policy agenda-setting

Within the agenda-setting approach, policy agenda is definitely less studied than parallel media and public agendas. Apparently, it is due to the complexity of the policy-making process and the fact that many policy or political decisions and behaviors are not accessible to researchers. Certainly, the study of the setting of the policy agenda as such is not the goal of the study (the agenda-setting theory would not be sufficient, and there are many other approaches, e.g. the rational approach, political decision making, and collective political behavior). Instead, the paper focuses on the relationship between media and policy agendas; that is, it seeks to establish how media coverage about issues can affect (and often change) the way the policies are being created and implemented. Also, the opposite direction of influence, i.e. policy agenda in relation to media agenda, is not the subject matter of the study, not only because it would be too difficult to analyze such an extensive field of research in a single paper, but also because of the author's conviction that media influence on policy making is much more strategic and strongly connected with the mediatization of political (public) life. What is more, the studies devoted both to the media-to-politics and politics-to-media effects as well as those focused on the reciprocal effects, e.g. L. Van Noije et al. (2008) and S. Walgrave et al. (2008), proved that the political agenda co-determines the media agenda but the media have greater significance to politics than vice versa (Van Aelst and Walgrave, 2011: 297-298).

A starting point for the analysis of policy agenda-setting is the study of R. W. Cobb and C. D. Elder (1971). They proposed seeing the process of policy-making as strongly connected with agenda-building (a term meaning basically the same as agenda-setting (McCombs, 2008: 168-169). Cobb and Elder raise several basic questions: where do public policy issues come from and what determines the agenda for political controversy within a community. They identify sources of political bias within systemic and institutional agendas that shape the process of agenda building and help explain why some issues receive the attention of decision makers and others do not. The first source of bias is so-called 'older items', items that "have previously reached the agenda but that either have never been resolved or having been resolved are subject to periodic alternation" (Cobb and Elder, 1971: 906-907). The tendency of decision makers to give priority to older issues can be easily observed. The second source of bias in an institutional agenda is the decision makers themselves; if the issue is a concern of some key (strategic) decision makers, then its prospects for inclusion on the agenda grow considerably. The third and fourth sources of bias are related to political party organizations and the media. Political parties play a crucial role in translating issues into agenda items. The media play a significant role in promoting the issue to the systemic agenda and increasing its prospects to become part of the agenda. Similar finding were presented by a group of scholars in 1983 (Cook et al., 1983: 16). Using an experimental design built around a single media event, they came to the conclusion that policy changes were not the result of changes in public opinion but rather resulted from collaboration between journalists and government staff members. Cobb and Elder provide a contemporary example: "Dr Martin Luther King, Jr. once said, 'I have a dream,' but today he is history. Black students today will not come to you and say, 'We have a dream.' We have an agenda. At the top of our agenda is an end to racism and its immediate manifestation, white skin privilege" (Cobb and Elder, 1971: 905).

Subsequently, the empirical study of Linsky (1986) made a significant contribution to policy agenda studies. His work, based on six case studies (interviews with Washington officials), revealed the crucial role of media (coverage) in the process of policy making. Firstly, he indicates that a majority of politicians can be described as 'heavy viewers'; what is more, they consider the most important and popular issues of media reports as equally important for the public (Linsky, 1986: 87; compare: Kepplinger, 2007: 16). Secondly, the policymakers are dependent on media logic in their activities—if they want to achieve their goals they have to ensure positive media coverage for themselves. M. Linsky concludes that "the press have a huge and identifiable impact" (Linsky, 1986: 87), mainly in defining the issue and determining how it is understood.

Many other scholars have also detected significant media impact on making politics, e.g. S. Iyengar and R. Reeves (1997), H. W. Schulz (1997), J. Street (2001), M. J. Rozell (2003), T. E. Cook (2005), M. Kepplinger (2007), and S. Michalczyk (2010). The expanded theoretical basis for research on media-policy agenda was established by J. W. Dearing and E. M. Rogers (1996) and developed further by S. N. Soroka (2002), J. Curran, J. Seaton (2003), S. Walgrave, P. Van Aelst (2006, 2011), T. A. Birkland (2007), and H. M. Kepplinger (2007) et al.

J. W. Dearing and E. M. Rogers proposed a dependency and incompatibility model of relationships between journalists and policymakers (1996: 74; compare: Kepplinger, 2007: 3-32). The mutual dependency brings together the sources of information (politicians) and the mediators of coverage (journalists). The incompatibility results from different time perspectives; policymakers usually need a long period to introduce their procedures, whereas journalists need immediacy to create fresh news. The authors explained the types of influence the news media have on policy making: "The mass media often has a direct influence on the policy agenda-setting process, in addition to their indirect influence through the public agenda-setting process" (Dearing and Rogers, 1996: 74). However, J. W. Dearing and E. M. Rogers see the agenda-setting as a non-linear process of circulation of issues. This model includes certain general directional relationships and influences, i.e. the media on the public and policy makers, but also assumes a recursive feedback, i.e. the public on policy makers (compare: Soroka, 2002: 11).

The opinions of scholars and their research results about the media's influence on politics are not always consistent and are often contradictory. Also, the studies which use agenda-setting theory and its methods often yield inconsistent results. This is partly because media scholars and political science scholars do not unite their efforts (Walgrave and Van Aelst, 2006: 89), but also because they use different methods and different data sets (for example different political agendas such as parliamentary, governmental, and presidential) that can give distinct outcomes. For example, T. E. Patterson says:

> "Journalists are increasingly influential political actors. Their heightened power is partly attributable to changes in communication, chiefly the emergence of television as a major medium. Journalists have also gained influence from changes in politics, particularly a weakening in the grassroots strength of the political parties." (Patterson, 2008: 32)

On the other hand, S. Koch-Baumgartner and K. Voltmer (2010: 218) identify several arguments for why the media hardly influence policy making. First of all, because media coverage is usually incidental and does not pay attention to an issue for a long period, while policymaking needs weeks, months or years to be successful. Secondly, media are more often (or even as a rule) interested in people (personalities), whereas policymaking is devoted to particular fields and problems. Thirdly, media agenda is generally driven by newsworthiness and visual attractiveness, whereas policy agenda is driven by specific problems that need to be solved (Patterson, 2008: 32).

By asking similar questions S. Walgrave and J. Lefevere found evidence that media matters for party manifestos: "Especially the level of attention media and parties devote to issues is correlated, but a change in media attention hardly seems to lead to a subsequent change in party attention" (Walgrave and Lefevere, 2010: 62). They also established that the impact on party manifestos is rather long-term than short-term, and is stronger when it comes to opposition parties than government parties.

Yet N. T. Gavin, who explored unemployment policy, found that the influence of televised unemployment news has only a weak and elliptical agenda-setting impact. Gavin also claims that "When it comes to the relationship between the media, the political agenda and the policy process, we certainly ought to be skeptical of one-dimensional models of cause-and-effect that run in uniform directions" (Gavin, 2010: 80).

Detailed research devoted to media and policy agendas has been conducted by F. R. Baumgartner and B. D. Jones (1993). They found some significant but unstable media effects. They took three fields into account: pesticides, smoking, and automobile safety. Their main finding is that the impact of the media depends mostly on the way the coverage is being framed (Baumgartner and Jones, 1993).

S. N. Soroka (2002), similar to J. W. Dearing and E. M. Rogers (1996), presents a wide examination of the agenda-setting process, taking into account the relationship between three agendas (media, public, and policy), devoting special attention to the policy agenda. He claims that "[…] past models—illustrated or implied—tend not to adequately accommodate the vast agenda-setting literature, however. Perhaps more important, most are based on a view of causal links between the various agendas that is too restrictive" (2002: 9). Consequently, we probably should not consider the influence of media over policymaking or policy issue over the media agenda as linear. Instead, many links and directions of reciprocal impact can be noticed. Accordingly, S. N. Soroka proposes 'the multidirectionality of the media-policy link' and argues for

> "(...) the significant role policymakers play as media sources—journalists often rely on government spokesperson and bureaucrats for quick, reliable information. […]. As a consequence there is the distinct possibility that policymakers can affect the media content. Analyses of the policy process, on the other hand, suggest that the media play a role in setting policy agendas [...]. Accumulated evidence, then, suggests that there is no single direction of influence between the media and policy agendas." (Soroka, 2002: 10)

Figure 1. An expanded model of the agenda-setting process

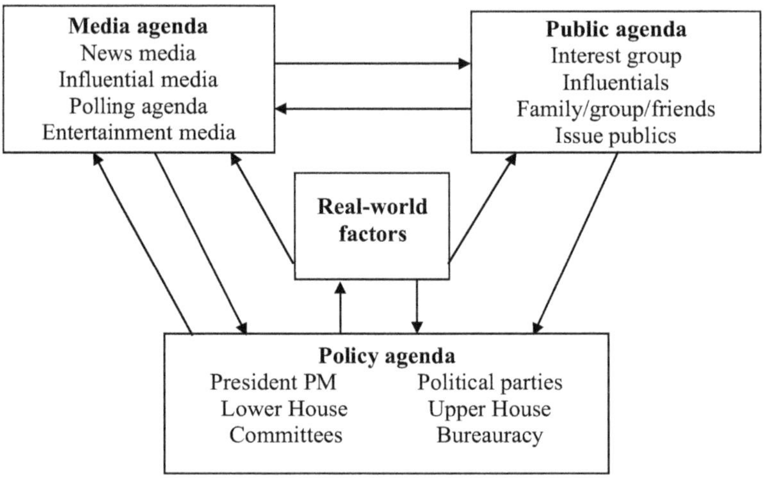

Source: Soroka 2002, p. 11.

The model of agenda-setting presented above includes real-world factors and 'subagendas', which are frequently omitted or underestimated in the literature. These 'subagendas', as elements of a certain type of agenda, enable a new form of analysis named 'inter-agenda-setting' research, for example ones devoted to the impact of broadsheet press (e.g. *New York Times* over 24-hour television news channels). The model intentionally disregards causal links between policy and the public agenda. S. N. Soroka claims that in this relationship generally there is not any direct contact and interaction; media coverage is necessary to play the role of mediator. It seems that this idea is justified with respect to the national level of politics, but not at the local level where citizens within small communities are able to interact and influence, or be influenced by, their deputies directly. Nonetheless, the expanded model seems to be a very useful tool to examine various types of agenda-setting processes and to make "an assumption about direction of causality, emphasizing the possibility of multidirectional agenda-setting and suggesting a structure for empirical investigation" (Soroka, 2002: 11).

One of the latest studies devoted to the media-policy agenda relationship was prepared by P. Van Aelst and S. Walgrave (2011), who made a comprehensive review of the existing body of literature. First, they found only nineteen studies dealing with the shifting salience between media and policy agendas. Second, many of those studies detected considerable impact of the media on policy agenda (eight), four found some impact, and seven only weak or no media impact. Although the literature is not very encouraging about media impact on policy making, some further findings presented by the two scholars provide us with a different picture of the problem:

> "However, these objective findings contrast with how politicians themselves perceive media's impact. An earlier survey of MPs in Belgium (Flanders) showed that these actors consider the mass media to be one of the most dominant political agenda setters […]. To be able to generalize these findings, the Belgian survey was replicated among MPs in Denmark, Netherlands and Sweden. […] almost two-thirds of MPs in our sample totally agrees with the proposition that the media set the political agenda more than politics itself. There are significant differences between countries […]. An overwhelming majority of MPs (80%) indicated that radio and TV often manage to set new issues on top of the political agenda, and two-thirds believe the written press has this power. […]. MPs tend to attribute more power to especially TV than to newspapers as well. TV is largely considered to be the most important medium in general." (Van Aelst and Walgrave, 2011: 298)

What is more, traditional political actors (Prime Minister, ministers, political parties, interest groups, MPs) do not always prevail as policy agenda setters over the media, which means that media possess greater power than political actors in shaping the policy agenda in Belgium, Denmark, the Netherlands and Sweden. Sometimes the power of the media and of politicians is equal and sometimes the power of politicians is even weaker:

> "The media matter a lot even in comparison with the traditional political powers. Only one actor seems to outweigh: the Prime Minister (PM). In all countries the PM sets the agenda more frequently than the written press and in two countries the PM also overshadows radio and TV. But even the PM's agenda-setting power does not systematically prevail over the impact of radio and TV—in Sweden and in the Netherlands the media are considered more powerful (or the PM as weaker)." (Van Aelst and Walgrave, 2011: 300)

The authors' state that, generally, "media matter for policy agenda, when media cover certain issues, chance increases that these issues will also pop up the political agenda afterwards" (Van Aelst and Walgrave, 2011: 296).

It is very difficult to make a cohesive conclusion that summarizes these studies and results. What we can state is that the media as a rule do not affect policy making directly (though there are some exceptions). Indirect impact occurs more often, but only under some specific circumstances and conditions. Nevertheless, as J. Kingdon claims (1984: 77), the media have an indirect impact on making politics quite often by setting the public agenda. Sometimes direct influence on political decisions is possible (CNN-effect concept, compare: Protess and McCombs, 1991; Willis, 2007; Robinson, 2002).

'Going public' with issues is a strategy employed by media or politicians to deal with issues immediately but avoid engaging in any routine procedures: "While the media's influence is significantly constrained by policy institutions, under some circumstances their involvement in the policy process can also change existing institutional arrangements" (Voltmer and Koch-Baumgarten, 2010: 8). Consequently, it is especially useful to establish the circumstances and conditions necessary for the media to impact policies.

Media influence on policy-making—the circumstances and conditions

The media effect on policy-making depends first of all on the type of political or policy (sub)agenda is being considered. D. Pritchard and D. Berkowitz enumerate two types of political agendas, the symbolic agenda and the resource agenda: "Symbolic agendas are those lists of issues that require visible, but not necessarily substantive, action on the part of policy makers […]. Resource agendas are those lists of issues that require substantive action, including the possible allocation of resources" (Berkowitz, 1993: 86). The symbolic political agenda can include parliamentary speeches and hearings (the PM exposé, the deputee questions or interpellations) and the agenda of political parties when these performances do not entail any political expenditures. The resource agenda incorporates the agenda of the government (decisions about policies and/or government spending) or the legislative agenda of the parliament. Apparently, it is easier to influence the symbolic political agenda because it does not entail any serious personal or financial costs. Media coverage of such issues usually means that the public is interested in them, and that is why politicians often devote their speeches to them or produce sound bites referring to them. On the contrary, evoking substantial changes in the policy agenda requires significant engagement of human resources and often financial resources (e.g. experts, money, time, structural changes). For this reason it is relatively rare that media coverage substantially affects policy-making.

Apart from the type of political agenda, the type of political actor (and its agenda) is also significant. As was mentioned above, it matters whether it is the agenda of the parliament, the president, the government, political parties or interest groups. Some studies recognize the budgetary issue and the political institution spending or resources engaged in solving the problem as a sort of policy agenda (Baumgartner and Jones, 1993; Soroka, 2002).

J. Kingdon (1984) proposes looking at political agenda setting through the 'window of opportunity'. This window opens (the issue moves from the media to the political or policy agenda) when three streams of condition come together: the political stream—the views of political elites and the public about the issue; the policy stream—the set of actual, possible solutions of the issue; and the problem stream—the nature (attributes) of the issue, the potential it has to become a public concern, and the possibility of solving the problem in a fixed situation. According to Kingdon, "If these three streams have prepared comfortable conditions (environment) for dealing with the problem within an issue, it makes the possibility for political change to occur" (although this 'window of opportunity' does not guarantee that policy change will happen; Kingdon, 1984: 166). However, the weakness of this concept is that there are too many conditions for the 'window of opportunity', so empirical operationalization can be very difficult.

The potential of the media to influence political decision making also depends on the field of policy. Those policy fields which are likely to generate news are possible areas of media impact. They include law and order, crime, family issues, defense, and social welfare (Koch-Baumgartner and Voltmer, 2010: 215-224). Empirical studies about the relationship between media, policy and public agendas have revealed that the policy field has great significance. For example, environmental issues are an area where the media become the agenda setter; inflation and unemployment issues—under the impact of real world indicators and debt/deficit issues—are definitely driven by the government (Soroka, 2002: 97).

The other significant factor shaping media impact is the stage where political decisions are settled. The greatest media influence can emerge at the early stage of deciding about policy, i.e. problem definition or problem formulation (Livingston, 1997: 292-293; compare: Walgrave, Van Aelst, Bennett, et. al., 2010: 2). If media attention at the stage of policy definition or formulation is very strong, it can be a causal factor and precede a policy change. If media attention at this stage is weak, it usually follows a policy change. At the stage of policy definition or formulation, media coverage can become the 'agenda-setting agent', especially when TV news channels broadcast news and commentaries that are emotional or compelling (for example about humanitarian crises), potentially reordering some policy priorities. On the other hand, intense media coverage at the stage of policy implementation accelerates policy, but generally only shortens the time it takes to make a decision without provoking any policy changes.

Some detailed findings about the structure of the political environment and certain regularities which favor media impact on policy agenda and policy making are presented by P. Van Aelst and S. Walgrave (2011: 303), C. Eilders (2000), E. Noelle-Neumann (1973), J. Strömbäck (2008), R. Vliegenthart and S. Walgrave (2011):

– self-propelling mechanism of intermedia agenda-setting: "While individual media outlets may not be very influential as such, the mass media as a whole certainly are a tremendous force for individual MPs, especially when the coverage is consonant across outlets and when the mass media are in "stampede mode";

- focusing/consonance framing/persistence (long-term coverage)—if various media report the same issue in a similar way for a relatively (noticeable) long time, then it becomes possible to influence political behavior and decisions (but this happens relatively rarely) (Walgrave and Van Aelst, 2006; Eilders, 2000; Noelle-Neumann, 1973);
- media role in 'spinning' the issue—although politicians are usually the initiators of the issue, by forwarding the information to the press or TV, they are often unable to develop it into 'breaking news': "political actors set the agenda by initiating certain issues but [...] journalists become more important in the second phase when those issues are discussed and defined. [...] the media rarely initiate the coverage of political stories but do play a role in amplifying and structuring them" (Van Aelst and Walgrave, 2011: 303);
- political actors' responsibility: "The clearer a political actor's responsibility regarding an issue, the greater the chance that media coverage on that issue will urge that agency to act, while diffuse and shared responsibilities breed little political action" (Walgrave and Van Aelst, 2006: 93);
- characteristics of the political actors (personalities)—they may be more or less susceptible to media influence (Walgrave and Van Aelst, 2006: 92);
- party characteristics (party size, ruling or opposition party, issue ownership)—for example, small, opposition parties specializing in an issue which is the subject of given media reports are more susceptible to media impact (Vliegenthart and Walgrave, 2010: 321-342).

Taking into account the complex environment of media outlet and many conditions of media impact, S. Walgrave and P. Van Aelst (2006) proposed a contingency model of mass media's political agenda-setting power. They treat media impact on policy making as a political process, determined by: issue type (i.e. obtrusive vs. unobtrusive, but also connected with policy field), media outlet (e.g. the type of medium—television, press or internet; at the same time the more media channels, press titles, internet webs are engaged, the more probable media impact is) and coverage type, whether positive or negative (the type of frame can also be meaningful). The factors connected with the media and its coverage are subsequently filtered by political context, specific to the time, country and political market (election and routine times, institutional rules, internal functioning, political configuration, and personal traits). This complexity of factors within the media and political context yields multi-dimensional pictures of political effects on the final stage of the process, i.e. political adoption.

The effects can be both symbolic and substantial, fast and slow. No one effect even seems to be more frequent. Does the model explain anything about the mass media's agenda setting power? Probably it does, because it makes some kind of categorization of possible media effects. It seems that the model's shortcoming is the absence of a real world factor, something that needs to be taken into account when media power on policy making is considered. The power of real world events sometimes prevails over the media and political contexts. The so called 'focusing event,' embodying the power of the real world factor, is defined as "[...] an event that is sudden, relatively rare, can be reasonably defined as harmful or revealing the possibility of potentially greater future harms, inflicts harms or suggests potential harms that are or could be concentrated on a definable geographical area or community of interest, and that is known to policy makers and the public virtually simultaneously" (Birkland, 2007: 22). Such events can achieve and exercise agenda setting power, due to their nature and specific features. Changes in agenda setting hierarchy, which are caused by focusing events, can change policy in in certain circumstances.

However, S. Walgrave and P. Van Aelst's model is necessary to reliably establish anything about mass media's agenda setting power. If somebody claims there is no media effect over policy agenda, he or she should at least be asked: which agenda (symbolic/substantial) or which reaction (slow/fast) is being taken into consideration?

Figure 2. Walgrave and Van Aelst's contingency model of mass media's political agenda-setting power

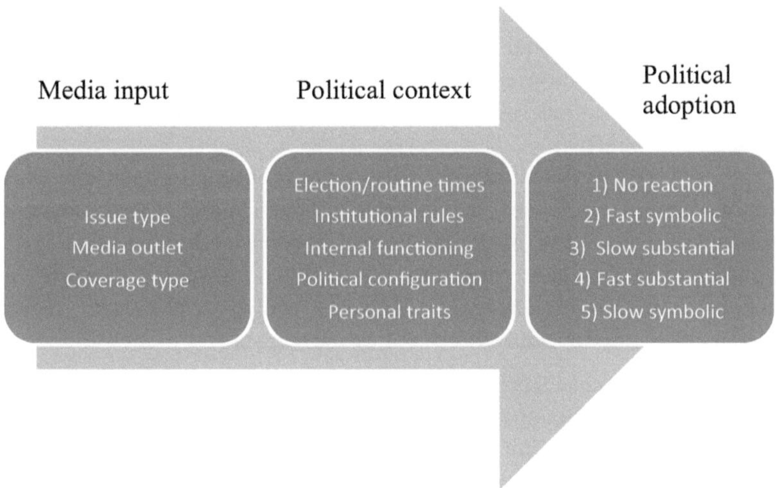

Source: Walgrave, Van Aelst, 2006, p. 104.

Materials and methods

Taking into account the considerations above, several hypotheses are proposed:

H1: Media impact on governmental policy making (substantial governmental agenda) does not occur very often, but when it emerges it is important due to the social consequences within the given policy field;

H2: Media impact on policy agenda is rather long-term than short-term;

H3: The media put issues onto the governmental agenda when coverage of the issue is consistent over a noticeably long period—the self-propelling mechanism of intermedia agenda-setting.

The following choices were made to test these hypotheses:

- the choice of media agenda—TV agenda; the research data includes four Polish TV (public and private) news programs broadcast in prime time each day in 2010, "Wiadomości" TVP1, "Panorama" TVP2, "Wydarzenia" Polsat, and "Fakty" TVN; the data set includes all prime time evening programs broadcast in 2010; the data are divided into two sets of issues: the first includes 'general issues'—the number of news stories devoted to the issue categories presented below; the second set of data contains the detailed category of issues, i.e. specific problems that news was devoted to; the 'general issues' set was subjected to statistical analysis; the 'detailed issues' set enables content analysis and conclusions about causality;
- the choice of policy agenda—substantial governmental agenda; the data set includes all formal decisions, i.e. acts, bills, decrees, dispositions and the amendments to these deeds taken by the Polish government in 2010;
- the choice of time related method—cross-sectional analysis;
- time lag—in multi-optional version (one month, two months, six months);
- non-election vs. election period—generally non-election period (with the exception of one month within the research period when the presidential campaign was held);
- the choice of policy fields: health, infrastructure, internal affairs and administration; 'national defense', 'environment', 'science and higher education', 'national education', and 'sport and tourism' ('justice administration');
- the choice of media issue: 'medicine and health', 'transport and roads', 'administration and safety services', 'defense', 'ecology and nature', 'science and education', 'sport', and 'tourism' ('crime, courts').

The policy fields were selected according to the consistency with 'fields' and subjects of issues within media agenda. The media issues called 'politics', 'history', 'church, religion, ethics', 'culture and entertainment' and 'curiosity, were rejected as impossible to assign to elements on the governmental agenda. On the other hand, the fields (departments) of government policy are too vast or too specific to be comparable with media agenda (for example, the departments and fields of economy, labor and social policy, foreign affairs, state treasury, and finance). In the first version of statistical analysis, the field of justice administration was included, but it was rejected in the second because of the disproportionate number of media reports about crime in comparison with the governmental agenda.

Results and discussion

The data analyzed in the paper include one year of governmental policy decisions and one year of TV news broadcasts, which is in accordance with the cross-sectional analysis model (compare: Cook et al., 1983; Soroka, 2002; Walgrave and Deswert, 2004). It is one of the first attempts to establish a relationship between media and policy agendas, especially with respect to the substantial policy agenda. The choice of substantial governmental agenda, which is directly connected with legislative process and the actual control over the country, was motivated by the very purpose of this research. The goal was to establish how strong the media agenda-setting power is in actual policy making. Because of data restrictions and some methodological problems, this aim was fulfilled only partially. The only media agenda accessible for the research consisted of TV news programs from one year (2010), so an extensive statistical analysis was not possible. However, apart from general categories of issues within media agenda, the data about the detailed categories of issues (particular subjects in the news) were also available, enabling the qualitative analyses devoted to the impact of media coverage on the government (how reporting specific objects by the news media in a given month influenced governmental decisions one, two or six month later).

Figure 3. Media agenda to governmental agenda—one month lag (the issue: Justice and Administration—Criminality/Courts included)

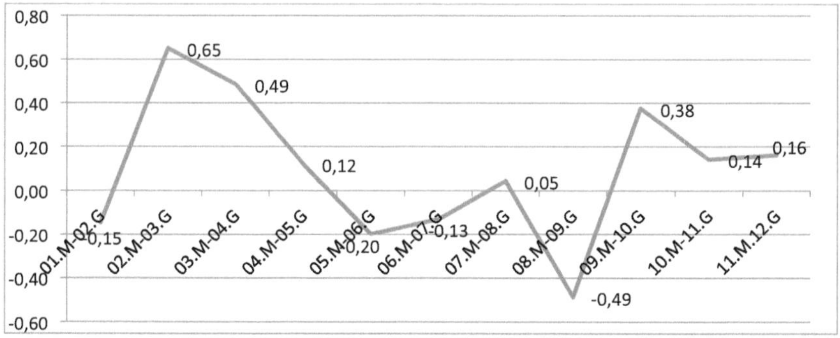

Source: Own study (01.M-02.G: January in media agenda—February in governmental agenda and so on).

Figure 4. *Media agenda to governmental agenda—six months lags (the issue: Justice and Administration—Criminality/Courts excluded)*

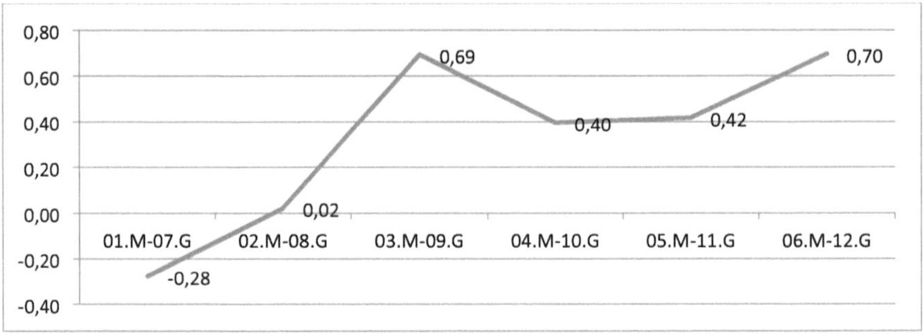

Source: Own study

Figure 5. *Media agenda to governmental agenda—two months lag (the issue: Justice and Administration—Criminality/Courts excluded)*

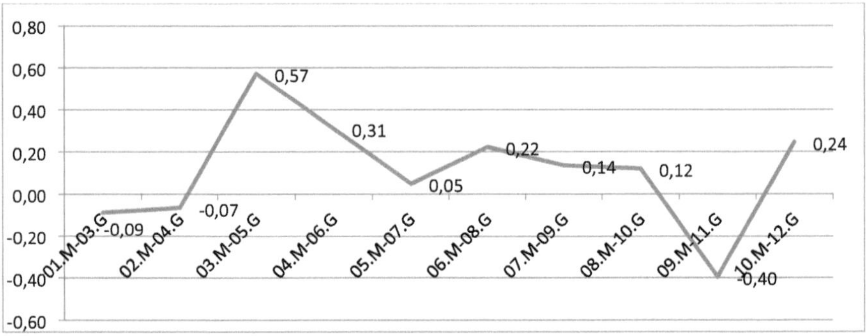

Source: Own study.

Figure 6. *Media agenda to governmental agenda—one month lag (the issue: Justice and Administration—Criminality/Courts excluded)*

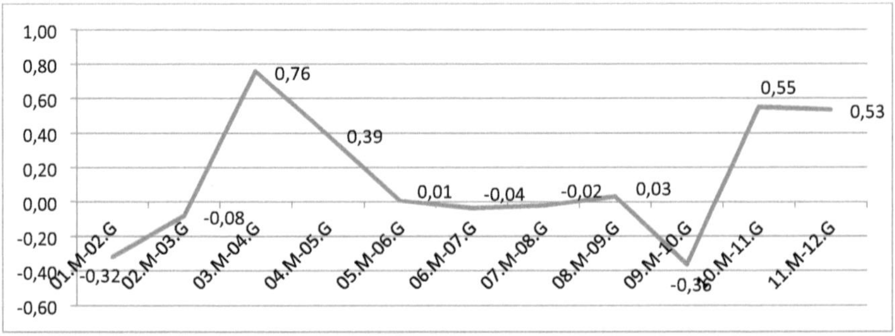

Source: Own study.

The results of the statistical analysis, i.e. the Pearson correlation, presented in the figures above are ambiguous. Generally, it cannot be asserted that, taking into account a one, two or six months' lag time, media coverage definitely, permanently and continuously impacts policy making, which is in accordance with the studies mentioned above. Nevertheless, media impact emerges in some of the periods. Medium and high levels of the Pearson's correlation factor were found in both cases—one and two months lag time:

- March in media agenda—April in governmental agenda—0,76
- October in media agenda—November in governmental agenda—0,55
- November in media agenda—December in governmental agenda—0,53
- March in media agenda—May in governmental agenda—0,57
- April in media agenda—June in governmental agenda—0,31

A higher factor of correlation was found when a six-month lag time was applied; a medium or high level of correlation occurred in four cases:

- March in media agenda—September in governmental agenda—0.69
- April in media agenda—October in governmental agenda—0,40
- May in media agenda—November in governmental agenda—0.42
- June in media agenda—December in governmental agenda—0,70

Also when the 'justice administration' issue in policy agenda and 'criminality/courts' issue in the media agenda were included (one month time lag), the correlation was noticeable:

- February in media agenda—March in governmental agenda—0,65
- March in media agenda—April in governmental agenda—0,49
- September in media agenda—October in governmental agenda—0,38

The total correlation factor is significant only in the case of six month lag (0,32) and low for one (0,13) and two months (0,11). This means that media coverage is very rarely a sufficient factor to make a policy outcome (McQuail, 2008: 448). It is very difficult to assess the actual media impact and isolate it in a policy environment; however, even preliminary statistical analysis indicates that this impact exists and should not be ignored. For this reason, it seems that the attachment of qualitative content analysis can be useful as a method appropriate for identifying a particular media impact. In the study, the cases in which the correlation was significant were subject to further analysis, which resulted in isolating three incidences of plausible media impact on policy decision-making:

1) February in media agenda—March in governmental agenda—0,65 (one month lag; justice administration issue in policy agenda and criminality/courts issue in media agenda included):
    - In February 2010 Polish news media devoted many reports and time (almost 2% of total coverage in February, the eighth issue out of 20 in

rating) to a policeman's murder, an assault in the center of Warsaw. When an off-duty policeman responded to acts of hooliganism, the young offenders (18-year old) stabbed him. As a result, 42 year-old Andrzej Struj died. In response, on 30 March 2010 the Polish government made two decisions connected with the case of the policeman: the approval of amendments to the Criminal Code and to the Police Act (they toughened the punishment for an attack on a functionary);

2) September in media agenda—October in governmental agenda—0,38 (one month lag; justice administration issue in policy agenda and criminality/courts issue in media agenda included):
   - In September 2010 one of the most popular issues in the Polish news media (the sixth issue out of 20 in rating, about 1,5% of total number of news) was the drug issue, particularly the problem of chemical stimulant (doping) substances (the afterburners) used by young people. Some fatal effects of the use of these afterburners were reported dramatically. In the next month the Minister of Health Care prepared an amendment to the drug addiction act, which was accepted at the cabinet meeting on the 5th October 2010. In this case the media impact seems to be very possible, as the problem of doping substances used as drugs was not legally controlled in Poland before that time.
3) June in media agenda—December in governmental agenda—0,70 (six month lag; justice administration issue in policy agenda and criminality/courts issue in media agenda excluded):
   - In June 2010 over 2% of monthly total news coverage of Polish news programs was devoted to the defense issue (the sixth issue out of 16 in rating), particularly to the operation of the Polish army in Iraq and Afghanistan. Six months later, in December 2010, a bill affecting soldiers and veterans was introduced, discussed and accepted at the meeting of the Polish cabinet. Of course, we cannot speak about the intense media coverage as the only reason which brought about the preparation of the bill devoted to veterans. However, taking into consideration the high correlation factor, it seems that media reports were not without influence. What is more, other resources corroborate this assumption; that is, there were press releases about the prolonged preparation process of the bill—the bill was stuck between organizational and institutional consultation (Górka, 2010: 6; Kowalska, 2010: 8). It can be presumed, then, that media coverage played the role of accelerant in the legislative process.

The results presented above allow an evaluation of the hypotheses. The first hypothesis, that media impact on governmental policy making (substantial governmental agenda), while not very frequent, is important when it does emerge should be regarded as entirely confirmed. As the statistical analysis indicated, there is no such tendency as stable media impact on making politics, especially when it comes to governmental policy. However, in the observed period, considerable evidence of the media's impact was detected. It was connected with the changes in the legal system, produced by the government under pressure and, at least partially, in response to the intense media coverage broadcast between one and several months earlier. All these changes were devoted to the serious problems of citizens' health or life—drug and war fatalities and violence against functionaries. These findings support not only the popular conviction that, in the cases when a media picture of force and death is especially expressive, the media agenda-setting power is stronger (than in the cases without human fatalities; Birkland, 2007), but also the less common assumption (Robinson, 2002; Willis, 2007) that media coverage can be a compelling stimulus for policy makers to regard an issue as important.

The second hypothesis, that media impact on policy agenda is rather more long-term than short-term, has also been confirmed. The higher correlation between media and policy agenda was found when the lag time of six months was applied. Nevertheless, the lag of one month turned out to be more favorable to media impact than the two months' lag. It seems that the time necessary to prepare some institutional or legal changes depends on the procedures operating within a given policy field or given issue.

The third hypothesis, that the media put issues into governmental agenda when media coverage about an issue is consistent during a noticeably long period (the self-propelling mechanism of intermedia agenda-setting), was partially confirmed, as the data of the study (media agenda) include the coverage of the four most established Polish TV news programs. However, press, Internet and radio coverage was not taken into account. The choice of TV news is justified by the still dominant role of TV in informing the public about politics, with the limitation of the Internet's constantly growing role.

Conclusion

This study was prepared with a conviction that policy agenda-setting research is one of the most interesting and least empirically explored fields of contemporary political communication. The investigation confirmed the presence of media impact on making politics as far as TV news agenda and governmental agenda are concerned. Still, it is more appropriate to speak about the 'emerging' media effect on making policy decisions than the stable and constantly functioning media impact. An irregularly appearing media effect can be described as a 'news effect' because of the news features, e.g. the occurence of human victims and fatalities, long-time coverage and the self-propelling mechanism of intermedia agenda-setting. These features bring power to the news, decisively influencing policy agenda.

The idea of a 'news effect' is in accordance with the hypothesis of the non-linearity of media effects on public policies confirmed in the most recent Western European studies (Boydstun, Hardy, Vliegenthart and Walgrave, 2012). Both concepts indicate that the rise in media attention does not always and does not in every situation cause the strong and visible reaction of public opinion and political elites. To create and intensify political tension and to evoke a policy decision, it is necessary for news to go beyond the threshold of media storm. Media storms happen relatively rarely, but if they take place, the impact of the media agenda on the policy agenda is strong and meaningful for policy change.

Media storms usually happen when an issue is framed as a scandal, a crisis or a large-scale fraud and particularly when the mainstream media attention to the issue grows rapidly (exceeding the usual level of attention by over 100%). The media-politics tension evokes the shifting of public policy priorities. As a result, rash and hasty decisions take effect and a casual law is established. This does not mean that the media are the only agenda setters; they rather create an important part of the political conditions when the decisions are made. The media logic which is applied in public policy making is also described as 'media reflexivity', that is the situation when politicians are not simply influenced by specific media content but rather adapt to the way the media operates. In this sense the media act as a part of almost every political decision and as a kind of anticipatory constraint limiting political actors' maneuvering space (Strombäck, 2008; Van Aelst and Walgrave, 2011: 295-313).

The analysis is preliminary and not sufficient to make definite conclusions about the media effect on policy making. However, taking into account the cohesion of its empirical research results in relation to the predominant outcomes of the policy agenda-setting research, it seems the results of this stream apply at least to Polish conditions.

References:

Baumgartner F. R., and Jones Bryan D. (1993). *Agendas and instability in American politics.* Chicago: University of Chicago Press.

Birkland T. A. (2007). *After Disaster: Agenda Setting, Public Policy and Focusing Event.* Washington: Georgetown University Press.

Boydstun A., Hardy A., Vliegenthart R. and Walgrave S. (2012). *The Non-Linear Effect of Media Coverage on Public and Governmental Attention.* Paper presented at the Annual Meeting of the Comparative Agendas Project, Reims 2012.

Cobb R. W. and Elder Charles D. (1971). The politics of Agenda-Building: An Alternative Perspective for Modern Democratic Theory. *The Journal of Politics*, 33, 892-915.

Cook F. L., Tyler T. R., Goetz E. G., Gordon M. T., Protess D. and Leff D. R. (1983). Media and agenda setting: Effects on the public, interest group leaders, policy makers, and Policy. *Public Opinion Quarterly*, 47(1), 16-35.

Cook T. E. (2005). *Governing with the News. The News Media as a Political Institution*. Chicago and London: The University of Chicago Press.

Curran J. and Seaton J. (2003). *Power without Responsibility. The Press, Broadcasting and New media in Britain*. New York: Routledge.

Dearing J. W. and Rogers E. M. (1996). *Agenda-Setting. Communication Concepts 6*. Thousand Oaks-London-New Delhi: Sage.

Eilders C. (2000). *Media as political actors? Issue focusing and selective emphasis in the German quality press*. "German Politics", 9(3), 181–206.

Gavin N. T. (2010). Closing the circle. A case study in the role of spin in the policy cycle. In K. Voltmer, S. Koch-Baumgarten (Eds.), *Public Policy and Mass Media. The interplay of mass communication and political decision making*. New York: Routledge, Taylor and Francis Group, 65-85.

Górka M. (2010). *Weterani czekają na pomoc i ustawę*. „Gazeta Wyborcza", 05.02.10.

Graber D. A., McQuail D. and Norris P. (2008). Introduction: The Politics of News in a Democracy. In D. A. Graber, D. McQuail, P. Norris (Eds.), *The Politics of News. The News of Politics*. Washington: CQ Press, 1-19.

Iyengar S. and Reeves R. (Eds). (1997). *Do the Media Govern? Politicians, Voters and Reporters in America*. London: Sage.

Kepplinger H. M. (2007). *Demontaż polityki w społeczeństwie informacyjnym*. Kraków: Wydawnictwo Uniwersytetu Jagiellońskiego.

Kingdon J. W. (1984). *Agendas, Alternatives, and Public Policies*. Boston: Little, Brown.

Koch-Baumgartner S. and Voltmer K. (2010). Conclusion. The interplay of mass communication and political decision making—policy matters. In S. Koch-Baumgartner, K. Voltmer. *Public Policy and Mass Media. The interplay of mass communication and political decision making*. New York: Routledge Taylor and Francis Group, 215-227.

Kowalska A. (2010). *Pokaleczeni*. „Gazeta Wyborcza", 09.11.2010.

Linsky M. (1986). *Impact: How the Press Affects Federal Policy Making*. New York: W. W. Norton.

Livingston S. (1997). Beyond the "CNN Effect. The Media-Foreign Policy Dynamic. In P. Norris (Ed.), *Politics and the Press. The News Media and their Influences*. London: Lynner Rienner Publishers Inc., 291-318.

McCombs M. (2008). *Ustanawianie agendy. Media masowe i opinia publiczna*. Kraków: Wydawnictwo Uniwersytetu Jagiellońskiego.

Michalczyk S. (2010). *Demokracja medialna. Teoretyczna analiza problemu*. Toruń: Wydawnictwo Adam Marszałek.

Noelle-Neumann E. (1973). Kumulation, Konsinanz und Őffentlichkaeitseffekt. Ein neuer Ansatz zur Analyse der Wirkung der Massenmedien. *Publizistic*,18, 26-55.

Patterson T. E. (2008). Political Roles of the Journalists. In D. A. Graber, D. McQuail, P. Norris (Eds.), *The Politics of News. The News of Politics*. Washington: CQ Press, 23-39.

Pritchard D. and Berkowitz D. (1993). The Limits of Agenda-setting: the Press and Political Responses to Crime in the United States, 1950-1980. *International Journal of Public Opinion Research*, 5(1), 86-91.

Protess D. L. and McCombs M. E. (1991). *Agenda-setting: Readings on media, public opinion and policymaking*. Hillsdale: Lawrence Erlbaum.

Robinson P. (2002). *The CNN Effect. The Myth of news, foreign policy and intervention*. London-New York: Routledge.

Rozell M. J. (Ed.). (2003). *Media Power. Media Politics*. Lanham: Rowman and Littlefield Publishers.

Schulz W. (1997). *Politische Komunikation. 1. Auflage*. Wiesbaden: VS Verlag für Sozialwissentschaften.

Soroka S. N. (2002*). Agenda-setting dynamics in Canada*. Vancouver: UBC Press.

Street J. (2001). *Mass Media, Politics and Democracy*. New York: Palgrave Macmillan.

Strömbäck J. (2008). Four Phases of Mediatization: An Analysis of the Mediatization of Politics. *The International Journal of Press/Politics*,13(3), 228-246.

Van Aelst P. and Walgrave S. (2011). Minimal or Massive? The Political Agenda-Setting Power of the Mass Media According to different Methods. *The International Journal of Press/Politics*, 16(3), 295-313.

Van Noije L., Oegema D. and Kleinnijenhuis J. (2008). Loss of Parliamentary Control Due to Mediatization and Europeanization: A Longitudinal and Cross-Sectional Analysis of Agenda Building in the United Kingdom and the Netherlands. *British Journal of Political Science*, 38(3), 455-478.

Vliegenthart R. and Walgrave S. (2011). When the Media Matter for Politics: Partisan Moderators of the Mass Media's Agenda-setting Influence on parliament in Belgium. *Party Politics*, 17(3), 321-342.

Voltmer K. and Koch-Baumgarten S. (2010). Introduction. Mass media and public policy—is there a link?. In K. Nuytemans, S. Koch-Baumgarten (Eds.) *Public Policy and Mass Media. The interplay of mass communication and political decision making*. New York: Routledge, Taylor and Francis Group, 1-14.

Walgrave S., Soroka S., and Nuytemans M. (2008). The Mass Media's Political Agenda-Setting Power. A Longitudinal Analysis of Media, Parliament and Government in Belgium (1993-2000). *Comparative Political Studies*, 41(6), 814-836.

Walgrave S. and Lefevere J. (2010*). Do the media shape parties' agenda references? An empirical study of party manifestos in Belgium (1987-2003).* In K. Voltmer, S. Koch-Baumgarten (Eds.). *Public Policy and Mass Media. The interplay of mass communication and political decision making*. New York: Routledge, Taylor and Francis Group, 44-64.

Walgrave S. and Van Aelst P. (2004). *The Mass Media's Political Agenda-Setting Power. Toward an Integration of the Available Evidence*. Paper prepared for delivery at the APSA Political Communication pre-conference, 2004 Chicago.

Walgrave S. and Van Aelst P. (2006). The Contingency of the Mass Media's Political Agenda Setting Power: Toward a Preliminary Theory. *Journal of Communication*, 56, 88-109.

Walgrave S., Van Aelst P. and Bennett L. (2010). *Towards a broader theory of agenda interactions between political actors and the mass media*. Paper prepared for the APSA Annual Meeting, Washington.

Willis J. (2007). *The Media Effect. How the News Influences Politics and Government*. London: Praeger.

14. Billboards in Municipal Elections in Slovakia: Unexpected Contexts

Łukasz Wojciechowski
Peter Mikuláš
Katarína Fichnová
Constantine the Philosopher University in Nitra, Slovakia

Abstract: This paper deals with one of the most important characteristics of new media: interactivity and its applications in outdoor political campaigns. The authors believe that an outdoor ad, as a form of traditional media, can be interactive and its structure may encourage the audience's reactions or even interventions. The durability of such interventions is extended in connection with new media by means of presentation on the Internet. The authors present the results of the visual and content analysis which suggest that the advertisements were supplemented either by the environment in which they were placed or by the recipients themselves. Such additions are almost always in contradiction to the originally intended message of communication. The entities responsible for the communication of political parties should consider the creation of a new position: a communication auditor.

Key words: media, outdoor media, political communication, visual analysis

Introduction

Visual advertising is among the most frequently used communication tools in political campaigns—this is not a surprising statement regarding visualization and visual culture as signs of the postmodern tendency to visualize our existence (Mirzoeff, 1999). An understanding of the world as a text is being replaced by an understanding the world as a picture (Kratochvíl and Šedík, 2007; Feriancová and Mikuláš, 2012). According to these authors, it is important to approach pictures not as a subsidiary form of communication but as an equal tool because pictures have the potential to create and communicate meanings that cannot be communicated otherwise. We believe that images are also faster to read, may represent the whole story, and enable quicker understanding of the story for the individual in comparison to written texts. These advantages of visual communication are used in old as well as in new media practice.

New media includes new forms of communication between the media and the audience: they are more interactive and more actual (Kalčoková, 2010). In new media, people are consumers of information and at the same time sources of information (Gero, 2004).

* The paper was supported by a grant for scientific project VEGA No. 1/0195/11 "Stereotyped genderisation of media space".

The "old media" usually means the "print media" (McQuail, 2007; Gero, 2004; Martinec and Salway, 2005). A billboard could be considered as one of the main means of print media, especially in political campaigns. A billboard, in its full range, cannot compete with new media in terms of interactivity with the audience; it is usually marked as a very asymmetric medium. However, we believe that despite this generally prevailing view, billboards possess the potential to stimulate audience activity and especially interactivity. An audience member can make, and even often does make, direct interventions to billboards. The recipient may supplement the meanings of billboard messages, leave feedback for the communicator, or communicate with other recipients such that he or she is in a certain form of interaction with the medium itself. In contrast to the new media audience, this is an audience that is not well situated (economically) and often does not have access to new technologies.

There is often a certain level of intersection between the new and old media in practical communication because new media often duplicate and disseminate messages emerging from old media forms. In our case, billboards used in political communication as a part of outdoor communication campaigns are also presented on the websites of particular political parties, or in blogs, comments, or e-versions of newspapers. Billboards are usually transformed into new media in the form of photographs or videos. This kind of digital conservation ensures open access to the billboards' messages, as opposed to the limited presence of billboards in their natural outdoor environment (subject to deterioration and being pasted over). We can call this a phenomenon of multiplication of the old media in the new media. This form of interaction undoubtedly enriches new media communication and at the same time not only preserves but also enhances unexpected communication possibilities of the old media. This might be one of the reasons why billboards are still such popular tools of communication with voters and supporters of political ideas, programs, and the promotion of political parties.

On the most general level, Johnston and Kaid (2002) distinguish two categories of visual political advertising: image advertisements and issue-oriented advertisements. Image advertisements are based on the candidate's public presentation and projected humanization. This type of political advertising emphasizes the strong visualization of the candidate, while text is generally reduced to a very short and easily understandable message. Issue-oriented advertisements provide the public with the attitudes of the candidate regarding election topics, while secondary advertisements from this category communicate the attitude of the political party, on the behalf of which candidate is speaking. In some cases in these types of advertisements the message is impersonal, meaning that it lacks an identifiable sender.

The billboard is a medium that has somehow become a synonym for any marketing or political communication and its forms are being improved and modernized with the emergence of new technologies (e.g. city lights, kinetic ads, ambient marketing ads, and traffic ads). Maybe we are not too far from the social billboards presented in sci-fi movies (e.g. a billboard personally talking to the passer-by in Minority Report).

In connection to the election campaigns in Slovakia, the billboard is considered to be a very popular medium, intensively used by almost all political parties. The billboard can even be regarded as one of the primary communication media in political marketing, despite its high content restrictions, because outdoor advertisements have never been under the moratorium. Political parties in Slovakia also use other traditional media (television, radio and newspapers) in their pre-election campaigns. Alternative media like social networks have begun to be used more extensively only since the pre-election campaign of 2008. The billboard is an interesting communication media with the ability to share social contexts, especially in connection with its location: placed in the streets, the living space of the audience, which has a large impact on its reception as well as perception. Location together with the possibility of interference within the text (both visual and written) creates a significant potential for changes, sometimes even a complete reversal of the original message's meaning. Outdoor advertising is in close contact with street life; moreover, it often substantially co-creates the street as a social and physical space that has quite a long time ago attracted the attention of avant-garde art groups seeking a space and form of protest against the advertising and consumer culture. Ordinary people of the streets have also started to interact with these new elements of communication in many different ways. In 1970s, the billboard become one of the main battlegrounds of the semiotic war led by many activist groups and also by thousands of individuals, a war against a commercial simulacrum growing to a monstrous size. All around the world, anti-advertising movements that also gave their names to the techniques of this war have been established (Kera and Kočička, 2004): commerce jamming, billboard alteration, fake advertisement, media activism, adbusting, billboard bandits, guerrilla theater, culture jamming and subvertising. The objectives of these semiotic wars varied: they were a recovery of "sell-out" areas on the streets, the reintroduction of the streets to its residents, but also fights against particular advertising clients, including numbers of those with political content. An understanding of this phenomenon takes into account the ideologically unjustified interaction of recipients with billboards (e.g. satirical incentives), interventions to outdoor advertising through their being pasted over, their juxtaposition to other elements, their surroundings, their location, and the creation of context with other elements such as competing advertisements. In Slovakia, according to the information available, we cannot talk in this context about the activism of groups, as individuals are responsible for almost all activities of the guerilla resistance aimed against mass announcements.

Only one group is known, the so-called Fanatic Four, which makes actions against the billboards of various political parties and publishes them as photographs on Facebook. The situation is slightly different in the neighboring Czech Republic. During the municipal election campaign in 2010, outdoor advertising space was purposely attacked by an unknown group, which focused on dozens of billboards in Brno (see http://contexts.weebly.com/02.html)[1].

An example from the Czech Republic indicates that usually the strongest political parties, those very often presented on billboards (in the Czech Republic it was mainly ODS and ČSSD), are the target subjects of activities leading to the deconstruction of political advertising. Moreover, the communication of these subjects is, because of their frequent public appearance, most often a part of contexts that are semiotically open with the surrounding environment and other (competing) advertisements. This paper, in its research section, deals with the uncovering of some of the possible reasons for text and image deconstruction.

The campaign leading up to Slovak parliamentary elections in 2010 was up to two times more expensive than the previous one. Still, it was not very creative as it missed strong and dominant themes that could have been carried across the political spectrum. The parties were presented very vaguely, although there has been enough material for so-called thematic posters presenting selected topics and issues. Most often, the aim of advertising was focused on the presentation of the selected candidate, a slogan and some graphic characters (e.g. the political party). Similar experiences are described by K. Gajdka (2009), who states in his analysis of political campaigns in Poland a permanently unprecedented usage of schematic conventional rules of political posters constructing. These findings correspond to occurences of other non-original, non-creative outdoor communications frequently used by political parties and candidates, who count on these approved and even compulsory procedures (Gajdka, 2009: 128). This initiates repeated devaluation of strong agitation elements that should be an unforgettable indicator of brand knowledge and brand benefits in concordance with the brand itself, as it is in our case towards a political party or its candidate. In this context, it was inspiring for us to identify how these trends were reflected in the municipal election campaign in Slovakia.

Among the monitored factors was the phenomenon of the situational context as already described by J. Mistrík (1997: 277), which according to him has to be counted as a part of the text contents although it is far from the language component. The author states that it is needed to include contexts such as temporal, spatial

1 This act is considered a crime of defamation and activists as members of organized group face up to three years of imprisonment.

and historical moments, the recipient's personality, the relationship with the author and all situational physical and psychological moments. Thus the text of the broadly understood political communication output is grounded in a nonlinear communication context in the environment in which it is located as an analogy to the digital logic of new media, built in the linguistic and extra-linguistic milieu. Information published on a billboard does not communicate only "inside the frame"; all elements of communication incidentally communicate also with its surroundings ("outside the frame"). Not only in relation to the recipient in the traditional abstract line of communication (author—message—receiver), but also in the case of political outdoor advertising, it is important to add other components that have not been primarily planned and which re-create and re-expand the original communication while the information is not passive but is being actively co-created by the location context or, for example, by the technique of collage, drawing or painting. This knowledge is also associated with the popular informal, non-conformist movement called culture jamming. The creative approaches of this movement are on the one hand placed in the sphere of artistic activity with a strong satirical accent, or on the other hand they also act as an official political billboard allusion. A good example can be seen in Figure 1. It is a caricature of politician Róbert Fico. The author's nickname is Shooty and he works for the broadsheet newspaper SME.

Figure 1: Original billboard and caricature of politician Róbert Fico used in pre-election billboard made by Shooty (Original text: Certainty in difficult times. New text: The certainty of difficult times)

Source: http://www.infovolby.sk/data/_media/parl2010_smer_35.jpg>; <http://1.bp.blogspot.com/_FQcEcgkbNds/TBJQO4694vI/AAAAAAAAABg/7mkwWnap1fw/s1600/28551_1383014349832_1666191864_882678_5850203_n.jpg>. Retrieved Nov. 12, 2010

The election slogan "Certainty in difficult times" has been transformed to "The certainty of difficult times". Moreover, the logo has been transformed by the synesthetic principle from the smell of roses to the excrements, which are expressed through the image association of logos. The combination of the two meanings (certainty of difficult times—security—but intended ironically) shows that the positive and negative poles meet in the ad, but the negative one is predominant. Interventions are often nothing more than acts of vandalism through the destruction of original advertisements as an expression of disagreement with the authors' political culture or opinions as opposed to products of creative processes. All these factors co-create the new, unplanned facultative semantization of the image by the text (Čmejrková 2000: 138; Szabo, 2009; Feriancová, Mikuláš, 2010) (see http://contexts.weebly.com/03.html and http://contexts.weebly.com/04.html).

The original image often acquires bizarre contexts in connection with the other layers of the environment in which the image is located; accordingly, it is read as a new text which could have for the author of the original message some unwanted consequences. The fulfillment of the communication objective followed by the authors of the campaign is very often influenced by various factors. Therefore, it is necessary to calculate not only the intended effects of communication but also those not originally intended.

According to theories of creativity, it is more likely for people with a higher level of creativity to be able to recognize such a nexus (ad Guilford, 1975; Satková, 2008; Szobiová, 2004). Creative individuals themselves enter non-invasively the original intention of the authors of communication and even when they do not add anything to the original structure of billboard, its message is being converted. Their creativity is usually unplanned and it is based on the new context (contextual creativity) from the understanding of a new nexus, sometimes even unplanned by the author himself. Even when the original billboards do not exist anymore, part of these new contexts is recorded and spread via the Internet.

These factors are relatively quite predictable, but the change of meaning can be also caused by direct interventions of an "active audience" that feels addressed (by the slogan, idea, image or other co-acting element) to the transformation of their own communication message into the existing one. Above all this, the personality of the person involved has certainly a significant share regarding a wide range of cognitive and non-cognitive structures—attitudes, beliefs, and motivational structures. We believe, however, that the structure of a billboard is another contributory factor besides the political opinion and personality variables mentioned above. According creativity theory, unstructured or poorly structured tasks stimulate creative individuals to shape, expand, assemble or transform the original stimulus (e.g. Torrance, 1975, 1990; Jurčová, 1981). As described by J. P. Guilford (1975), it is also known that individuals with creative abilities have (besides the frame of divergent thinking) a so-called sensibility, the ability to see and fill in the gaps in solutions. They have well-developed skills and sensitivity in finding problems and insufficiencies or imperfections, while they also show the effort to fix gaps and imperfections that have been found. The research of individuals who make interventions to billboards is methodologically very difficult as they are anonymous artists who do not want to be debunked. A partial answer to the question "Why are some billboards supplemented by drawings or texts?" can be given by the structure of the billboard itself. In addition to the personality factors mentioned above, and the political views held, there are also situational variables (e.g. opportunity, position of billboard, and susceptibility to risk) operating. However, this study focuses primarily on the impetuses related to the billboard advertisement.

In the past, Adidas used the billboard surface as an open medium for the creativity of the recipients (see http://contexts.weebly.com/05.html). Firstly, the company rented billboards and pasted a blank poster on them that begged, with its eye-catching purity and lack of structure, to be filled in by the creations of people who felt addressed by this kind of communication. After anonymous creative individuals reacted to this open semiotic space, a second layer of billboard was added, framing the sprayed signs into the shape of shoe.

Even though the Adidas campaign anticipated the interventions (of pictorial or verbal character) of anonymous individuals, there are many cases when the communicator does not expect any such interventions. Clients usually prevent such unwanted interference by agreements with renters that any damaged billboard has to be immediately replaced. For this reason, agencies usually order approximately 10% more copies than the total number of billboards.

Although 10% does not seem like a large amount, whatever the intention of the intervening persons, such interventions undoubtedly affect the processing of the original message. The percentage may significantly increase because particularly funny or interesting interventions are usually spread virally or through the principle of buzz (via e-mails or social networks) and spread the message further—all this not in congruence with the original intention of the communication.

Research

Research problem: Considering the above-mentioned facts, we ask the following questions:

- Which new meanings are added to the billboards (or other forms of outdoor advertising (Ziarko, 2011)[2] by the intervening persons?

---

2 Like A. Ziarko (2011) we also focused on all outdoor types of advertising (i.e. billboards, citylights, and posters). In the previous text we paid special attention to the billboard as the most representative type of outdoor advertisements. All types of outdoor advertisements, however, share many common elements and characters. In the following text, we use the term only to simplify the billboard, but it also represents the media of poster and citylight.

- How does the surrounding of billboards enter the communication? In which cases?
- What elements in the structure of outdoor advertisements (except political opinion) predispose them to supplementation (visual or textual)?
- Is it possible to identify the relationship between the structure of the billboard and the elements added (both visual and textual)?

The method for identifying research variables

In the study, we used two research tools: quantified content analysis (Scherer, 2004) and visual analysis (Trampota and Vojtěchovská, 2010). In quantified content analysis we focused on textual elements of outdoor advertisements (e.g. slogans), while in visual analysis we dealt with visual aspects (figural[3] elements, etc.).

A core set of units and selection of material

The structure of the sample was prepared according to A. Strauss, J. Corbin (1998) and J. Hendl (2005) and based on the formulated questions. According to the types of sampling in qualitative research, we chose homogeneous sampling with elements of stratified sampling. The research material consists of billboards or other types of outdoor advertising from the municipal political campaign of 2010 in Slovakia. The basic unit for the purposes of analysis was a billboard or another type of outdoor advertising, its visual elements and its direct surroundings, in the case that they changed or influenced the meaning in terms of image (visual analysis), and the textual part as texts having been supplemented or otherwise changed (content analysis).

We used the types of technical and symbolic codes for visual analysis, as in Hansen et. al. (1998). Categories for image analysis were developed by the authors G. Rose (2001), V. Leeuwen et. al. (2004), T. Trampota, M. Vojtěchovská (2010) and G. Janková (2009). Categories corresponding to the elements that occur only in audio-visual records were omitted. The categories included are presented in table 1.

The basic set consisted of political billboards, posters, and citylights used in the municipal election campaign in Slovakia in 2010. The sample consisted of 225 photographs of outdoor advertisements, used in the municipal election campaign in Slovakia in 2010, collected from 19 towns (Banská Bystrica, Bardejov, Bratislava,

3 The term *figural* indicates any visually displayed reality.

Bytča, Handlová, Hlohovec, Komárno, Košice, Levice, Nitra, Nitrianske, Hrnčiarovce, Partizánske, Považská Bystrica, Prievidza, Sliač, Spišské Podhradie, Svidník, Zvolen, Žiar nad Hronom). Large, but also smaller, towns from all Slovak regions were included. The selection process is described above.

Units of analysis were outdoor advertisements: more precisely, billboard, poster, citylight and their visual components and surroundings, if they affected the meaning of the image (visual) or the text in the slogan. Advertisements examined were photographed by digital camera. As it was a municipal election, each city had its own specific outdoor set of commercials promoting relevant regional candidates.

Table 1: Categories of visual analysis according to T. Trampota a M. Vojtěchovská (2010, pp. 159-162) with other variables added by authors

Analysis of technical codes	
Field size	1. extreme close-up
	2. close-up
	3. bust or the medium shot
	4. full shot
Perspective	1. direct
	2. worm's-eye view
	3. bird's-eye view
Angle of view	1. Wide-angle lenses
	2. Standard lenses
	3. Long focus lenses
Lighting	1. Natural lighting
	2. Artificial lighting
Analysis of symbolic codes	
Color	1. black-white
	2. warm colors
	3. cold colors
	4. balanced colors
Representative processes and interactions	
Representative processes	1. conceptual
	2. symbolic
Roles	1. actor

	2. goal
	3. interactor
	4. carrier
Interaction with the audience	1. direct view
	2. front view
	3. view from profile
	4. view from behind
Interventions:	
in text	
in image	
Removal	
Context	

The method of data processing was analysis by scientific triangulation. Materials obtained by visual and content analysis were quantified and processed by descriptive statistics (frequency analysis) and then we applied factor analysis to identify hidden relations between variables. We used Varimax rotation.

Results

The sample was suitable for the procedures of qualitative analysis. The range of data was sufficient for factor analysis procedures. We studied the frequency of the various categories in political billboards.

Results of visual analysis

The following categories were the most frequent:

a) One of the most frequently represented was the category of technical code, which concerns perspective, the angle of gaze and whether photo lens is at the eye level of the depicted person. The photo lens was at the eye level of the person on the billboard of the pre-election municipal political campaign in 98% of cases. The persons displayed (usually politicians, but also sometimes their sympathizers) kept direct eye contact with the potential recipient. This would invoke an atmosphere of sincerity and direct contact. In some cases, eye contact was also verbally stressed ("we can look into your eyes."). Politicians want to be seen as direct and honest personalities. In this context, T. Trampota and M. Vojtěchovská (2010: 162) stated: *"With a direct gaze at recipients the picture creates the impression that the person is looking straight into the eyes of the reader. Thus, on a symbolic level, the depicted person asks the viewer for direct action."*

b) Another category revised was labeled "Representative processes" and it had one of the most frequent appearances. As a part of this category we had defined several subcategories that could be found in table 1. The subcategory labeled "Representative processes and interactions—carrier, conceptual" occurred in 97% of the research material. It was an understandable declaration of affiliation to the promoted party. R. Zamora (2010) stresses that the politician is the brand presented in its human form.

c) Following the category of Technical codes, the category often implemented was the type of lighting, where artificial lighting was detected in 95% of all analyzed photographs of billboards. Artificial lighting means studio lighting, whereby light can stylize reality and thus induce a flattering and positive visual effect, which could be seen as an effort to please the recipient of communication.

d) Concerning the category of Technical codes focused on the optics used, the most frequent was the utilization of a standard lens identified in 96% of billboards analyzed. This type of lens produces relatively natural-looking images, with the same proportions as human eyes perceive. (Trampota and Vojtěchovská, 2010).

e) In the category of Technical codes we focused also on the field size and size of portrayed person. A bust (depiction of the upper part of the human figure—the face, part of the arms and the shoulders) was identified in 76% of analyzed material.

Bust as a type of view is in our cultural conditions associated with visual presentation on official documents, but it is also a popular way of visually representing prominent figures from the sphere of arts, culture and history (and not only in two-dimensional, but often in three-dimensional, design—a bust). It is most likely for politicians to want to be associated with these connotations.

f) The meanings of the messages may be affected by other billboards, signs or subjects located in the immediate vicinity. This was identified in 39% of the research material and it suggests that over one third of billboards may be affected (positively or negatively) by the context and placement.

Unlike in parliamentary elections in Slovakia (analyzed in our earlier work; see Wojciechowski, Mikuláš and Fichnová, 2012), extreme close-ups of candidates (16% vs. 0%) were not presented in the municipal campaign, text was supplemented to a lesser degree than image (17% vs. 10%), and images were less frequently sketched-in (17% vs. 9%). There were not very many new contexts emerging from placement or surroundings (63% vs. 39%); however, there were more cases of images being torn down in the municipal campaign than in the parliamentary one (3% vs. 9%).

The following changes of the message meaning were identified as the most frequent ones:

1.) Inappropriate context—surroundings in which outdoor advertisements were placed.

The results are: the contradictory meaning, mockery, and interpretations other than those originally intended (for some typical examples see picture 2, http://contexts.weebly.com/06.html and http://contexts.weebly.com/01.html).

2.) Another type of unplanned transformation of the meaning: changes caused by the removal of a particular poster part(s). This is a very simple and effective way to prevent the message from meeting the recipient and changing the intended meaning (see picture 3).

The most commonly removed elements (scraped off or torn off) were: a) Eyes—the reasons may vary from, for example, allusions to their impertinency or the suppression of identification. Eyes are an important part of nonverbal communication-disabling communication. Pupil absence or significant reduction indicates unfriendliness. b) Mouth and nose—additional identifiers of the persons displayed and also the equipment by which they communicate or receive information from the environment. Removal of the mouth indicates a desire to silence actors, disagreement with what they say, as well as a conviction that their message is not worth hearing or it is a lie. A removal of the nose suggests that the intervening persons do not want to provide information about themselves. In addition, a distorted face becomes less recognizable in its individual features. In Slovakia, if we want to emphasize that we are confident that something will happen as anticipated, we use the phrase "I have a nose for it". The nose destruction and its removal suggests that someone (e.g. the politician) is wrong if he or she thinks that he or she will be successful; accordingly it suggests that he or she is wrong in everything and that he or she does not have the ability to anticipate and plan the future (i.e. does not have a nose for it).

Anthropologists claim that when someone starts to be unattractive (unlikeable) to us, we will register it at first on an extra-linguistic level—the person stops "smelling good" to us.

Finally, removal of body parts recalls medieval punishments for delinquency, lies, or thievery.

Picture 2: Poster message is semantically linked to its location

Sources: Photo by Smatanová Mária (Hlohovec, 2010)

Picture 3: Décollage—part of billboard is ripped off (image source listed in references).

Source: Photo by Nagy Michal (Nitra, 2010)

3.) The elements added may result in modifications of the information presented. In the research material it occurred in the following forms:

3.1.) Supplementation of material (e.g. with bubble gum, snow, mud, or paint). Material added influenced the visual aspect of the billboard or other kind of outdoor advertising. For example, one of the candidates had gum stuck to his lips in a way which made his lips seem comically big. Another billboard with a candidate had been covered with mud so that it looked from a distance like a photograph that had not been retouched to remove adolescent pimples (potentially a reference to the candidate's immature behavior). In another case mud on the image looked like a headshot. There were also billboards splashed with paint; in some cases red was used to seem like blood seeping from the candidate's mouth, evoking the notion that the candidate will "suck the blood" out of the city.

3.2.) Pre-prepared supplementation of the text. An example of this type of supplementation are yellow papers with the text "For how much?" glued to the billboard of the candidate PG, an independent candidate whose chances of winning were diffused by other candidates. They, however, gave up their candidacies in his favor, and it was said that the purpose of this act was to eliminate his strongest opponent LV. "For how much?" is thus a provocative question, which should most likely indicate that the PG paid other candidates to do so.

3.3.) Spontaneous supplementation of the text, e.g. with spray paint. This is a spontaneous reaction (not prepared in advance). In this case, interventions are made by adding textual messages to billboards with sprays or other writing tools available. Examples of text supplementation are as follows: "Stop chit-chatting!", "Liar!", "Thief!", but also "Mafioso!", or various stronger or weaker versions of swear words.

3.4.) Supplementation of the image. Voters often etch images into different parts of the face, most often different kinds of moustache (regular, twisted, Hitler's) not only on male candidates' faces but females' to the same extent. Beards, eyebrows, black teeth, big ears, or donkey ears were also drawn, but with less frequency.

3.5.) Combination of the aforementioned. An example is one billboard with a candidate and a claim—"People of Petržalka (note: Petržalka is a sector of Bratislava), you are at home here"—modified with spray paint to the form of a filthy rhombus symbol.

These supplementations influence the message communicated in billboards, so the original intention of the communicators is not only modified but sometimes completely changed. T. Duncan (1997) in his Integrated Marketing Communication Message Typology adds to the four types of messages "unplanned messages". In this case the term applies to journalists, notices of interest consumer groups, product pull-outs, the gossip of employees and crises, but not to the supplementation of meaning by the recipients or context.

C. Grönroos (2000) includes within the category of unplanned messages in political communication word-of-mouth, referrals, references, news stories, gossip, and internet chat groups, though he does not omit other kinds of unplanned messages. Ch. H. Patti, E. Luck, and S. Chapman (2003) point to the vulnerability caused by unplanned messages in political communication, thinking about political communication in terms of talk shows or information from the news. None of the authors mentioned above refer to unplanned communication as a result of recipient activity, when recipients actively append, recreate and even modify the messages originally intended in outdoor campaigns. Secondly, these messages are afterwards communicated by other recipients and usually spread also via the Internet to other recipients virally via blogs and other media.

Table 2: Results of factor analysis of monitored categories in the political advertisements (Municipal election campaign in Slovakia, 2010)

Factors	1	2	3	4	5	6	7
Representative processes and interactions (RpaI)_Roles_3_interactor	.875						
RpaI_Representative processes_4_symbolic	.761						
Analysis of the technical codes_ Angle of view_1_Wide-angle lenses	.637						
RpaI_Representative processes_3_ conceptual_analytical	.634						
RpaI_Representative processes_2_ conceptual_classification	-.600	.0477	-.423				
Analysis of the technical codes _Lighting_ 2. Artificial lighting		.891					
RpaI_Interaction with the audience_1_direct view		.862					
Representative processes and interactions _Roles_4_carrier		.637	-.493				
Representative processes and interactions_ Representative processes_1_narative			.788				
Analysis of the technical codes_ Field size_5_full shot			.762				
Representative processes and interactions_ Roles_1_actor			.680				
Analysis of the technical codes_Perspective_1_direct				.804			
Analysis of the technical codes_Perspective_3_bird's-eye view				-.724			
Analysis of the technical codes _Field size_4_full shot	.412			-.582			

Analysis of the technical codes _Field size_3_medium shot	-.374		-.301	.579			
Analysis of symbolic codes_Colour_4_balanced colors				.409		-.357	
Analysis of symbolic codes_Colour_3_ cold colors					-.870		
AoSC__Colour _2_warm colors					.730		
Analysis of the technical codes_Field size _2_close-up					.376		
Representative processes and interactions_Interaction with the audience_2_from front		-.312				.618	
AoSC _Colour_1_ black-white						.449	
Analysis of the technical codes_Angle of view_2_Normal, or Standard lenses	.388					-.409	
Analysis of the technical codes_Lighting_1_Natural lighting		-.381					.634
Supplements_context							.511
Supplements_of text							-.499
Supplements_of image							-.487

Legend:
RpaI: Representative processes and interactions
AoSC: Analysis of symbolic codes_Colour
A source: Wojciechowski, Ł.; Fichnová, K,; Mikuláš, P., 2010

A very important part of our research was oriented to the questions of whether elements in the structure of pre-election billboards predispose them to be supplemented graphically or textually and whether it is possible to identify the relationship between the structure and elements of advertisements and the supplementation of text or visual elements.[4] We tried to answer these questions by identifying the forces of mutual correlations between individual categories, and then we applied factor analysis (table 2). The results showed that:

- intervention did not occur when actors were presented in natural lighting

4 The authors of this paper are aware that the supplementation of billboards goes beyond the political opinion of recipient and that the structure of billboards is stimulated also by a number of other factors related to personality of intervening person (e.g. age, susceptibility to risk, creativity, commitment, ethics and social norms) and situational factors (e.g. availability, opportunity, and billboard location).

- in contrast, interventions were more frequent when artificial lighting had been used
- artificiality and uniformity almost always caused supplementation of the text or image
- campaigns without interesting ideas usually stimulated interventions, which is consistent with the findings of psychologists working in the field of creativity (Torrance, 1975, 1990; Jurčová, 1981; Gulilford, 1975; and others), because the lack of creativity of authors (in our case copywriters) provoke creative individuals to shape their imperfect and weak work
- if new meanings were not created by context (placement or surroundings), they were often supplemented by a drawing or text

Based on the results and findings described above, we attempted to summarize these factors in "The typology of the media text factors co-creating aims of communication" (see figure 1).

Figure 1: The typology of the media text factors co-creating aims of communication.

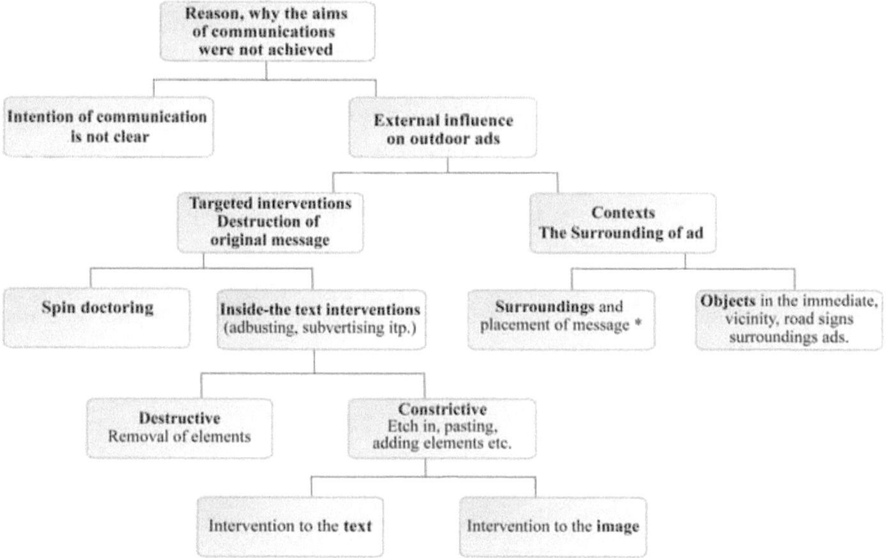

Source: Wojciechowski, Ł., Fichnová, K. and Mikuláš, P. (2010)

* placement and environment are often intentionally selected factors in new forms of marketing communications

Conclusions

The results presented above can be summarized as follows:

- The meanings of outdoor advertisements were changed either by their surroundings or by the recipients themselves. New contexts are created actively or passively. Active changes are represented by the intervention of passers-by, critics of the political situation or vandals. Passive changes develop from context in relation to the surrounding ambient.
- Possible reasons for intervention on a billboard lie in its structure, the visual presentation of the actor and the location of the billboard in the environment.
- Interventions almost always oppose the originally intended message; in a broader context we could understand this as a part of codetermination culture (Debord, 1994; Inštitorisová, 2009).
- Departments responsible for the communication of political parties should consider the creation of the position of auditor, a person responsible for the implementation of communication in real terms, or they should make use of the opportunity to ask external communication specialists
- In the context of categories of visual political advertising of Johnston and Kaid (2002), it should be noted that almost all billboards intervened upon are those of the image type; only one example of the issue-oriented type was identified (see http://contexts.weebly.com/06.html), and even that one was just a surrounding for other billboards placed nearby. This result shows that image ads may be at higher risk in terms of potential assaults.
- In the next stage it will be important to add other categories of analysis, for example in the category of "interaction with the audience" are needed half-profile items (different views), hand position (the presence of gestures), facial expression, clothing and the level of formality, the second plan, and the number of displayed persons.

As stated above, even though several authors suggest that every political communication leads to planned messages as well as to unplanned ones, none of the authors (Duncan, Duncan and Moriarty, 1997; Grönroos, 2000; Patti, Luck and Chapman, 2003; and others) seek the potential of unplanned messages in the context to which outdoor political advertising is exposed (the synergy of environmental elements) or the context of completion or alteration of the message by recipients themselves, followed by the further dissemination of this altered (and unplanned) message—whether in original outdoor form or via the Internet.

E. Anduiza, M. Cantijoch, and A. Gallego (2007) claim that the Internet (when browsed without a specific aim) can lead a priori to unplanned exposure to political or social content; nevertheless, these authors do not take account of the viral spreading of communication altered by an individual recipient.

Both variants of altered message spreading (in terms of outdoor advertising changed by the recipient, as well as its subsequent spreading via the Internet) interfere with the primary communication intentions of political parties and stress the known fact that the recipient is not a passive consumer of communication (see e.g. Mody, 1992; Vybíral, 2009); moreover, he actively enters the process of message perception (subjective perception), changing the message and spreading it further as elaborated in this chapter.

Interactivity[5] and interaction[6] with marketing billboards occur not only today, but also in classical movies from the genre of science fiction, e.g. Blade Runner (1982, directed by Ridley Scott) or Minority Report (2002, directed by Steven Spielberg), and in commercial advertising such as a Honda billboard with SMS and Bluetooth interaction, McDonald's Piccadilly Circus Sign, the Big in Japan campaign, Nikon, Nokia, Adobe CS3, or the HBO / Big Love: Audio Billboards. These are the examples of the dialogue directed from the sender to a recipient who can interact in a manner expected by the author. In an era of significant viewer participation, if an individual participates in the communication, his "share" could also inform the critical view and make adjustments that have as a goal the modification of the communication content, such that the original message changes and the sender is insulted or mocked.

Communication teams preparing political communication for political parties should think about this potential, not only in the phase of making a decision about the kind of message they will communicate and what specific claims would be suitable to use (in case they leave a slogan ripe for unwanted modification), but also in the phase of the realization of an outdoor campaign in certain environmental conditions, in order to prevent situations in which the environmental context negatively interferes with the intended message.

We believe that these findings could be inspirational for further, more detailed and more extensive research. It would be very interesting to compare our research with similar studies conducted in other countries. A comparison of results could show the broader context of political communication habits, e.g. the cultural perception of advertisements, the activity or passivity of the audience, the quality of marketers' advertisement preparation, and the creativity of all the agents in the communication process.

5 Interactivity in the sense of simultaneous operating.
6 Interaction in the meaning of mutual influences and stimulating activity

References

Anduiza, A., Cantijoch, M. and Gallego, A. (2007). Political Participation And The Internet: Descriptive Hypotheses and Causal Mechanisms. In *Paper to be presented at the Symposium "Changing politics through digital networks: The role of ICTs in the formation of new social and political actors and actions"*, Florence, 5-6 October 2007. 25 p. Retrieved April 24, 2011 from http://www.regione.toscana.it/regione/multimedia/RT/documents/1211883108709_ gallego.pdf

Čmejrková, S. (2000). *Reklama v češtině. Čeština v reklamě*. Praha: Leda

Debord, G. (1994). *The Society of Spectacle*. New York..

Duncan, T., Duncan, T. R. and Moriarty, S. (1997). *Driving Brand Value: Using Integrated Marketing to Manage Profitable Shareholder Relationships*. Medford, OR, U.S.A.: McGraw-Hill Companies

Feriancová, A. and Mikuláš, P. (2012). Manipulácia v historických kontextoch—príklad fotografie. In Fichnová (ed.) *(Ko)médiá. Vedecké a odborné štúdie zamerané na mediálnu a marketingovú komunikáciu* Nitra: UKF.

Fichnová, K., Wojciechowski, L.P. and Mikuláš, P (2012). Photography in political campaign: goals and reality. The case of the parliament campaign in Slovakia in 2010. In *Annales Universitatis Paedagogicae Cracoviensis: Studia de Cultura III.* Vol. 3, No. 112 (2012), 38-55.

Gajdka, K. (2009). Nowe trendy w samorządowych kampaniach wyborczych. In: A. Adamus Matuszyński: *Budovanie społecności lokalnej. Jak rozwijać trwałe relacje pomiędzy samorządem a jego społecznym otoczeniem?* Katowice: Wydawnictwo Akademii Ekonomicznej, 123–166

Gero, Š. (2004). Vzťah obrazu a textu v masmediálnej komunikácii. In V. Patráš (Eds.), *Súčasná jazyková komunikácia v interdisciplinárnych súvislostiach* [Contemporary Language Communication with Intedisciplinary Connections]. Banská Bystrica: Univerzita Mateja Bela, Fakulta humanitných vied; Pedagogická fakulta, 249-256

Grönroos, C. (2000). Creating a relationship dialogue: communication, interaction, value. In: *Marketing Rewiew*. Vol. 1, No. 1, 5-14.

Guilford, J. P. (1975). Creativity: A Quarter Century of Progress. In I. A. Taylor, J. W. Getzels (Eds.), *Perspectives in Creativity.*Chicago: Aldine Publishing Company, 37-59

Hansen, A. et. al. (1998). *Mass Communication Research Methods.* London: MacMillan Press.

Hendl, J. (2005). *Kvalitatívny výskum*. Praha: Portál

Inštitorisová, D. (2009). Úvod, In. D. Inštitorisová (Eds.) *Divadlo—interaktivita, insceno-vanosť, diskurz*. Nitra: UKF, 19-31

Janková, G. (2009). Analýza farieb vo vnímaní reklamy. In E. Bútorová and E. Kováčová (Eds.), *Veda v praxi—prax vo vede: zborník konferenčných príspevkov z vedeckej konferencie interných a externých doktorandov a mladých vedeckých pracovníkov, konanej pri príležitosti "Týždňa vedy a techniky na Slovensku" v dňoch 12.-18. novembra 2007.* Nitra: UKF, 252-258

Johnston, A. and Kaid L. L. (2002). Image Ads and Issue Ads in U.S. Presidential Advertising: Using Videostyle to Explore Stylistic Differences in Televised Political Ads from 1952 to 2000. *Journal of Communication*, 52 (2), 281-300.

Jurčová, M. (1981). *Psychologické charakteristiky úloh tvorivého charakteru. Jednotná škola,* 33, 7, 644-659.

Kaid, L. L. (2004). *Handbook Of Political Communication Research.* New Jersey: Lawrence Erlbaum Associates Publishers.

Kalčoková, B. (2010). *Nové médiá—nová závislosť?* uverejnené 2010. Retrieved october 01.2011 from: http://mediaetika.longtail.sk/?p=561.

Kera, D. and Kočička, P. (2004). *About a group of castrates with impotent equipment Fascination with a public space.* In: Typo12, 2004. Retrieved october 12.2010 from http://www.svettisku.cz/buxus/generate_page.php?page_id=1095.

Kratochvil, M. and Šedík, M. (2007). *Význam a funkcie vizuálnej komunikácie v e-learningu.* Banská Bystrica: Univerzita Mateja Bela v Banskej Bystrici Pedagogická fakulta Katedra prírodovedy a Uakom Umb.

Láb, F. and Turek, J. (2009). *Fotografie po fotografii.* Praha: Karolinum

Leeuwen Van, Th. and Jewitt C. (2004). *The Handbook of Visual Analysis.* London: Sage publications Ltd.

Martinec, R., and Salway, A. (2005). A system for image–text relations in new (and old) media. *Visual Communication.* 4, 3; 337-371.

McQuail, D. (2007). *Úvod do teórie masové komunikace.* Praha: Portál

Mirzoeff, N. (1999). *An Introduction to Visual Culture.* London, New York: Routledge

Mistrík, J. (1997). *Štylistika.* Bratislava: SPN.

Mody, B. (1992). Energizing the Communication Component in extension: A case for new pilot projects. 1992. In *12th World Bank Agricultural Symposium, 1992.* Retrieved may 30. 2010 from: http://www.rrojasdatabank.info/12agrisym/agrisym89-104.pdf

Patti, Ch. H. , Luck, E.and Chapman, S. (2003). Building A Brand Relationship With Voters: The Need For Imc Within Political Parties. In *ANZMAC 2003 Conference Proceedings Adelaide 1-3* December 2003, 2019-2025.

Pospíšil, F. (2010). *Jen tak si stříknout. A2.* Číslo 21. Retrieved october 10.2010 from http://www.advojka.cz/archiv/2010/21/jen-tak-si-striknout

Płażewski, J. (2008). *Język filmu.* Warszawa: Książka i Wiedza

Rose, G. (2001). *Visual Methodologies: An Introduction to the Interpretation of Visual Materials.* London: Sage publications Ltd.

Satková, J. (2008). Výtvarná tvorba inšpirovaná médiami a individualita, In M. Žilková (Eds.) *Slovo—obraz zvuk II: duchovný rozmer súčasnej kultúry* (pp. 242-244). Nitra: UKF

Scherer, H. (2004). Úvod do metody obsahové analýzy. In Schulz, W., Reifová, I. a kol., *Analýza obsahu mediálních sdělení.* UK Praha: Karolinum, 29-50.

Strauss, A., Corbin, J., (1998). *Basics of Qualitative Research: Grounded Theory Procedures and Technique.* London: Sage publications Ltd.

Šramová, B., Spálová, L.and Mikuláš, P., (2010). *Diskriminačné komunikačné stratégie politickej strany v predvolebnej kampani 2010 v sr.* Príspevok prezentovaný na vedeckej konferencii „Demokracie jako hodnota a problém", Liberec. (in press)

Szabo, P. (2009). Text a obraz—o niektorých princípoch uplatňujúcich sa v printovej reklame. In *Masmediálna komunikácia a realita III: marketingová komunikácia. Vedecká konferencia, Trnava 29.-30. apríl 2009.* Trnava: UCM, 111-125.

Szobiová, E. (2004). *Tvorivosť, od záhady k poznaniu.* Stimul: Bratislava.

Tódová, M. (2009). *Martináková sa hnevá na Markízu.* Published 10.2.2009. Retrieved may 30. 2010 from http://volby.sme.sk/c/4301569/martinakova-sa-hneva-na-markizu.html.

Torrance, E. P. (1975). Creativity Research in Education: Still Alive. In *Perspectives in Creativity* (pp. 278-296). Chicago: Aldine Publishing Company.

Torrance, E. P. (1990). Creativity in the Classrom. In Woolfolk, A. E., (Ed.) *Educational Psychology.* New Jersley: Prentice-Hall, Inc. A Division of Simon andSchuster, 144 -146.

Trampota, T. and Vojtěchovská, M. (2010). *Metody výzkumu médií.* Praha: Portál

Vybíral, Z. (2009). *Psychologie komunikace*. Praha: Portál.

Zamora, R. (2010). *Local media and the "political brand" Candidates attributes portrayed on local media and their consequences on public perceptions. Central European Journal of Communication.* 3, 5,283-299.

Ziarko, A. (2011). Reklama wizualna w samorządowej kampanii wyborczej we Wrocławiu w 2006 roku. In B. Dobek-Ostrowska and K. Majdecka (eds.) *Studia empiryczne nad komunikowaniem politycznym w Polsce [Empirical studies in political communication.* Wrocław: Wydawnictwo Uniwersytetu Wrocławskiego, 99-121.

15. Comparative Media Discourse Analysis of a Selected Political Event in Slovakia

Peter Szabo
Peter Mikuláš
Lucia Spálová
University of Constantine the Philosopher in Nitra, Slovakia

Abstract: The following article deals with the possibilities for discourse analysis of printed media texts. The authors used discourse analysis to analyze media coverage of a specific media event: the visit of Hungarian President László Sólyom on the occasion of the unveiling of the statue of St. Stephen in Komárno, Slovakia. The event took place on August 21st, 2009. The results of the discourse analysis document basic differentiating discourses constructed by the media about the event in non-tabloid press outlets in Slovakia.

Keywords: discourse, discourse analysis, media event, dominant discourses, media ritual

Introduction

Media discourse is an important component of modern culture. The mass media present concise yet selective images of culture. It is difficult to separate the media discourse from everyday discourse and at the same time to evaluate the extent of their influence. Both discourses react to each other in a complex network of interactions; however, media offers to its recipients "expertise", "authority" and "access to resources", which may imply higher objectivity. In today's information environment we note the predominance of passive forms of receiving information by uncommitted recipients, resulting in an increase of the media impact on everyday life. From this point of view, we may consider the degree of influence of media discourse on the individual as important and current. The media offers discourses which create the basis for orientation in the world, form the world and also "serve as a crucial source of standards, models and norms" (McQuail, 2002).

* The paper was supported by scientific project VEGA No. 1/0399/11: Opportunities and dangers internet media communication grant.

Media coverage of events generally tends to neglect a general view on the mediated events. In the context of the event analyzed, the visit of the Hungarian president on the occasion of unveiling a statue of St. Stephen in Komárno, the mass media only briefly mentioned the important fact that the Hungarian president has already attended a similar event in Komárno. On October 2nd, 2007 L. Sólyom took part in an unofficial visit of Komárno, where he lectured at Selye János University. Although the event was declared as a private visit, Sólyom lectured on the problems of Slovak-Hungarian relations; in particular he was very critical of the Slovak declaration of the unchangeability of the Beneš Decrees. Slovak politicians interpreted this attitude as clearly crossing the bounds of an unofficial visit by a foreign political representative in the Slovak Republic. Moreover, Sólyom participated in several unofficial visits to Slovakia, such as celebrations of St. Stephen's day in Diakovce (August 19th, 2007, Hungarian National Holiday). The Hungarian president also faced criticism of other countries, Serbia and Romania, which he had also visited with the status of private person. On the other hand, it is necessary to add that this attitude of the Hungarian president has its critics in some circles in Hungary as well. The newspaper Népszava cites Mátyás Eörs, a foreign policy expert for the liberal democrats: "Sólyom should consider the reactions of residents in neighboring countries when he has celebrated every Hungarian National Holiday abroad for the past several years" ("Pravda", August 25th, 2009: 2).

To answer the question why the Hungarian president puts such an importance on his presence in the border areas of neighboring countries, we have to go back almost a century. The Hungarians feel the separation of the nation after WWI was unjust in areas where ethnic Hungarians were absorbed by other nationalities within the new state borders.

One of the recurring themes of similar events is that, in the case of international confrontation between Slovakia and Hungary, the representatives of Komárno tend to support the attitudes of Hungarian representatives in official statements. A similar attitude was assumed by Hungarian national political parties operating in Slovakia (SMK, Most-Híd) and by political scientists of Hungarian nationality in Slovakia.

Specification of the media event studies

The topic analyzed is particularly characterized by the following facts: the media brought the story from start to finish (developing the story), the culmination of events had a theatrical audio-visual character, and two relatively autonomous levels were mixed: the president as a representative of the country and the president as a private individual (personal and public sphere).

The visit of L. Sólyom was a frequently mediated topic. Slovak media discussed the event for several days, identifying the whole event as a diplomatic confrontation or a diplomatic shootout. The story focusing on the visit of the Hungarian president had a structure and was played out strictly under the spotlight of journalists. The dramatic climax in the form of the theatrical performances of President Sólyom on Komárno Bridge was also part of the story. This theatrical aspect became a major information source about the event, both at home and abroad. In accordance with the views of many media theorists (Abercombie, 1996; Featherstone, 1991; Feriancová and Mikuláš, 2012) the primary active component for media recipients is visual communication, not the spoken word or written text. This fact is reinforced by the media, because they "let" images to speak for themselves, without adequate reflection in the text component (both due to spatial and ideological reasons). Ignacio Ramonet (2003) stresses the fact that not all (socially relevant) events have an adequate representation in the media environment. Each event by its occurrence in reality determines both media interest (out-of-text construction or the surroundings of the text) and the forms of treatment in the media text (inside-the-text construction). If PR specialists choose to prefer image and action to depict attractive, possibly conflicting situations, they direct events in order to provide media (as required by them) with sufficient material. Some events tend to move into the sphere of so-called media rituals. N. Couldry (2003: 57) underlines one aspect of media rituals as presenting oneself to the media without any realistic expectations regarding the proclaimed intentions of the participant. In the above-mentioned story, Sólyom assumed a diplomatic note issued by the Slovak Ministry of Foreign Affairs right in the middle of the Komárno Bridge. The note stated that the Hungarian president was an unwanted person in Slovakia, at the day of the anniversary of the occupation of (Czecho)Slovakia which took place in 1968. Sólyom used mass media to communicate a clear message, a shock caused by the Slovak diplomatic procedure. He interpreted the whole event as an unwelcome surprise, something he did not expect at all. Thanks to the professional timing and localization, his assumption of the note happened right in front of a large number of media. The event, the march across the bridge, became a perfect audio-visual event for these reasons:

- None of it happened outside the camera lenses of journalists.
- None of it was left open; the Hungarian president pushed the action to an absurd climax, at the end of which he was stopped by the diplomatic note.

- A diplomatic shootout was materialized through the media. The march across the bridge provided an interpretative framework for representing the entire series of events in the media.

Research problem

The main thematic area of our research is Slovak-Hungarian relations in media discourse. These relations (at least on the official inter-state level) have long been marked with tensions, and events that occur between the two countries are unprecedented in the European context. One of the recent events of contradictory nature was the visit of the Hungarian president László Sólyom in Slovakia in 2009. A visit took place on the occasion of the unveiling of the statue of St. Stephen in Komárno. The main topic of our research is the analysis of the event in terms of the context given and the presentation of this event in the media. Due to the above-mentioned facts, we wondered how those media events were presented in non-tabloid newspapers published in the Slovak and Hungarian languages within Slovakia.

Due to the mixed nature of the research we ask wider based research questions and hypotheses.

Research questions:

1. Which dominant discourses of the event do the newspapers studied indicate?
2. To what extent did the newspapers studied deal with the analyzed topic?
3. In what genre of classification would we place the newspapers that were informed of the subject of the visit of the Hungarian president at the unveiling of the statue of St. Stephen?
4. What type of photos framed the articles about the events analyzed?

Hypotheses:

H1: Evaluation of Hungarian president's intent is statistically significant in terms of information variance between the Slovak and Hungarian newspapers.

H2: Evaluation of the Komárno representatives' plan depends on the country of origin of the newspaper.

H3: The difference between Slovak and Hungarian newspapers in the evaluation of Slovak officials' plan to prevent the entry of the Hungarian president into Slovakia is statistically significant.

H4: The types of event framing in titles are different in Slovak and Hungarian newspapers.

H5: The types of event framing in articles are different in Slovak and Hungarian newspapers.

Research material

The selection of the research material was carried out according to the recommendations of A. Strauss, J. Corbin (1999) and J. Hendl (2005). The selection of the materials was determined by the circulation and readership of the non-tabloid newspapers in Slovakia. We have selected three Slovak newspapers: "SME", "Pravda", and "Hospodárske noviny", a newspaper for the Hungarian minority published in Slovakia. The number of newspapers in Slovak and Hungarian could not have been balanced, because there is only one newspaper in Slovakia published in the Hungarian language—"Új Szó". Due to the wider choice of Slovak newspapers, we created a methodology to ensure accurate identification of the dominant discourse in their content. The basic units of analysis were relevant newspaper articles. Considering the recommendation of O. Holsti (in Janoušek, 2007), we analyzed media discourses constructed in the articles before the event, on the day of the event and after the event (August 20th, 2009—August 22th, 2009). The newspaper "Hospodárske noviny" does not have a Saturday edition, so we decided to analyze its Monday, August 24 issue. Together we analyzed 29 articles ("SME"—7, "Pravda"—8, "Hospodárske noviny"—4, "Új Szó"—10).

Method

The most common method used when analyzing media is content analysis. Media research commonly uses quantitative content analysis, which is more descriptive and proceeds "top-down"—that is, the meaning is created by researchers and might be considered subjective. Quantitative content analysis allows the registration of certain terms and concepts in the media text, but does not answer questions about their actual meaning or individual or social significance. These are the major reasons for criticism of the quantitative approach by researchers working with an alternative paradigm using a qualitative approach to content analysis. Therefore, an increasing number of researchers propose different research approaches in order to maintain relevance and validate their research. Many approaches have been proposed (e.g. Miessler, 2007; Pavelka, 2007; Janoušek, 2007; Urbánek, 2007; Fichnová, Wojciechowski and Polakevičová, 2010). E. Hradiská (2004) recommends using quantitative analysis to obtain a first orientation in the data; according to her it should serve as an introduction or a starting point for deeper analysis. An opponent of this approach, J. Miessler (2007), suggests making a detailed critical discourse analysis on a smaller amount of relevant texts—this way the meaning is not lost in categorization. The last step is the application of the quantitative content analysis based on the large number of texts.

In our research we started off with deeper qualitative analysis and those results subsequently became the basis for determining relevant categories in the quantitative approach. This eliminated the loss of meaning contained in the media text. Mixed approaches improve the quality of the methodological approach by reflecting the social sciences methodology and simultaneously accentuating the desirable transdisciplinary approach to media research.

In the interests of this methodological pluralism we will try to outline the possibilities of discourse analysis in broader political and social contexts with the case of media discourse arising from the visit of the Hungarian president on the occasion of the unveiling of a statue of St. Stephen in Komárno in 2009 from the perspective of the Slovak media differentiated nationally.

Our basic methodological approach formed the principles of discourse analysis that put a spotlight on explicit language in social situations (spoken word as well as written text) and its enrichment of the socio-critical aspect. The term "discourse" in a broad sense includes all forms of spoken interaction and written texts of all kinds (Edwards and Potter, 1992). Discourse is characterized by three dimensions: situational placement—with a focus on the place of the communication process; action orientation—organizing various social practices; and structure—discourse is constructed and at the same time it is constructing internal and external experience of the world. In discourse analysis we do not focus on the core, the nature of discourse, but on the construction of discourse itself and its role in communication. The specific event acquires its meaning through the discourse, the bears no moral value or particular significance itself, and is open to different interpretations in different discourses. Within the discourse there is a temporary fixing of the importance and the value of a particular event through its placement into the overall context and value system of the discourse. There are many different conceptions of discursive analysis. Our analysis is based on the perception of discourse inspired by M.A.K. Halliday (1985). A specific approach is characterized by critical discursive analysis (CDA), emphasizing "the language as a form of social practice" (M. Foucault, 2002; Fairclough, 2006). CDA focuses on uncovering the structures of subjectivity—submission to certain dominant discourse in society and also on the deconstruction of identity. Critical discursive analysis targets the role of discourse in the re/production and questioning of political domination.

We have chosen the principle of free coding (Strauss and Corbin, 1999). This inductive method looks for general categories which are able to explain the main topics of the phenomenon studied. The process of data analysis takes place at several levels in an increasing level of abstraction, with the aim of identifying the central categories and putting them into relationships with other categories in the wider context.

In this study we present a qualitative and quantitative level of discursive analysis. In defining the categories of content analysis, we applied the qualitative approach in order to preserve the importance of the events analyzed. Consequently, we quantified the categories for identifying the predominant framing of the event by tracking logs. To determine the significance of differences between the Slovak Republic and Hungary, we used the nonparametric statistical method of $\chi 2$-test and contingency coefficient C. The chosen significance level was $\alpha = 0.05$. The calculations were carried out using SPSS and Excel software.

Results of qualitative analysis

Linguistic and psychological analysis of communication

In this section of analysis, we have used an approach to discourse analysis described by M. A. K. Halliday (1985) in joint authorship with R. Hasan, who described three metafunctions of language. The most common term used to describe this feature is "register". Register is actually a set of dimensions or levels of discourse: interpersonal, textual and ideational.

Another important concept besides register is "genre". It is a specific type of text that reflects the type of social context and accesses a steady pattern of meanings. It is a structured, goal-oriented social process. In our analysis, the genre is determined by the type of newspaper analyzed and the placement of stories (e.g. comment, message, or social section).

Interpersonal and ideational level of discourse: tenor

When analyzing the interpersonal level of language, it is important to characterize participants of the communication, their status and (social) roles, and the types of their relationships. On the ideational level the emphasis is given to analysis of the social activities undertaken by language users that have an impact on the final act of communication.

After projecting the described model on the specific case of communication between Slovak and Hungarian political representation at the existing level of relations between them (tenor) and conducted discourse, we may talk about contradiction, conflict and tension. A newly introduced language law in Slovakia and several contentious issues from the past at the international level (e.g. the issue of dual citizenship for Slovak citizens of Hungarian nationality and the description of the territory of Slovakia as Felvedék[1] by Hungarian politicians) form the background and context of the diplomatic squabble between the two countries. However, the fact is that Slovak political representatives were just responding to conflict and tensions caused by the Hungarian side. In particular, László Sólyom was the initiator of the announced visit at the unveiling of the statue of St. Stephen, the first Hungarian King. Slovak representatives responded to his initiative. Apart from the different interpretations concerning the intentions of the Hungarian president, the fact remains that this type of visit by a neighboring country ultimately enters the realm of diplomacy and should be treated as a specific ritual with a prescribed protocol. This sentiment was expressed by Rudolf Chmel, former Ambassador of the Slovak Republic to Hungary:

"For the vote on whether to invite the president of the Slovak Republic Ivan Gašparovič also, the result was 5:0 in opposition of the invitation. This outcome has explanatory value and may reflect the game with the so-called Hungarian card in the last presidential election. If I could draw attention of organizers to anything, I would remind them that with this action they entered the international field and should adjust their behavior accordingly." ("Pravda", August 22nd, 2009: 3)

Rudolf Chmel's opinion is just one of many similar statements from both Slovak and Hungarian politicians (of course, not all are either positive or negative). By analyzing a large number of articles we will try to determine the predominant (or dominant) discourse prevailing in a particular newspaper.

Textual level of discourse: mode

This type of analysis describes the specific role of language itself, what users of the language expect from it, and the symbolic role of the text and its status in the social context; that is, we analyze the context of direct or metaphorical expression of communicants. The object of analysis is the structure of the text.

According to the above-mentioned facts, we will take a closer look at the language of discourse participants. These include not only the major players (Slovak constitutional representatives, the Hungarian president) but also broader discourse participants, i.e. other politicians and political commentators who evaluated the event. Many of their comments also reflect the focus of particular newspapers. Comparisons of the specific statements of politicians as well as

1 "The upland" or "Upstate"

those of journalists (e.g. columns, opinions, comments) are of significant importance in terms of positive or negative evaluations. The assessment of the planned visit of the Hungarian president at the unveiling of the statue of St. Stephen in Komárno was expressed also by politician Milan Urbányi. However, he also mentioned the Slovak side: "A mistake was made in both Slovak and Hungarian diplomacy. If Sólyom went to Banská Bystrica to celebrate someone's birthday, that would be called a private visit. But he has gone to Komárno and today is the anniversary of occupation of Czechoslovakia by the armies of Warsaw Pact; this is bad timing" ("Új Szó", August 22nd, 2009: 2).

Similarly, Slovak Prime Minister Robert Fico negatively assessed the intention of the Hungarian president prior to his visit to Slovakia: "None of the leading Slovak representatives will be there because no one has been invited. It's sort of an attempt to celebrate Hungarian statehood on Slovak territory. The Hungarian president is engaging in an act of gross provocation, which may have far reaching consequences for the Hungarian-Slovak relations" ("SME", August 20th, 2009: 2). The expressions of the Slovak Prime minister were straightforward for the most part, including clear information; however they stimulated further interpretations in the media: "So Sólyom's action and the Slovak reaction to it only pour more oil on the fire that is the degradation of Slovak-Hungarian relations..." ("Pravda", August 21st, 2009: 12). The question of action and reaction is reflected also in the language, which both sides of this dispute used. While Prime Minister Robert Fico commented frankly, President Ivan Gašparovič chose a more careful or rather more diplomatic approach, although his comments show a resemblance to Robert Fico's statements: "I don't want to say that we should respond as Romanians and Serbs did. Maybe we should" ("Pravda", August 20th, 2009: 4).[2] In addition, President Ivan Gašparovic called Sólyom's activities "graceful rides around the countries of the former Kingdom of Hungary" ("Pravda", August 20th, 2009: 4). Comparing statements by the Prime Minister and the President, we may see essentially the same view regarding the announced visit of the Hungarian president, just expressed in two different ways. In the first case it is a direct indication of opinion. In the second case, it is an indirect (but also negative) assessment, which is expressed by the metaphor "graceful rides", a term connected with the armed military expeditions of Hussite troops from the medieval territory of Bohemia invading neighboring countries. This label for the activities of the Hungarian president points again to the evaluation of his intentions and highlights the contexts in which the visit was prepared.

---

2 It is known that the Serbian President banned Sólyom from entering the country, Romania's banned on aircraft flying over its airspace.

The specificity of this sign lies in the possibilities of metaphor: "The essence of metaphor is understanding and experiencing one kind of thing in terms of other thing" (Lakoff and Johnson, 2002: 17). Similarly, the intentions of Hungarian president were understood in the light of historical facts, showing affinity with his behavior in this matter. Furthermore, "the analogy plays a very important role in the creation and comprehension of speech, because it stands behind the metaphors" (Thagard, 2001: 96). Gašparovič´s expression thus contained a disguised criticism, which was expressed not directly but metaphorically. His evaluation of Sólyom's intention was negative, but diplomatic, as in this case: "I do not want to say that we should respond like Romanians and Serbs did. Maybe we should." ("Pravda", August 20th, 2009: 4). This expression also signifies at least a controversial attitude, if not criticism. The attitude of the Slovak president is obvious.

On the other hand, there is the evaluation of the whole matter by the Hungarian President Sólyom. In his response he described the statements of the Slovak constitutional representatives as undue hysteria. In fact he did not comment on the suspicions of Slovak representatives, who described his intentions as provocation.

Based on the results of the qualitative linguistic and psychological analysis of the presented media event—the announced visit of the Hungarian President on the occasion of the unveiling of a statue of St. Stephen in Komárno in 2009—we can answer the first research question, "Which dominant discourses of the event are indicated by the newspapers studied?" We identified different dominant media discourses about the event: the Slovak side interpreted the event mainly as a provocation by the Hungarians, while the Hungarian interpretation focused on the hysteria caused by Slovak officials and their diplomatic immaturity (smallness).

Results of quantitative analysis

Based on deeper qualitative analysis we distinguished different categories and subcategories of analysis at three levels of meaning. The first part of the analysis is focused on the location and genre classification of articles. This part of the descriptive analysis will help us identify the level of significance of the unit analyzed. In the second part of the analysis, we focused on visual aspects, the relationship between text and image, and the connotative function of the visual part of the articles. The most significant part of the analysis is the holistic analysis of the communicative intentions of the entities, in which we considered both implicit and metaphorical meanings of the events. The main criterion for selecting the particular units for analysis was in fact the degree to which they reflected on the events.

Location and genre classification of analysis units

In figure 1 we present the location and genre classification of the units analyzed: articles dealing with the topic of the visit of the Hungarian President Komárno in 2009 at the unveiling the statue of St. Stephen. According to the location and length of the articles, we can conclude that the event was given sufficient media attention. Since most of the articles were included in the news, we assumed a balanced framing of events in the newspapers.

Figure 1: Location and genre classification of analysis units

Categories	Subcategories	SME	Pravda	HN	Új Szó
Location of articles	Front-page	28%	0 **	25%	30%
	Pages 2-5	71%	62%	50%	40%
	Pages 6-10	0%	12%	25%	30%
	Pages 11-20	0%	25%	0%	0%
Length of articles	1 column articles	28%	12%	0%	10%
	2 column articles	0%	0%	25%	0%
	3 or more column articles	71%	87%	75%	90%
Sections	News	71%	62%	50%	60%
	Opinions and analysis	14%	12%	25%	40%
	Interviews	14%	25%	25%	0%

Note: If the article started on the front page and continued on other pages, we have identified it as the front-page article.
** Newspaper "Pravda" has a front-page photo and brief information about the events and informs the reader that the article appears on the second page.

Based on the results above (Figure 1) we can answer the second research question, "To what extent did the researched newspapers deal with the topic analyzed?" Significant space was devoted to the event on newspaper pages 2-5 (56%) and the articles about the events were large, mostly at 3 columns or more (81%). The answer to the 3rd research question ("In what genre classification did the newspapers studied inform readers of the visit of the Hungarian President at the unveiling of the statue of St. Stephen?") is as follows: most of the articles were included in the news section of the newspapers studied (61%).

Visual Analysis / relationship of text and image

As shown in figure 2, in the quantitative part of the visual analysis we focused on the relationship of the visual communications component of journalism to the text. We have set two basic categories: the appearance of photos in articles presenting the event and the presence of photographs on the front page of periodicals in the reviewed period. The highest frequency of images was recorded in "Hospodárske noviny": up to half of the published articles contained two or more photos. The lowest number of photos has been identified in "Új Szó", where no article contained two or more photos. Insignificant proportions between photos and the text were primarily caused by numerous journalistic genres used in this discourse in various newspapers (see fig. 1). For analytical genres such as comment, but also for short journalistic units such as column, it is not common to add a visual part to the journalistic text. The reason for this result can be explained by the fact that the sample did not include the tabloid media, which focuses on the presence of visual elements in texts with a much more developed strategy. However, the importance of the presence of photographs in the newspapers is outlined in the subcategory "Articles with photographs". It appears more clearly when we realize their connotative accent. We also quantified this aspect, based on initial semiotic segmentation. Most of the photographs had significant connotations. Photographs with slight connotations and illustrative photographs appeared seldom in newspapers "SME" and "Új Szó", but more often in the newspaper "Pravda". This result creates a fairly convincing picture of meaningful discourse about the events on a visual level. It should also be noted that the illustrative pictures dominated the content before the visit when there was a lack of visual material or visual representations had not been made available yet. Conversely, after the event happened, pictures with strong connotations dominated the media, as expected.

In the further part of the quantitative content analysis, we focused on the relationship between the text and the image presented on the front pages of the newspapers studied. We found that most articles about the event (with some exceptions in "SME" and "Új Szó") included both text and a photo. It seems that the event appears to move from the space inside the newspaper to the headlines on the front page, especially after it has been enriched with visual representation, i.e. visually materialized. The highest degree of balance in the relationship of text and photo was found in "Hospodárske noviny"; in quantitative terms it was also found in "SME". On the contrary, the dominance of pictures was observed in articles on the front pages of "Pravda". The event was presented in most articles on the front pages as a main report, which demonstrates its importance.

Figure 2 Visual Analysis / relationship of text and image

Categories	**Subcategories**		**SME**	**Prav-da**	**HN**	**Új Szó**
Photographs	Articles with photographs	No photo	57%	50%	25%	70%
		1 photo	28%	37%	25%	30%
		2 or more photos	14%	12%	50%	0%
	Photograph with a strong connotation		80%	57%	66%	66%
	Photograph with a weak connotation		20%	14%	0%	0%
	Photograph without connotative function		0%	28%	33%	33%
Front page	Contains only a text message		50%	0%	0%	25%
	Contains a text message together with a photograph	Text is dominant	25%	0%	0%	25%
		Text and photos in the balance	0%	0%	100%	25%
		Photo is dominant	25%	100%	0%	25%
	Location of the message (text or photos) on the front page	Main report	100%	100%	100%	67%
		Equally dominant as the main report	0%	0%	0%	0%
		Sideline report	0%	0%	0%	33%

Based on these results (Figure 2) we can answer the fourth research question, "What type of photos framed the articles about the events analyzed?" Articles about the events were mostly framed by photographs with strong connotations (67%).

Analysis of the intention of communication and type of framing

Figure 3 shows the dominant discourse on the events in different newspapers. From the quantitative representation of negative evaluations of the intentions of the Hungarian president, we may draw clear conclusions. 75% of the articles in "Pravda" and "Hospodárske noviny" contained negative evaluation; 57% of "SME's" coverage consisted of such articles. The newspaper "Új Szó" stood in contrast to the three Slovak newspapers. The intentions of the Hungarian president were assessed as positive in 60% of cases and only 10% of the articles contained negative evaluations. On the basis of this proportional representation we can draw the conclusion that the Slovak newspapers published articles with a substantially negative attitude towards the intention of president Sólyom in his visit to Komárno.

Figure 3 Analysis of the intention of communication and type of framing

Categories	Subcategories		SME	Pravda	HN	Új Szó
Intention of communication	Evaluation of the intentions of the Hungarian president	Positive	0%	0%	0%	60%
		Negative	57%	75%	75%	10%
		Neutral	28%	12%	25%	20%
		N/A	14%	12%	0%	10%
	Evaluation of the Komárno representatives' intentions	Positive	0%	0%	0%	0%
		Negative	86%	50%	25%	20%
		Neutral	0%	12%	0%	10%
		N/A	14%	38%	75%	70%
	Evaluation of Slovak political representatives' intention to prevent the entry of the Hungarian president	Positive	0%	12%	0%	0%
		Negative	57%	37%	25%	90%
		Neutral	28%	25%	25%	10%
		N/A	14%	25%	50%	0%
Framing of the message	Type of framing in the headlines	Provocation of L. Sólyom, resp. representatives of Komárno	43%	12%	50%	0%
		An undue / hysterical reaction of Slovakia	14%	25%	0%	50%
		Mixed / balanced type of framing	43%	62%	50%	50%
	Type of framing in the article	Provocation of L. Sólyom, resp. representatives of Komárno	43%	37%	75%	0%
		An undue / hysterical reaction of Slovakia	14%	37%	0%	70%
		Mixed / balanced type of framing	43%	25%	25%	30%

Source: Authors

The evaluation of the Komárno representatives' intentions confirmed differences between the three Slovak dailies and "Új Szó". Negative evaluations dominated the newspapers "Pravda" and "SME", while "Új Szó's" coverage was only 20% such articles. Among the articles in "Hospodárske noviny" only one contained a negative evaluation of the Komárno representatives' procedure in the planning of the event. The relatively small number of articles with a negative evaluation could be explained by the fact that there were only four articles in the "Hospodárske noviny" and only one of them contained a negative evaluation of the Komárno government's tactics.

The third subcategory, the evaluation of Slovak political representatives' intention to prevent the entry of the Hungarian president provides a slightly different picture of events. The steps of Slovak political leaders were framed as positive only by "Hospodárske noviny". Approximately a quarter of all articles in the newspapers (except "Új Szó") just provided information about this step by the Slovak side, but either did not include an evaluation or provided a rather balanced (neutral) one. Most articles in "Új Szó" condemned the intention not to allow the entry of the Hungarian President to Komárno, while Slovak newspapers represented some divergence from the established line and better balance in this direction.

Figure 4 shows a statistical data confrontation of holistic analysis focusing on the intentions of communication actors reflecting implicit and metaphorical meanings of the event's depiction in the media studied.

Figure 4 Values of χ2-test and the degree of dependence between two qualitative characteristics (contingency coefficient)

	The value of statistics χ^2	**The value of contingency coefficient C**	**P—value**
Evaluation of Hungarian president´s intention, depending on the country issuing the newspaper	16,037	0,597	**0,001*** **
Evaluation of Komárno representatives´ intention, depending on the country	3,804	0,341	0,149
Evaluation of Slovak officials´ intention to prevent the entry of Hungarian President, depending on the country	16,249	0,558	**0,0001*** **
Type of event framing in the title, depending on the country	8,880	0,484	**0,012** **
Type of event framing in the article, depending on the country	5,946	0,412	0,051

*** statistically significant difference in the frequency between nationally oriented newspapers at the significance level α=0,01

** statistically significant difference in the frequency between nationally oriented newspapers at the significance level α=0,05

Source: Authors

The analysis confirmed that differences in the presentation of the events were significant and were determined by the nationality of the writer. Subcategories of analysis, i.e. evaluations of the intentions of the Hungarian President and evaluations of Slovak political representatives' intentions, have considerable explanatory value. They show polarization and are determined by the political orientation of each newspaper: whether it is pro-Slovak or pro-Hungarian. In the case of the events analyzed it is simple because the differences in the presentation of the events are significant, being based on ethnicity. This basic finding is also a starting point for considering which of the newspapers provides a balanced view. Based on the differences in the presentation of these events it is important to examine how the intention of the Hungarian president was evaluated. There is a big difference in the reporting among newspapers regarding this aspect: "Pravda", "SME" and "Hospodárske noviny" in general evaluated Sólyom's intention as negative, while "Új Szó" treated it as positive. The qualitative analysis is also confirmed by statistical analysis of data. The first hypothesis (*H1*: *Evaluation of Hungarian president's intent is statistically significant in terms of information variance between the Slovak and Hungarian newspapers.*) was confirmed (C = 0.597 ***) at the significance level $\alpha = 0.01$. The differences in representation are also demonstrated by other criterion (evaluation of the Komárno representatives' intentions), where there are differences similar to those in the previous subcategory. The vast majority of articles in "SME", half of the articles in "Pravda", and one article in "Hospodárske noviny" included a negative evaluation. On the other hand, articles published in "Új Szó" were mostly neutral towards the organizers and only a minor proportion of the articles included negative evaluation. None of the articles evaluated their behavior as positive. On this basis, it can be concluded that this aspect of the event did not receive serious attention in newspapers. At the center of interest were the Hungarian president and the Slovak constitutional representatives, such that "Új Szó" reflected the antagonism between Slovakia and Hungary expressed by concrete personalities (by the Hungarian president and Slovak political representatives) in connection to the historical background of the diplomatic conflict. The qualitative analysis of the evaluation of the Komárno representatives' intention was not statistically confirmed (C = 0.341). The second hypothesis (*H2*: *Evaluation of the Komárno representatives' plan depends on the country of origin of the newspaper.*) has therefore been rejected. However, statistical confrontation of data confirmed the third hypothesis (*H3*: *The difference between Slovak and Hungarian newspapers in the evaluation of Slovak officials' plan to prevent the entry of the Hungarian president into Slovakia is statistically significant.*) (C= 0,558***).

The answer to the question concerning the balance of each newspaper is provided by the two additional subcategories: the framing type in the headlines and in the articles themselves. These categories offer a complete picture of representing events, since they reflect the context in which the events are evaluated but also interpret them with attention to the desired frame.

The framing of titles is quite balanced in all the newspapers. Half of the subtitles use a mixed or balanced type of framing. "Pravda" provides mostly balanced framing of the event, while "Új Szó" frames headlines mostly as the hysterical reaction of the Slovak side, thus affirming the one-sidedness of its representation of this significant event. The daily newspaper "SME" has the same percentage in both subcategories (43% provocation, 14% hysterical reaction and 43% mixed or balanced framing), presenting the event largely as a provocation but also using a balanced framing for the same number of headlines and articles. The ratio between the three subcategories shows that the newspapers "SME" and "Pravda" are well balanced in comparison with "Új Szó". Statistical analysis confirmed the fourth hypothesis (*H4: The types of event framing in titles are different in Slovak and Hungarian newspapers.*) ($C = 0{,}484$; $p=0{,}012$) on the significance level $\alpha=0{,}05$. The fifth hypothesis (*H5: The types of event framing in articles are different in Slovak and Hungarian newspapers.*) has been rejected ($C=0{,}412$; $p=0{,}051$).

Conclusions

Based on the results of the qualitative analysis of the event we identified various media discourses about the event: the Slovak side interpreted the incident as Hungarian provocation while the Hungarian interpretation focused on the hysteria caused by Slovak officials and their diplomatic immaturity. In the newspapers the event was presented in one of these two types of message framing. A balanced framing type was rare. An important role was played by the visual components of mediated messages which implicitly determined the communication. The event became a media event and the media followed the design features of the media ritual.

In deeper analysis of the communication intentions and the event framing types we have seen differences in the presentation of each newspaper. "SME" analyzed the event to the same degree as provocation of L. Sólyom and as the improper or hysterical reaction of Slovakia. A balanced type of framing occurred sporadically. The type of framing in the title matched the framing of the article. Since the vast majority of articles were included in the sections news, we had assumed dominance of a balanced type of framing. In "Pravda", the headlines were mostly balanced and unbiased; in the articles, however, we observed the dominance of one-sided framing, although it was proportionately symmetrical to both identified discourses. Most articles in "Pravda" were recognized as news stories. However, there was no lack of analysis, commentaries and interviews, which could explain the unilateral selective framing. "Hospodárske noviny" presented the event mostly as the provocation of the Hungarian side, which was more visible in contributions than in titles. Only half of the articles have the character of news. "Új Szó" placed articles primarily in news service but a significant number of contributions were included in commentaries and analysis. We noticed strong media discourse in the articles of "Új Szó", which marked the whole event as the improper, hysterical reaction of Slovakia, a trend more noticeable in contributions than in titles.

In a detailed analysis of the events we have identified clear differences in the presentation of the Slovak daily newspaper and the nationally oriented newspaper. The intention of the Komárno city's representatives was notably negatively rated by "SME" and "Pravda". For the most part "Hospodárske noviny" and "Új Szó" did not take an evaluative approach to this matter. Based on the analysis we may conclude that the best balance in the presentation was provided by the newspaper "Pravda", followed by "SME" and then by "Hospodárske noviny". "Új Szó" appeared a rather one-sided newspaper.

Statistical analysis of qualitative data (analyzed discourses) showed statistically significant differences in these elements: *1) the evaluation of Hungarian president's intention by Slovak and Hungarian newspapers; 2) the evaluation Slovak officials' intention to prevent the entry of the Hungarian president to Slovakia; 3) the type of event framing in the titles of Slovak and Hungarian newspapers.* These results lead us to the conclusion that the presentation of the event in the Slovak newspapers was better balanced and brought more objective framing than in "Új Szó".

References

Abercombie, N. (1996). *Television and Society.* Cambridge: Polity Press.

Edwards, D. and Potter, J. (1992). *Discursive Psychology.* London: Sage.

Fairclough, N. (2006). *Discourse and Social Change.* Cambridge, Malden: Polity Press.

Featherstone, M. (1991). *Consumer Culture and Postmodernism by Mike Featherstone.* London: Sage.

Feriancová, A. and Mikuláš, P. (2012). Manipulácia v historických kontextoch—príklad fotografie. In: K. Fichnová (ed.) *(Ko)médiá. Vedecké a odborné štúdie zamerané na mediálnu a marketingovú komunikáciu* Nitra: UKF.

Fichnová, K., Wojciechowski, L.and Polakevičová, I. (2010). *Subiektywne postrzeganie przez dojrzewającą młodzież pojęć oznaczających media*. In W. Kwiatkowska. Media w edukacji—poglądy, zastosowania, społeczne spostrzeganie. Toruń: Wydawnictwo Adam Marszałek, 305-325.

Foucault, M. (2002). *Archeologie vědění*. Praha: Herrmannand synové.

Halliday, M. and Hasan, R. (1985). *Language, Context and Text: Aspects of Language in a Social-semiotic perspective*. Oxford: Oxford University Press.

Hendl, J. (2005). *Kvalitativní výzkum: základní metody a aplikace*. Praha: Portál.

Hradiská, E. (2004). *Metódy analýzy produktov*. In T. Kolárik and E. Sollárová (Eds.), Metódy sociálno psychologickej praxe. Bratislava: Ikar, 35-42.

Janoušek, J. (2007). *Verbální komunikace a lidská psychika*. Praha: Grada.

Lakoff, G., and Johnson, M. (2002). *Metafory, kterými žijeme*. Brno: HOST.

McQuail, D. (2009). *Úvod do teorie masové komunikace*. Praha: Portál

Miessler, J. (2007). *Kritická diskurzivní analýza (CDA) a velké množství masmediálních textů*.In M. Bočák and J. Rusnák (Eds.), Médiá a text II. Prešov: Filozofická fakulta Prešovskej university, 116-123

Pavelka, J. (2008). *Možnosti a limity sémiotické a naratologické analýzy jako nástrojů interpretace*. In M. Bočák and J. Rusnák (Eds.). Médiá a text II. Prešov: Filozofická fakulta Prešovskej university, 156-170

Ramonet, I. (2003). *Tyranie médií*. Praha: Mladá fronta.

Strauss, A. and Corbin, J. (1999). *Základy kvalitativního výzkumu*. Boskovice: Albert.

Thagard, P. (2001). *Úvod do kognitivní vědy. Mysl a myšlení*. Praha: Portál.

Urbánek, T. (2007). Přístupy k analýze textových dat v psychologii. *Československá psychologie*, 3, 290-300.

Index

Notes of contributors

Editores

Bogusława Dobek-Ostrowska, Ph.D., Professor of communication and media at the University of Wroclaw, Poland. She is the founder and president of the Polish Communication Association and the editor of "Central European Journal of Communication". She was the president of the International Federation of Communication on Associations. She serves on the editorial boards of many journals, including "Communication Theory". She is an author and editor of many books and articles, including *The Mass Media and Political Actors in Political Communication Studies* (2004), *Polish Media System at a Crossroad. Media in politics, politics in media* (2011).
E-mail: dobek@uni.wroc.pl

Jan Garlicki, Ph.D., Full Professor and Head of the Department of Sociology and Psychology of Politics at the Institute of Political Science, University of Warsaw. His scientific and research interests include sociology of politics, political marketing and marketing research. He specializes in the issues of political culture and political participation. He is a founding member and since 2003 an honorary member of the Polish Society of Market and Opinion Researchers (PTBRiO) as well as a member of the Polish Sociological Association (PTS). He is an author of many publications, including *Democracy and European Integration* (2005) and was the editor of three volumes of "Political Studies": the *Political Marketing Strategies and Mechanisms* (vol. 16, 2010), the *Political Culture of Internauts in Poland* (vol. 21, 2011), the *Political elites and Internet Users* (vol. 26, 2012).
E-mail: jgarlicki@uw.edu.pl

Authors

Silke Adam is Professor of Communication studies at the University of Bern, Switzerland, where she directs the Institute of Communication and Media Studies. Her research focuses on European communication, network analysis and media systems impact.
E-mail: silke.adam@ikmb.unibe.ch

Tendai Joseph Chari, University of Venda, South Africa, is a Lecturer at the University of Venda, South Africa, where he teaches Media Studies. His research interests are political communication, new media, media representation

and media ethics. Some of his most recent publications have appeared in the *Journal of African Media Studies*, *Ecquid Novi* and *African Identity*.
E-mail: tendai.chari@yahoo.com

Brian Collins studies popular culture and political science at Bowling Green State University in Ohio.
E-mail: bricoll@bgsu.edu

German Espino Sanchez is Professor of the University Autonomous of Queretaro, Mexico. He earned a PhD in Political Science with a particular focus on Political Communication. He has authored three books in Spanish about Political Communication, the latest on New Technologies and Political Communication in Mexico.
E-mail: yomeros666@hotmail.com

Katarína Fichnová, Ph.D., Constantine the Philosopher University in Nitra, Slovakia, is an expert in social communication, media communication and persuasion. The focus of her research is application of methodical concepts of mixed approach in applied media research of communicators with an emphasis on perception of communicators in target communities. She also deals with the transdiciplinary character of social research with regard to suitable academic and methodological approaches used in social studies, critical social psychology and discourse philology.
E-mail: kfichnova@ukf.sk

Ilona Grzywińska is a PhD student and a Research Fellow at the Institute of Political Science, University of Warsaw. Her field of research includes the impact of social media on political communication and agenda setting theory. She received a Fulbright Scholarship within which she conducted research at University of Florida, USA.
E-mail: ilonagrzywinska@gmail.com

David J. Jackson, is Associate Professor in the Department of Political Science at Bowling Green State University in Ohio. He is the author of Entertainment and Politics: The Influence of Pop Culture on Young Adult Political Socialization and Classrooms and Barrooms: An American in Poland.
E-mail: jacksod@bgsu.edu

Ewa Krzątała-Jaworska, Ph.D., Candidate and Teaching Assistant in the Department of Political Science at Paris 1 Panthéon-Sorbonne University in Paris. In cooperation with Turin University and Stanford University, she coordinates the international research program entitled "Is Representative Democracy in Crisis?

Research Review and Research Perspectives". She is member of the Research Network "Electronic Democracy" (DEL). She cooperates with University of Milan. Her research interests include the Internet and political engagement, citizen participation and e-participation in policy-making as well as social capital.
E-mail: ewakj@yahoo.fr

Daniel Mider, Ph.D., Assistant Professor at the Department of Sociology and Psychology of Politics at the Institute of Political Science, University of Warsaw. He specializes in teaching sociology, research methods and techniques in political science, statistics and marketing on the Internet. His research interests include the sociology of the Internet, theory of democracy and methodology of quantitative and qualitative researches, in particular in the field of political science. He is author of several monographs including *Political Participation on the Internet. Study in the Field of Political Science* (2008).
E-mail: d.mider@uw.edu.pl

Peter Mikuláš, Ph.D., Constantine the Philosopher University in Nitra (Slovakia), is an expert in media communication theory and media analysis. In his theoretical work and research he deals with the genre categorization of media products, especially television and new media. Another part of his research deals with marketing aspects of media production and visual communication, especially political photography as part of a political PR and also other marketing aspects of political communication. He also focuses on new media and online social networking and the use of mobile technologies in social networks.
E-mail: pmikulas@ukf.sk

James Moir, University of Abertay Dundee, United Kingdom, is a senior Lecturer in Sociology at the University of Abertay Dundee, Scotland, UK. His research focuses on the application of discourse analysis to a wide range of socio-psychological issues, including political communication and opinion polling as an ideological framing of opinionation.
E-mail: J.Moir@abertay.ac.uk

Antonio Momoc, Ph.D., post-doctoral researcher in sociology at University of Bucharest, Romania. He has a degree in journalism, a master of arts in communication sciences and another one in political science. He studies the way in which politicians in Romania relate to new communication technologies. He has published books about communism and about the interwar period. He participated as political communication specialist in the electoral campaigns of the Liberal Party in 2008 and of the Green Party in 2009.
E-mail: antoniomomoc@yahoo.com

Ewa Nowak, Ph.D., University of Maria Curie-Sklodowska in Lublin, Poland, Ph. D. in political science, graduated from Maria Curie-Skłodowska University in Lublin, lecturer in Political Science Faculty of. Her academic and research activity focuses on political communication, media effect, agenda-setting, electoral behaviour, civil society, and Europeanization or the European public sphere.
E-mail: terewa@gmail.com

Jakub Nowak, Ph.D. lecturer in Faculty of Political Science of Maria Curie-Skłodowska University in Lublin, Areas of research: social and culture aspects of new media; communication theories, and political communication.
E-mail: nowakkuba@gazeta.pl

Barbara Pfetsch is Professor of Communication Theory and Media Effects Research at the Institute of Communication and Media Studies at the Freie Universität Berlin, Germany. Her research focuses on the comparative study of political communication and the public sphere.
E-mail: Pfetsch@zedat.fu-berlin.de

Lucia Spálová, Ph.D., University of Constantine the Philosopher in Nitra (Slovakia), is an expert in social communication, media communication and persuasion. The focus of her research is the application of methodical concepts of mixed approach in applied media research of communicators with an emphasis on the perception of communicators in target communities. She also deals with transdiciplinary character of social research with regard to suitable academic and methodogical approaches used in social studies, critical social psychology and discourse philology.
E-mail: lspalova@ukf.sk

Peter Szabo, Ph.D., University of Constantine the Philosopher in Nitra (Slovakia) is an expert on language communication, the semiotics of media communication and advertising and the interaction between media and marketing communications. The focus of his research and theoretical interest is communication theory, semiotics and linguistic context. In addition, his research area includes analysis of literary texts and their forays into different contexts (advertising texts, film adaptations of literary works, intertextuality, etc.).
E-mail: pszabo@ukf.sk

Jürgen Wilke, Ph.D., Professor at Johannes Gutenberg-Universität Mainz, Germany. He has published widely in media history and media structure, political communication, international communication, and news analysis (particularly news agencies). Wilke is former President of the German Association of

Communication Research, former member of the International Council of IAMCR and Head of its History Section, Prof. h.c. Lomonossow University Moscow (Russia) and Corresponding Member of the Austrian Academy of Sciences (Vienna).
Homepage: juergen-wilke.net; E-mail: juergen.wilke@uni-mainz.de

Łukasz Wojciechowski, Ph.D., Constantine the Philosopher University in Nitra (Slovakia) deals with the issues of creativity, stereotypes and gender in media and marketing texts. His research is oriented around mass media, particularly electronic, visual semiotics, photography and movies. He also focuses on current questions of visual and content analysis of mass media communication in political campaigns.
E-mail: lwojciechowski@ukf.sk

Studies in Communication and Politics

Edited by Bogusława Dobek-Ostrowska and Michał Głowacki

Vol. 1 Bogusława Dobek-Ostrowska / Jan Garlicki (eds.): Political Communication in the Era of New Technologies. 2013.

www.peterlang.com

www.ingramcontent.com/pod-product-compliance
Ingram Content Group UK Ltd.
Pitfield, Milton Keynes, MK11 3LW, UK
UKHW041826100926
8556IPUK00002B/45